The MYTH *of the*
SUPERHERO

The MYTH *of the* SUPERHERO

Marco Arnaudo

Translated by
Jamie Richards

THE JOHNS HOPKINS UNIVERSITY PRESS
Baltimore

Originally published as *Il fumetto supereroico: Mito, etica e strategie narrative*.
© 2010 Marco Arnaudo/Tunué S.r.l. Published by arrangement with Tunué S.r.l.
All rights reserved.

© 2013 The Johns Hopkins University Press
All rights reserved. Published 2013
Printed in the United States of America on acid-free paper
2 4 6 8 9 7 5 3 1

The Johns Hopkins University Press
2715 North Charles Street
Baltimore, Maryland 21218-4363
www.press.jhu.edu

Library of Congress Cataloging-in-Publication Data
Arnaudo, Marco.
[Fumetto supereroico. English]
The myth of the superhero / Marco Arnaudo ; translated by Jamie Richards.
p. cm.
ISBN 978-1-4214-0910-8 (hdbk. : acid-free paper) — ISBN 978-1-4214-0953-5
(pbk. : acid-free paper) — ISBN 1-4214-0910-0 (hdbk. : acid-free paper) —
ISBN 1-4214-0953-4 (pbk. : acid-free paper)
Includes bibliographical references and index.
1. Superhero comic books, strips, etc.—History and criticism.
2. Superheroes in literature. I. Richards, Jamie. II. Title.
741.5'9—dc23   2012036697

A catalog record for this book is available from the British Library.

*Special discounts are available for bulk purchases of this book. For more information,
please contact Special Sales at 410-516-6936 or specialsales@press.jhu.edu.*

The Johns Hopkins University Press uses environmentally friendly book materials,
including recycled text paper that is composed of at least 30 percent
post-consumer waste, whenever possible.

Contents

Acknowledgments   *vii*

Introduction   1

Chapter 1. Myth and Religion   11

Chapter 2. Ethics and Society   63

Chapter 3. Epic and Neobaroque   117

Conclusion   156

Notes   *159*
Bibliography   *183*
Index   *197*

Acknowledgments

I'd like to thank Giuseppe Gazzola, Paolo Di Tonno, Simona Micali, and Marco Pellitteri for their invaluable suggestions for revisions to the Italian version of this text. I would also like to thank translator Jamie Richards and Johns Hopkins University Press manuscript editor Michele Callaghan for all their help in making the book accessible to an American audience.

This book is dedicated to all my students, in recognition of the discussions that gave me so many new ideas and kept me from being content to rest on the old ones.

The MYTH *of the*
SUPERHERO

INTRODUCTION

Since the 1930s, a certain type of comic book has made its way through publishing houses and cultures all over the planet. It is a genre that has spread faster than a speeding bullet, has struck the collective imagination more powerfully than a locomotive, and has managed to leap the most remote national barriers in a single bound to reach a vast number of readers.

The genre is, of course, the superhero comic, which launched in 1938 with publication of the first Superman story (by Jerry Siegel and Joe Shuster). It was destined for a path full of obstacles and transformations, as even a brief examination of its development will demonstrate.[1] Superman's huge, immediate success spurred other authors to get in on the action, and they created an enormous number of superheroes in stories that used very simple (if not rudimentary) narrative techniques, were aimed primarily at a preadolescent audience, and were often inspired by the anxieties of World War II (frequently with Axis saboteurs as villains).[2] In the 1950s, the genre was attacked by an army of psychologists and educators. To defend the art form from accusations of alleged immorality, its authors transformed the superhero comic into a fantasy completely disengaged from reality. Still, their texts and drawings had become more refined and often employed remarkable solutions, with delightfully innovative results.

Comics publisher Marvel began to orient superhero comic books toward young adults in the 1960s,[3] presenting controversial storylines and themes that attracted the same students who were listening to Bob Dylan and protesting the Vietnam War.[4] The "comic" preadolescent and early adolescent branch of comics continued to coexist with the "serious" young adult titles for at least another decade. By that time, the repressive

1

climate of the fifties had lost ground. Comics with more mature themes and dramatic storylines, such as thrillers or in some cases even horror, had begun to dominate the genre. Another factor in this change was that between the seventies and eighties the audience for superhero fare, now more likely to be adult, was essentially transforming into the reader of today: that is, not so much (or not exclusively) an adolescent boy on the lookout for escapist thrills, but a highly specialized fan, a demanding enthusiast who was increasingly knowledgeable about the developments of various series and the stylistic differences among authors.

In the nineties, the genre was revolutionized by a group of new independent publishers. Among these, one standout is Image,[5] which introduced a spectacular, violent style founded on graphic excess, which forced the genre's main publishers, Marvel and DC,[6] to refashion themselves in turn. At the beginning of the new millennium, the superhero comic book is still changing, moving away from the narrative and graphic extremes of the nineties and also gaining increased visibility because of a spate of highly successful Hollywood films.

In one form or another, for one audience or another, the figure of the superhero has been able to reinvent itself and endure for seventy-five years and counting, not only entering the lives of countless readers but also, because of film and television adaptations, becoming a shared cultural heritage even for people who have never read the original comics. This sort of phenomenon couldn't help but attract the attention of many scholars, who have produced a substantial body of work, analyzing superhero comics in anthropological, sociological, pedagogical, and semiotic terms.

In this vast array of scholarship, I want to clarify the intentions of the present work, which addresses the superhero genre's relationship to myth, religion, society, literary genre, and epistemological frameworks—all topics that have already been explored so extensively that it might be surprising to find them amassed here in such a relatively short book. Neither is it my intention to offer a "crib note" on the subject, a presentation of what is common knowledge among scholars about the superhero genre as a cultural fact. Rather, I aim to construct a discourse that builds on all the aforementioned (and oft-discussed) topics in order to identify certain symptomatic characteristics of the superhero comic that converge in my overall thesis. My belief is that this thesis can provide a deep understanding of the nature of the superhero comic and its possible role in contemporary society (especially, though not exclusively, in the United States). As in the best of the "cliffhanger" tradition so dear to comics, I won't disclose this thesis here and will instead let the reader discover it over the course of the book. However, I ought to mention that, despite the vastly heterogeneous topics discussed in the three sections of this work, the book does not digress from its basic aims and instead builds on its argument as it proceeds.

Superhero Seriality

Analysis of a cultural product must always respect the historical, formal, and material components of its object. Like any form of expression, the comic possesses its own modes of communication that must be understood as such, both to do justice to the work of its authors and to better appreciate its most original and successful creations, or at the very least, discard those that are inferior to an informed reader. To give a general definition, we could describe the comic as a form of artistic expression that tells a story in a series of still images that are rendered most often through drawing, usually but not necessarily include written text, and create an impression of temporal continuity and movement that enables the development of a narrative. The comic's visual and narrative components, therefore, are absolutely interdependent. One can never be neglected in favor of the other.

The comic appears in (but cannot be identified with) various genres, styles, and forms of publication, which can be roughly subdivided into three groups:

- individual self-contained narratives—such as a free-standing comic book or graphic novel (a "one-shot" story or comic strip with characters that only appear once);
- self-contained serial narratives—such as strips with consistent characters but without continuity or series of graphic novels that always have the same characters (as is quite common in European comics); and
- continuous serial narratives, in which each issue brings together the previous events and prepares the ground for the next issue, potentially ad infinitum—as it happens for superhero stories in comic books or daily strips.

Only in the last form of narrative is it necessary to have knowledge of the context external to the work being read to fully appreciate the present story. Also, the order of the various narrative segments cannot be changed without creating serious incongruities in the storyline.

In this book I deal almost exclusively with this form, not only because it predominates in the superhero genre but also because through Marvel and DC it has developed expressive potential and artistic results that are completely unique. In fact, to the best of anyone's knowledge, there is no other example of a narrative in which *one* story like Superman's or Batman's, which first appeared in the 1930s, has been regularly and consistently followed without interruption for so long, resulting in such a volume of stories at such a fast pace, and with dozens of authors, each inserting himself into the collective work by adding his own touch.

In addition, the individual titles of Superman's publisher, DC Comics, are in turn only single elements in an immense narrative universe, in which the characters continually interact and the events and timeline in one title must be compatible with those of all the others, past and present. Put simply, if Superman gets married in May, no DC title can represent him as a bachelor in June. Today's readers are sometimes shocked to discover that Superman, whom they know to be against homicide, sometimes killed people during World War II. This reaction, clearly, wouldn't even be imaginable if the character narrated in the stories of the twenty-first century weren't perceived as being the same individual as before.

We can, therefore, legitimately say that the real story, the ultimate work, is determined by the cumulative biographies of each character on a single fictional plane, and it coincides with the entire DC Universe (or that of Marvel, whose comics work in the same way). If this is true, what we have before us is a collective narrative millions of pages long that has developed over several decades, and, as a result, has taken a particular path, encountered particular challenges, and articulated certain responses in a way that has no parallel in any other form of modern narrative.

This is why I find it reductive to discuss Batman or Superman as if they were Leopold Bloom or Holden Caulfield (as many do)—in other words, as manifestations of narrative intent that are self-contained in a single work—or to equate superheroes of a seventy-five-year-old tradition with the protagonists of nineteenth-century serial novels, who were ultimately still polished by the author and contained in *one* book. Tempting but equally superficial is the comparison between superheroes and characters from film and television series like *Rambo* or *Buffy the Vampire Slayer*, which continue for an often high but still limited number of episodes. Even if a new *Rambo* film were to be made, it would only put off ending the story arc by some months or years. To have an accurate parallel with the super-heroes of Marvel or DC would require a Rambo series with hundreds of new films all connected in a great big Ramboverse and coming out in theaters every Wednesday for decades. What can never be overempha-sized, then, is that a story that has continued to branch for so long, a story that is potentially endless (as long as readers continue to support it), compared with a shorter, concluded narrative, doesn't just change in length but also in narrative structure, in how it treats its subject matter, in its pace of presentation and choice of themes. And if publishing history has had many serial forms, especially in the past two centuries, in no other instance has seriality been able to develop, grow, learn its strengths, deal with its weaknesses, and openly bare its mechanisms as it does in the Mar-vel and DC superhero comics. Consequently, in the pages that follow, I frequently underline how the relationship between the superhero genre and the serial form has resulted in certain effects that are not found in other forms, creating advantages that serve to counterbalance its equally specific limitations.

Selection of the Material

The approach described above has influenced my choice of material in several ways. First, the most logical step was limiting myself to the super-heroes of DC and Marvel, which, as I have stated, have developed fea-tures that are still unique to them today. I have excluded more recent publishers, such as Dark Horse and Image, for the simple reason that they have not yet produced a comparable critical mass of stories.[7] For the sake of simplicity, therefore, "superhero comic" will henceforth refer exclu-sively to Marvel and DC comics. It will be up to readers, if they so choose, to test if and how my claims also apply to works from other publishers. At the same time, to the extent possible I have kept to a minimum all refer-ences to comics, even from Marvel or DC, that are somewhat indepen-dent of regular superhero titles, like self-contained stories or entire series that are parallel to "canonical" narrative universes and have little or no bearing on their development.

A significant consequence of this choice was the almost total exclu-sion of works that are usually considered the gems of the superhero genre, such as *Watchmen, The Dark Knight Returns, Marvels, Astro City,* the entire Vertigo line, and so on.[8] This has actually turned out to be an advantage for various reasons. First, because these are the works that have been studied the most, I felt that it was less necessary to make another contribution to the already existing scholarship; second, the studies that focus on these "peripheral" examples outside of regular series often seem to suggest (perhaps even unintentionally) the dearth of critical interest in the "official" superhero genre, as if only its "eccentric" or "deviant" manifestations were redeemable. This is to an extent what happened with Art Spiegelman's *Maus* in terms of the non-superhero graphic novel.[9] The extraordinary fanfare that surrounded Spiegelman's work didn't increase general attention to the medium as a whole. On the contrary, it created the distorted impression that *Maus* is the only masterpiece in an otherwise negligible panorama—to the extent that, sadly, *Maus* has become the token comic for those who don't read comics otherwise.[10] My hope is that an investigation of the mainstream, of the "majors" that publish for the large audience of faithful comics readers, can restore to the superhero genre the dignity it deserves. It deserves this not only because of the excellence and inventiveness of many of its works but also because of the role that (as we will see) it plays in American society as well as abroad, since the genre's international popularity demonstrates that other cultures also are able to relate to it. Yet I don't aim to go so far as to suggest the paradox that the mainstream is per se "better" than masterpieces like *Watchmen* but simply to point out that successful serial titles contain specific elements of interest that cannot be found in shorter, self-contained comics publications, even if they're considered more "highbrow."

The problem such a focus creates, however, is narrowing down material to base my argument on from Marvel and DC's immense production. In a chat with my trusty comic book seller, I was able to learn that Marvel and DC combined publish between 130 and 150 new superhero issues per month. If you calculate that one issue spans an average of 22 pages, a reader would hypothetically had to have read between 2,860 and 3,300 pages a month just to keep up with what's going on in the superhero world. And what about back issues? How big, in terms of pages, is the narrative universe composed of the single titles of the two publishing houses? Here we venture even further into dangerous territory. From the late 1930s to the 2000s, the sales and success of superhero comics have fluctuated enormously, from the astronomical figures of the early forties to

THE MYTH OF THE SUPERHERO

the meager revenues—as in the near death of the genre—of the fifties. Purely for the sake of simplification, to have at least a very general idea, let's say that the positive and negative fluctuations are about even and cancel each other out. If we take today's rate of publication over a twelve-month period and multiply that figure by the number of years from 1938 (the year that marked the launch of Superman and the explosive kick-off of the Golden Age of comics) to 2010, the number of pages adds up to somewhere between 2,471,040 and 2,851,200.

This calculation is very rough; yet even so, one can see that the sum of all the text—which I will refer to as the metatext or macrotext—of the superhero world of Marvel and DC constitutes a massive work that no one has ever read in its entirely and that would be virtually impossible to read. The situation appears even more hopeless if we consider that most libraries do not hold large quantities of superhero comics (especially those issues that were never collected into volumes) and that many old comics are extremely hard to find and expensive to purchase, making even the physical reality of the complete superhero macrotext virtually inaccessible to almost every reader. This mass of stories ungraspable in its entirety is the frame of reference that we must always insert into each new issue of a Marvel or DC superhero comic. If one doesn't feel overwhelmed or have a sense of reverential awe at the prospect of a multimillion-page narrative, one cannot form a clear idea of how much this art form has to offer.

It's easy to see how deciding what the most relevant examples in the genre are is like trying to take a water sample from a tsunami. It's also understandable why some scholars give in to the temptation to oversimplify matters and describe the nature of the superhero genre or of a specific character using just a few critically acclaimed, self-contained stories (such as *The Dark Knight Returns* for Batman). Yet understanding the logic behind the practical reasons that lead to this sort of arbitrary delimitation of the field doesn't necessarily mean condoning it. In fact, to be honest, I think that any closed view of the superhero comic should be rejected as inadequate and distorted. In contrast to this hyperselectivity, the opposite methodological option, which is also widely practiced, consists of accumulating as many examples as possible in what inevitably turns out to be an A to Z dictionary or a history of the genre. These might be very useful tools, but they can seldom help the reader identify the genre's specific techniques, trends, constants, and variations.

Parameters of the Discussion

This book falls in between the above approaches. My methodological take can be exemplified by the historical map, which marks solely those components of the landscape that enable the representation of the dynamics of past events, as in a map that spatially depicts the development of battles in a war. A representation of this sort preselects its focal points based on its own logic and its particular aims. It would be silly to accuse it of incompleteness when whatever isn't there was omitted on purpose to show more clearly what is meant to be shown. Similarly, my explorations of superhero comics led me to identify certain fundamental concepts that must be brought into relief to show the development of certain ideas.

In case the reader thinks of texts outside my selection that seem just as useful and wonders why I didn't mention them, I candidly admit that when choosing between examples I considered to be of analogous importance, an inscrutable element of personal taste came into play, though I stress it was limited to the range of interchangeable options. In other cases, it may be apparent that I am simply not aware of this other example that seems superior in comparison to my mediocre one. If so, I can only refer back to the above calculations and say that the scholar of superhero comics doesn't enjoy the certainties relied on by experts in other areas (Shakespeare scholars, for example), who don't encounter any problems reading all the primary texts before starting to write.

In other cases, examples may come to mind that directly contradict my claims. This too is inevitable, is certain to happen. In fact, I'll go one step further and clarify that I too know several such examples, but if I have neglected them in this book it isn't for the sake of argument. The fact is, given the mass of available material, the number of authors who have contributed to it, and the decades over which the entire superhero macrotext has developed, I'd actually be suspicious of anyone who claimed to have found the interpretative key that would work for *every* instance of the subject at hand, without exception. What interests me, then, is showing some of the principal trends within, around, and against which a notable number of authors have responded and discussing how this has influenced the identity of the genre and its relationship with society and readers. To go back to the metaphor of the map depicting a historical battle, it's about seeing where the rows of soldiers went and where the

THE MYTH OF THE SUPERHERO

fights took place. If, in the confusion of the moment, a few isolated groups went running in the opposite direction, surrendered to the enemy, or hid in the bushes, that obviously doesn't contradict the bigger picture. To avoid weighing down the text with excessive repetition, I chose not to use the formula "with the necessary exceptions" every time I make a general statement, but please note: everything that follows should be considered "with the necessary exceptions."

The reader will undoubtedly notice a heavy concentration on the primary texts (comics) and, conversely, a limited (or more limited, compared with the "average" in comics criticism) referencing of sociological, semiotic, or anthropological sources. This can be explained by the fact that, if these disciplinary areas have undoubtedly made crucial contributions to our understanding of mass culture and of superhero comics, I hope to minimize the risk inherent to interdisciplinary works of losing sight of the main subject. In other words, I will only make use of tools from other disciplines when they serve to shed light on the subject, so that it remains completely clear that this is a study of comics criticism applied to the superhero genre and not a sociological or semiological study that takes its examples from comics. This approach, however, does not exclude the possibility of other applications. It simply reasserts that a work of comics criticism aware of its own objectives ought to reveal above all those characteristics of its subject that do not pertain to research from the perspective of other disciplines, so that its specificities are presented in a reliable discourse that can then be offered to the scholarly community as a basis for further inquiry.

One last note regarding method. Particularly in chapter 2 of this book, I refer to past racial and ethnic representations that to our contemporary sensibility can seem excessively stereotypical and perhaps troubling. I completely agree that, from the point of view of contemporary society, we must acknowledge the intrinsically stereotypical nature of these representations to better appreciate how far we have come and to remind us of the type of cultural tradition we would not want to go back to. At the same time, in a historical and critical investigation such as this, I believe it's also important to point out what certain stereotypical expressions signified in their *original cultural context*. In this view, there might be representations that are more stereotypical than those of today but still less stereotypical than the *commonly accepted* average in the historical period. John Stuart Mill's remarks on the topic remain pertinent: "To find fault with our ancestors for not having annual parliaments, universal suffrage, and vote by ballot, would be like quarrelling with the Greeks and Romans for not using steam navigation, when we know it is so safe and expeditious [...]. It was necessary that many other things should be thought and done, before [...] it was possible that steam navigation should be thought of. Human nature must proceed step by step."[11] Applying this idea to the critical and historical analyses conducted in this book, I often point out precisely these gradual and "intermediate" (from the perspective of our historical context) steps. If, therefore, I speak positively of narrative elements that are chock-full of dated stereotypes, it isn't because I endorse them per se or because I don't realize how dated they are, but because I consider it necessary for the sake of historical accuracy to understand the contributions that were in some way *advanced* compared with the standards of their time. Especially because it was often these little changes that made up the long, difficult, and complex path that has led us to the less than perfect but certainly more sensitive, tolerant, and respectful society of today.

⚡ 1 ⚡

MYTH and RELIGION

From Classical Myth to the Superhero

From the very beginning, the superhero comic has maintained such a strong relationship with myth and religion that Richard Reynolds, referring to the genre as a whole, saw fit to define it "a modern mythology."[1] The gods of the Norse tradition, like Thor and Loki, are an integral part of the superhero universe, along with less prominent yet nonetheless significant appearances from Greek and Roman figures such as Hercules, Ares (Mars), and Eros (Cupid), the gods of ancient Egypt (generally portrayed as villains), spirits from Native American cultures, and divine beings from practically every other pantheon that the human race has ever devised.

The motivation behind these elements, at least initially, can be linked to the fairly pedestrian issue of copyright. After Siegel and Shuster published the first Superman story in 1938, the character's extraordinary success led many other authors to produce an enormous number of comics with similar characters within a very short time, creating the superhero genre in a furious race to come up with new ideas and to succeed on the same scale. The problem with inventing new superheroes was justifying their powers without encountering legal problems such as plagiarizing Superman or other new heroes. In this regard, ancient mythology offered an inexhaustible reserve of superhuman personalities and adventurous deeds that weren't the exclusive property of anyone. This, however, only explains why characters from mythology were present at the beginning but not their constant presence in the genre. Indeed, it is unlikely that mythological heroes would have remained a constant source for superhero comics if there had not been particular narrative or symbolic affinities between the ancient stories and the new ones.

The most obvious commonality lies in the strength and extraordinary abilities that superheroes and mythological heroes share. On the narrative level, there is a similar strong focus on conflict, both individual (duels) and collective (war), as well as the persistence of thematic archetypes such as the voyage or the test. These similarities in formula, however superficial they may seem, are actually so strong that authors of superhero comics sometimes turn to mythological models without even realizing it. Dennis O'Neil explains, discussing some of the Superman stories he wrote in the early seventies:

> A few days ago, just before beginning this reminiscence, I happened on a summary of the ancient Mesopotamian epic of Gilgamesh and realized, bemused, that this is my Superman story. Yet, to the best of my recollection, I'd never read Gilgamesh before, had never studied mythology in either high school or college.[2]

In order to delve into specifics, let us consider mythology scholar Joseph Campbell's classic description of heroic adventure, which he defines as *classic monomyth* and presents as the basic recurring plot of all mythologies in the world:

> A hero ventures forth from the world of common day into a region of supernatural wonder (x): fabulous forces are there encountered and a decisive victory is won (y): the hero comes back from this mysterious adventure with the power to bestow boons on his fellow man (z).[3]

Considering this formula, the similarities between the superhero genre and classical myth are truly remarkable—and, most important, more remarkable than they are between myth and any other popular contemporary genre. Whenever he dons a mask and costume and travels to another planet or even just to the tops of skyscrapers to defeat supercriminals, the superhero symbolically retraces the traditional journey of the mythical hero. Just like the hero of myth, after temporarily leaving behind the community familiar to the reader and the other characters, the modern superhero returns, mission accomplished, his common identity (Clark Kent, Peter Parker) restored, and the community rewarded with greater security (a criminal arrested, a threat averted) or the recovery of lost goods (stolen money, a kidnapping victim) or new knowledge (for example, when the hero brings back useful new technology from space that is unknown to

THE MYTH OF THE SUPERHERO

humans on Earth).[4] Thus, the superhero genre expands the traditional mythical model without contradicting it, yet also shows the hero's private affairs when he goes about his daily life. Given the way these elements are used by different authors, the superhero genre can be said to vacillate between the complete reproduction of classic monomyth, with the hero portrayed almost entirely in action and outside of society, and the opposite extreme, a soap opera with incursions into the world of magic.

In fact, even the serial form of superhero comics appears to bring the genre closer to the universe of myth. As Dennis O'Neil has written, collaborative writing produced according to the demanding pace of the market seems like

> a maniacally accelerated version of the folkloric process. As with fables and myths, Superman's stories were begun by one author but revised and altered by many others, and due to the constant need to produce, fill pages, meet deadlines, publish all that stuff, what would have taken generations in the pre-industrial era now happens within just a few years.[5]

A Modern Olympus

If the narrative and thematic analogies between myth and superhero comics enabled the transfer to the latter sphere from the former, it isn't surprising that authors found myth to be a rich source of inspiration for their stories from the very beginning. The year 1940 turned out to be a decisive one in this process. January 1940 marked the birth of the Flash, who had small wings on the helmet and boots of his costume and was introduced to us at the opening of the story as the "reincarnation of winged Mercury."[6] One month later, a story came out in which a magician gives the young Billy Batson the power to transform into Captain Marvel by saying the word "Shazam," an acrostic for the wisdom of Solomon, the strength of Hercules, the stamina of Atlas, the power of Zeus, the courage of Achilles, and the speed of Mercury.[7] May saw the debut of Doctor Fate, a potpourri of traditions, having learned the magic of Atlantis, Egypt, and Chaldea and fighting a villain called Wotan (the German name for Odin).[8] In August of that same year, Martin A. Burstein and Jack Kirby published the story "Mercury in the 20th Century," a title that epitomizes the interconnectedness between superheroes and mythology.[9] Here, Mercury, the ancient god himself, is sent to Earth by Jupiter to thwart Pluto—who

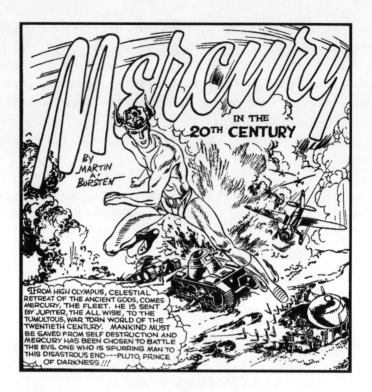

The god Mercury fights during World War II in a 1940 story by
Martin A. Bursten and Jack Kirby. © Pure Imagination

appears in the guise of the dictator Rudolph Hendler, a direct reference
to Adolf Hitler—and his plans of conquest.[10]

A groundbreaking period took place from late 1941 to early 1942,
when psychologist William Moulton Marston introduced the Wonder
Woman character to the superhero genre. The first episode begins with
a preliminary account of the history of the Amazons. After warring with
Hercules, who envied their physical prowess and skill as warriors, the
Amazons withdrew to Paradise Island, in reclusion from "Man's World."[11]
But then one fateful day in the present epoch Captain Steve Trevor lands
on the island after a dogfight with a Nazi plane and thus technology, the
media, and war violate the fixedness of the ancient mythological world.
Diana, daughter of the Amazonian queen Hippolyta, is chosen to take
Trevor back to Man's World, thus coming to the United States and start-
ing her career as Wonder Woman.

In the caption at the beginning of the second story, we are told that
Diana is as beautiful as Aphrodite, wise as Athena, swifter than Hermes,

THE MYTH OF THE SUPERHERO

Wonder Woman's birth in 1942 from a statue brought to life, just like the
Greek myth about the sculptor Pygmalion and his statue, Galatea.
© DC Comics

and stronger than Hercules (a subtitle that appears on the splash page of
Wonder Woman stories all the way up through the sixties).[12] A few
months later we learn that Diana was born from a little statue molded by
Hippolyta and worshiped by her, just as the sculptor Pygmalion worshipped his creation Galatea, and so fiercely so as to move Aphrodite to
infuse life into the small figure.[13]

But however well fleshed out the mythological scenario constructed
by the Wonder Woman authors, this back story often remained fairly
obscure in the early tales of the heroine. Once it fulfilled its purpose of
justifying her powers, the narrative could then freely concentrate on
contemporary adventures, with battles against mad scientists and Nazi
saboteurs. The presence of these cultural roots in the character's profile,
however, allows this element to be accentuated more or less depending
on the taste of the authors and readers. For example, in a story arc that
started in December 1968,[14] the authors decided to make their protagonist more realistic, so they had her lose her superpowers, dress according
to fashion rather than in her traditional costume, and learn karate to
fight crime. Yet, after a few months,[15] myth returned to the series in the
form of a war declared by Ares against the Amazons, to whose aid came
none other than the Valkyries of Norse mythology and the troops of the
paladin Roland of French medieval lore, in a classic example of the extent
of how permeable the boundaries among different traditions are in the
superhero universe.

Medieval hero Roland's troops join the Amazons and
Valkyries in the war against Ares. © DC Comics

In later years, mythology in Wonder Woman appeared most notably in
a story arc begun by George Pérez in 1987, in which Pérez tried to follow
solely the Greek tradition, excluding not only Valkyries and paladins but
Roman influences as well. In the early twenty-first century, writer Greg
Rucka again plunged the heroine back into her original mythological
world in a series of stories where, among other things, Wonder Woman
was pitted against Medusa, blinding herself so she wouldn't turn to stone
and later descending into Hades to seek a cure to restore her vision. This
story arc contained one of the most interesting examples of the hybrid-
ization of myth and the contemporary world when Wonder Woman
fights Medusa on live television in the middle of Yankee Stadium.[16]

This story perhaps best demonstrates the complete interchangeability
of historical epochs in the superhero universe, with a battle between
ancient figures that comes to stand for contemporary forms of sports
entertainment, the combatants armed with shields, swords, and hatchets

THE MYTH OF THE SUPERHERO

In an extraordinary meeting of classic and modern, Wonder Woman decapitates Medusa in a live broadcast from Yankee Stadium. © DC Comics

corresponding to players equipped with padding, helmets, and baseball bats. This situation seems to make the threat of Medusa more real and tangible, as though, if she were to beat Wonder Woman, she would look right into the camera and petrify the millions of spectators watching at home. Through the allegorical possibilities of myth, the story thus delves into the problematic fascination with the spectacle of violence that contributes to the success of so much modern media. Not just as readers of the story, but also as virtual spectators of the clash filmed by the TV cameras represented in the story, we are made to ask ourselves how long we can bear to watch. Up to the instant before Medusa's gaze? But if we make it that far, captivated by what we have already seen, will we really be able to avert our eyes and resist the temptation to look at that completely exclusive, new image that would constitute the climax of the spectacle? This example demonstrates how the use of mythological figures in the modern comic need not be merely for show or to add a sense of adventure but rather can construct complex messages that hit close to home, making antiquity relevant again in accordance with a principle of allegory that is relatively rare in the world of contemporary pop fiction.

The Power of the Shaman

As far back as the most remote periods of time, many of the world's cultures have had shaman figures. These figures may be profoundly different from one another but all share certain basic traits, such as the power to contact friendly spirits, the ability to enter the realm of the supernatural, and the duty to help people by defeating evil spirits in battle.[17]

The similarities to the superhero genre are already evident.[18] Like the shamans, superheroes also break through the dull cloud of everyday life to fight in the supernatural world for the benefit of human beings.[19] As with shamans, superhuman powers cause the community to have conflicted feelings of respect and fear toward the superhero, who could theoretically use his gifts to help as much as to hurt (which brings to mind the persecution of mutants in the Marvel Universe or the long defamation campaign against Spider-Man launched by the fictitious New York newspaper the *Daily Bugle*).[20] An even greater similarity, which puts the superhero even closer to the shaman than to the hero of myth, lies in the origins of their superpowers. As Campbell writes:

> the priest is the socially initiated, ceremonially inducted member of a recognized religious organization, where he holds a certain rank and functions as the tenant of an office that was held by others before him, while the shaman is one who, as a consequence of a personal psychological crisis, has gained a certain power of his own.[21]

Receiving shamanistic power does not follow a predictable chain of events with fixed rules, but rather it usually occurs after a traumatic experience that symbolically recalls a journey from death to rebirth. Tradition has passed down examples of shamans who acquired their powers after a serious illness, after being struck by lightning, or being bitten by a snake,[22] just as many comics characters transform into superheroes after profoundly dramatic experiences: the explosion of a gamma bomb for the Hulk, an incident with a truck transporting radioactive waste for Daredevil, a war injury for Iron Man, and so on. Billy Batson even summons a lightning bolt that strikes him whenever he turns into Captain Marvel. If we go back to the first superhero, we can see that even Superman barely escaped the explosion of his home planet—and if that is not a near-death experience, what is?

According to tradition, the shaman's initial shock and the subsequent process of initiation later leads to a physical modification that can include the insertion of an amulet inside the body, as in the cases in which the initiate's intestines are transformed into quartz crystals that can then be projected into other people to cure or wound them.[23] This metamorphosis signals the shaman's transition from human to superhuman through the attribution of a special "armored" body, just as happens in the superhero genre when a superpowered character incorporates a foreign element (such as Wolverine's skeleton bonding with the superstrong fictional metal "adamantium" or Silver Surfer's and Colossus' metal skin as equivalents for the quartz intestines), or when the character acquires the ability to project energy onto others (from Dazzler's lasers to Cyclops's optical rays, the Human Torch's flames, and so on).

Furthermore, let's not forget that, when he fulfills his specifically thaumaturgic functions, the shaman usually wears a mask and a costume or paints his body with particular symbols that serve both to mark and to generate special powers. For example, a shamanic costume decorated with feathers represents the bird spirits that will lend the shaman the power of flight.[24] Merely by virtue of putting on this kind of visual-symbolic apparatus, Mircea Eliade writes, the shaman "transcends profane space and prepares to enter into contact with the spiritual world,"[25] just as the shamanic costume transforms its wearer into a supernatural being, according to the rule common in the religious imaginary that "one becomes what one displays."[26] And if one considers the presence of "borrowed" animal traits and costumes that express and provide superhuman powers in superhero comics, the similarities between shamans and superheroes become immediately evident. We have Spider-Man and Spider-Woman, Batman, Catwoman, the Black Panther, the Wasp, Ant-Man, the Falcon, Hawkman and Hawkgirl, the Vulture, the Rhino, the Octopus, Scorpion, Armadillo, the entire Serpent Squad, Beast, Wolverine, Tigra, White Tiger, the half-fish Marrina and Aquaman, the monstrous rat-man Vermin, Snowbird (who can transform into all the arctic animals), and Animal Man (who can mimic the characteristics of any animal). The list could go on, with countless other heroes and criminals whose powers are literally or symbolically mediated through the animal world.[27] In short, no other genre of fiction comes so close to reproducing the world of shamanistic forces, in which mysteriously elected human beings channel animal powers that are helpful one minute, harmful the next, fighting an ongoing battle for the fate of the common people.

This parallel with the shaman, then, seems to provide the best explanation for the use of masks and costumes, which is absolutely essential and unique to the superhero genre and which is only partially explained in practical terms in the stories themselves. The reason often cited by authors is that the costume serves to protect the heroes' identities and to prevent the villains from exacting revenge against their families or friends. If the matter could be reduced to that, however, Spider-Man could wear a duck or harlequin mask and his identity would be concealed just as well. Even more problematic is the fact that the hero's identity is often completely public. Since the sixties, every resident of the Marvel Universe has known that the leader of the Fantastic Four is Reed Richards and that his partner is Sue Storm; nonetheless, when the two go into battle they still wear special costumes and take on the roles of Mister Fantastic and the Invisible Woman. In other words, on closer examination, keeping the heroes' identity secret seems more like an excuse elaborated after the fact than an explanation as to why the authors "sensed" from the very beginning that the superhero genre required masks, costumes, and, in general, the metamorphosis of a normal human into a supernatural being endowed with symbolic visual markers.

It is completely natural to wonder whether recycling this cultural matrix was really among Stan Lee's or Siegel and Shuster's intentions in creating their most successful characters. An affirmative response would be presumptuous and on further thought even unnecessary. Maybe creating interesting, powerful, and mysterious characters could have in itself led our authors to delve into the same zones of the human psyche that in different cultures and different times have been translated into the figure of the mystic healer. In other words, one could interpret the similarities between shamans and superheroes not in terms of direct reference to earlier mythic forms but as the result of a general convergence of intentions.

Yet it may also be the case that authors consciously noticed shamanistic elements in the figure of the superhero and chose to weave them explicitly in their stories. One example can be found as early as April 1941 with the debut of Miss Fury, created by Tarpe Mills. The story opens with the socialite Marla Drake getting ready for a costume ball. She decides to wear a panther skin (left to her by an uncle) that was originally the ceremonial robe of an African shaman.[28] On the way to the party, Marla encounters an escaped criminal, captures him, and from then on decides to start fighting crime as a costumed hero. Marla/Miss Fury doesn't have

THE MYTH OF THE SUPERHERO

Marla Drake starts fighting as Miss Fury when she is
attacked on her way to a costume ball. © Pure Imagination

superpowers per se, but she uses special weapons that are incorporated
into her costume, such as claws and a tail (used as a whip), and exhibits
the physical prowess that characterizes heroes like Batman and Catwoman. Here, the symbolic connection between the abilities of the superheroine, the energy of the panther, and the function of the shaman is
well established.

In one 1973 storyline, Ghost Rider fights two Apache shamans: Snake
Dance, a "classic" shaman, who, it seems, can invoke animal spirits and
turn into a snake,[29] and his daughter Linda Littletrees, who, at a moment

Ghost Rider goes up against Linda Littletrees, the daughter
of an Apache shaman turned Satanist. © Marvel

of lowered inhibitions during her college years, becomes a Satanist (!) and
as a result mixes Native American magic with supernatural elements of
Christian origin.[30] If the mystics of the Native American tradition are represented as villains in this story arc, it is never without an enormous

THE MYTH OF THE SUPERHERO

amount of sympathy. The stories in this cycle, in fact, constantly stress the miserable conditions that government policy has reduced the natives to (which in turn leads Snake Dance to rebel), while Linda's metamorphosis represents well the danger of the loss or of the corruption of one's roots faced by the native who enters white civilization. These stories end up showing the devastating dilemma of Native American culture at the time: either remain isolated and stuck in the past (like Snake Dance) or become part of the majority at the risk of losing one's true self or turning into a monstrous hybrid.

Later on, more shamanistic heroes began to appear. In 1975, Marvel introduced White Tiger, a hero whose powers, though still fairly generic, come from a tiger-shaped amulet.[31] In 1978 DC created Vixen, an African heroine in possession of an amulet that enables her to borrow powers from animal spirits.[32] One year later, the next step was Marvel's new character Shaman,[33] a member of the First Nations who, after studying Western surgery in medical school, learns the ways of shamanism from his grandfather's spirit and gains powers like control of the elements and the ability to contact spirits (in an optimistic integration of cultures that enables him to overcome Linda Littletrees's dilemma).[34] Shortly thereafter in the early 1980s, two Marvel characters with the name Talisman came on the scene: an Australian aborigine shaman and Shaman's daughter and heir to her father's powers.[35]

In more recent years, the shamanistic tradition has appeared not only localized within specific characters like those mentioned above but also as an influence on originally nonshamanistic superheroes.

In the five-part story arc *Shaman*, from 1989–90, Dennis O'Neil rewrote the origins of Batman in mystical terms,[36] though they had been realistically rewritten just a few years earlier in the famous *Batman: Year One* by Frank Miller and David Mazzucchelli. O'Neil's story returns to the events in *Year One* from up close but adds a slightly earlier adventure where Bruce Wayne almost freezes to death in Alaska, is saved by a local shaman, and has a vision of a mysterious bat god during a healing ritual. Later, after his first disastrous foray into avenging crime, Bruce Wayne sits in his study, bleeding and meditating on his uncertain future, when he recalls the face of the man who healed him and his bat mask. In this story, unlike most other origin stories of Batman, it is not simply a bat flying through the window but the memory of a shamanistic experience that determines Bruce's choice of secret identity.

As the story progresses, the character's fighting skills and his ability to dodge enemy bullets are connected quite explicitly to the shamanistic

The spirit of a bat appears to a young Bruce Wayne in
a rewriting of Batman's origin story. © DC Comics

powers that he seems to derive from wearing a bat mask.[37] O'Neil, in
short, noticed that the superhero Batman and the shaman share the same
characteristics that I have described above, with the animal costume as
the catalyst of power and the various traumas in Wayne's life (his parents' murder, his near death on his first mission) as steps in the shaman's
initiation. At that point, all it took was a few more scenes (the rescue in
Alaska, the vision, a ritual experienced by Bruce himself) to rewrite the
character in a new yet familiar way that linked the shamanic figure with
what we already knew of Batman. In this way, the author also became a
critic and interpreter, since his own contribution to the character's development revealed something previously latent in the series.

In a 1997 prequel to the *Superman* series, *The Kents*, we find out that in
1860 an ancestor of Clark Kent's Earth family, Nathaniel Kent, had come
into possession of an Iroquois healing blanket with the symbol we now

THE MYTH OF THE SUPERHERO

recognize as Superman's. As Mary Glenowen—who would later become Nathaniel's wife and is half Native American—explains:

> the five lines [the sides of the symbol] represent each of the five tribes of the [Iroquois] confederation [. . .]; the symbol inside is a snake . . . one of the medicine animals. It represents healing and making whole. Deganawidah, the lawgiver and prophet who helped form the Iroquois confederation, spoke of a great hero to come from the sky who would unite East and West into one nation. I believe this was to be his sign.[38]

In other words, we are meant to understand that Superman's symbols and powers are the same as those of the Iroquois shaman and that the coming of Superman from Krypton and his superheroic mission had in fact been prophesied in that culture.

The Superman symbol is presented on a shamanistic healing blanket that was given to Clark's ancestor, Nathaniel Kent, by his future wife. Shamanism, then, was at least part of the inspiration behind Superman's heroic mission.
© DC Comics

Ezekiel—a businessman who gained powers similar to Spider-Man's—makes the superhero consider the possibility that his powers derive from a totemic spirit. © Marvel

Finally, let us recall the Marvel character Ezekiel, a business tycoon who obtained powers like Peter Parker's through a mystical ritual performed by a Peruvian shaman.[39] In one installment, Ezekiel reveals a completely new version of the famous origin story based on the bite of a

THE MYTH OF THE SUPERHERO

radioactive spider, explaining to Peter that perhaps Spider-Man's powers derive from the totemic spirit of the spider and not, as previously believed, radioactivity:

> Who and what you are bridges the gap between spider and man. But you're not the first. There are totemic powers that go back to the dawn of time. Their presence remains with us, almost like a race memory. Ask a shaman or an Egyptian priest [...]. We tell stories, put on masks, build statues and say prayers to a memory. The memory that once, when the world was new, great forces walked the Earth. Forces that bridged the gap between humans and other species.[40]

Once again, the author (here J. Michael Straczynski) has identified shamanistic elements in the tradition of both the character of Peter Parker and the superhero genre as a whole, perhaps evoking Eliade's passage on the powers that shamans have derived from snakebites. At that point, all it took was emphasizing that shared symbolic potential to truly make Spider-Man a modern shaman with the spirit of a spider.

New Golems

Despite the high visibility of mythological figures such as Wonder Woman or Thor or the more or less direct import of shamanism, the traditions that have most profoundly made a mark on the development of the superhero genre are undoubtedly Judeo-Christian. This is obviously due to the weight these cultures carry in American society; therefore, they are as much in the background of the authors as of the readers. Indeed, the very existence of pagan divinities and beings with godlike powers in the superhero universe occasionally calls for a disclaimer to reassure readers (and sometimes their parents), who for the most part belong to the monotheistic religions of the West. As early as a 1968 episode of the *Fantastic Four*, when the Invisible Woman describes Silver Surfer as "all-powerful," a Watcher (an alien who also has great power) exclaims, "Omnipotent? There is only one who deserves that name. And His only weapon ... is love!"[41] In one 1974 story, Hellstorm comes to the "primordial matrix" the universe is modeled after, and, not knowing whether this is what people call God, he is answered, "No! Like everything else, it's his creation."[42] In 1989, the West Coast Avengers wonder if the mutant Scarlet Witch can create life ex nihilo, but the

Hellstorm, son of Satan, is awestruck before
the mysterious "primordial matrix." © Marvel

witch Agatha Harkness firmly denies the possibility: "that power is reserved
unto but one force in this universe."[43] In a more recent Thor story, the god
of thunder is approached by a little boy who says: "Mama, look, it's Thor!
He claims to be a god, but Father O'Toole says he isn't," at which Thor patiently explains:

Far away from here, there exists a home of gods, a realm of eternal wonder called Asgard. 'Tis a place of great majesty and beauty whose residents strive to live just and beneficial lives. 'Tis not, however, Heaven. Nor is it home to He whose radiance dwarfs e'en our own.[44]

In short, every so often the authors demonstrated a need to ward off potential religious critiques, alluding to monotheism by making it clear that, however extraordinary their characters may be, there is still always a semi-undefined divine One watching from above that believers can see through their own faith.[45]

With regard to specific monotheistic religions, Simcha Weinstein recalls the impressive number of Jewish authors who have made major contributions to the development of the superhero genre.[46] Nor can one fail to mention that Jerry Siegel and Joe Shuster, the two creators of Superman, were Jewish and that they were followed by Jewish cultural figures such as Bob Kane and Bill Finger (the creators of Batman), Will Eisner (author of *The Spirit* and tireless experimentalist in the medium), Jack Kirby and Joe Simon (the creators of Captain America), Stan Lee, the reinventor of the entire genre for Marvel, and Chris Claremont, the writer who brought the X-Men series so much popular success.[47] Given this, would it even be possible not to see the culture of these authors reflected in the superhero comics themselves?

In the case of early Superman, written and drawn by Siegel and Shuster, there are numerous significant points of contact between Jewish culture and the founding elements of the series.[48] Superhuman strength, which had almost no modern literary precedents before Superman, may have been at least partly inspired by the biblical Samson. This similarity became even stronger once kryptonite was introduced in the forties, which famously gave Superman a weakness just like Samson's hair was for him. An analogous role in the establishment of Superman's powers and limitations can be attributed to the folkloric figure of the golem, the stalwart clay giant particularly known from the legend surrounding Judah Loew, the sixteenth-century rabbi from Prague who was said to have created it to protect Jews from persecution.[49] Just like Superman, the golem possesses superhuman strength and labors for the safety of others; and just like Superman, he has a weakness that makes it possible to destroy him—by simply erasing the magic writing on his forehead or mouth (depending on the tradition).

Also, just as the Kryptonians face the threat of extinction through the destruction of their planet at the beginning of Superman's mythology, the Jews must face the pharaoh's order to drown every male child in the book of Exodus. And, as Moses' mother saves him by putting him in a basket and entrusting him to the waters of the Nile, so Kal-El's parents save their child by putting him in a rocket headed for the planet Earth.[50] In short, Superman's Kryptonian origins echo the Moses story so precisely that it seems highly likely that, whether consciously or otherwise, the Jewish background of the authors had at least some measure of influence.

Superman's very name, Kal-El, includes the suffix "El," which means "God" in Hebrew (an abbreviation of Elohim) and appears in the names of biblical figures such as Daniel, Samuel, and the angels Gabriel and Michael.[51] And the archangel Michael, the great warrior who opposes Satan in the Jewish tradition, seems in turn an appropriate precursor to a savior sent from Krypton to fight evil on Earth.[52] The symbolism and background story of Superman therefore revived ancient Jewish tradition in a particular period, the late 1930s, when the persecution of the Jews in Europe could have easily inspired the desire for a new guardian angel.

The presence of these activated or at least "activatable" Jewish roots in the Superman comics was also depicted in a storyline that continued through three issues of *Superman, Man of Steel* (#80–82, Summer 1998), in which the authors commemorated the character's sixtieth anniversary by projecting him, in a certain sense, back to his origins, in a sort of alternative past where he finds himself defending the persecuted Jews in Hitler-occupied Poland. At a certain point in this story arc, Superman sneaks into the Jewish ghetto, where he witnesses Nazi horrors and befriends two boys, Moishe and Baruch—a direct homage to Siegel and Shuster. In fact, the two have just created a heroic comic book savior in order to give themselves hope and to be able to endure their difficult reality. Moishe writes the stories and Baruch does the illustrations.[53] "Our angel," Moishe calls the hero, explaining the idea to Superman himself. Baruch's grandfather is a bit taken aback: "Such a muscular angel? And what's this on his chest?" "It's his magic symbol, see?" Moishe replies, referring to the emblem on the character's costume. "And he's strong so he can fight tanks and guns and . . . he would save us." At this, the grandfather remarks that the hero in question seems more like a golem than an angel. This is an extremely clear illustration of the idea that the figure of Superman as we see him in 1998 and as he was conceived in 1938 is at least compatible with Jewish angels and golems and can also legitimately be understood as having been derived from them.[54]

THE MYTH OF THE SUPERHERO

The young boys Moishe and Baruch create superhero comics to
help them get through anti-Semitic persecution. © DC Comics

That said, would it be legitimate to claim that Superman *is* Jewish or
that Superman's character represents a Jewish figure in any general and
absolute sense? Yes and no, I would say. Superman, just like any successful
superhero, exhibits a strong combination of iconicity and flexibility,[55] due
to two things: (1) strong visual and narrative signs such as masks,[56] symbols, costumes, gadgets, and special abilities—all factors that allow variations while still maintaining a recognizable identity solidly connected to
the character's previous incarnations—and (2) seriality, which over the
course of months or years allows the gradual but also great variation in
the character. Their story is constantly being written and rewritten by
many different authors, each of whom might have portrayed the character according to different religious or cultural interpretations.

For example, Superman's coming to Earth, which could certainly be understood as a transfiguration of the Moses story, could just as easily, with slight changes, become a retelling of the coming of Christ (as we will see later). And where Baruch and Moishe saw Superman as a Jewish angel, in a recent story written by Kurt Busiek we have a member of the Christian faith praying to Superman as her guardian angel.[57] The same thing happened with Wonder Woman. If in the forties she came to life from a statue as a gift from a Greek goddess, as in the myth of Pygmalion, in an eighties' retelling she came from a clay figurine animated by a mysterious spark that fell from the sky, thus taking on connotations from Genesis.[58]

It is therefore not a question of determining which reading is "right" or "wrong," but noting that the stories of Superman or Wonder Woman lend themselves equally well to various possibilities with equally valid meanings, different aspects of which different authors have chosen to emphasize in their stories. In other words, it would be absurd to argue over whether Superman ("all" of Superman, intrinsically) is a Jewish golem, a Christian redeemer, or an Iroquois shaman; rather, it is necessary to recognize that different interpretations of the same basic features make him one type of figure and then another. The accelerated folkloric process described by O'Neil has generated different Supermen who can be seen as Jewish and then Christian and then shamanistic.

In fact, since all the stories in a given narrative universe are to be considered as having the same degree of reality in terms of the truth value of the subject represented (irrespective of differences in quality or level of success of the stories themselves),[59] it only takes one story in which Superman points to shamanism, one in which he represents Moses, and one in which he represents Jesus for the hero not to able to be legitimately described in terms of any of these three sources alone but to be considered equally a hybrid of all of them.

Returning to our main thread, I would like to note that, in addition to Superman, there are several other cases in which Jewish culture can be traced back to the roots of characters in the superhero world. As Weinstein has pointed out, Captain America's symbols and costume (created in 1941 by Simon and Kirby, both Jews)[60] have a dual meaning that connects them equally to American culture (explicitly) and to Jewish culture (implicitly). Captain America's weapon, from the second issue of the comic on, is a round shield with a five-pointed star in the center,[61] which clearly refers to the American flag and the idea of defense and protection. At the same time, it also recalls the symbol of the Jewish culture and religion, the

THE MYTH OF THE SUPERHERO

Superman is mistaken for an angel sent to Earth to
protect a devout Christian. © DC Comics

In the retelling of Wonder Woman's origin story in the 1980s, the heroine is made out of clay and brought to life by a mysterious spark from the sky and not by Aphrodite. © DC Comics

Star of David, or more precisely, the "Shield of David" characterized by the star (even if six-pointed). Similarly, Weinstein notes, the "A" on Captain America's mask can be seen not only as the initial of "America" but also as a reference to the aleph, the first letter of the word written on a golem's forehead to activate it. This connection is even more interesting, given that it is precisely when Captain America puts on his mask—thereby putting the A/aleph on his forehead—that he ceases to be a mere civilian and is "activated" as a superhero and defender of the community.[62]

The theme of the persecution of the Jews also serves as a subtext for many X-Men stories and for Marvel mutant stories in general. In this fictional universe, the characters who obtain their powers through technology or some sort of accident are known as "mutates" and are often admired and celebrated as heroes (like the Fantastic Four), whereas the ones who develop special abilities due to genetic mutation are called "mutants." The mutants are seen as "different" and are often the object of discrimination and hostility from the public.[63] When the X-Men originated amid the social tensions of the sixties and the growing visibility and

Captain America's shield, which has been round virtually since the character's origins, recalls David's shield and is used to fight the Anti-Semites (i.e., Nazis) in this comic from 1941. © Marvel

coming-to-consciousness of oppressed minorities, the difference between humans and mutants seems to have been established essentially to tap into the mood of the time and to acknowledge the theme of the "different" as persecuted. As the series evolved, the authors began to see this element of discrimination as an opportunity to connect the characters' persecution with anti-Semitism in general and the tragedy of the Holocaust more specifically.

The gradual transformation of archvillain Magneto must be read in this light. Leader of the evil mutants, initially described as a megalomaniac and general opponent of mutant oppression, Magneto was later "retconned"— retroactively changed—into a Jewish Auschwitz survivor whose plan to dominate humanity was a way to prevent a new Holocaust (of mutants) and deal with his guilt over not having been able to intervene during the Nazi exterminations (since his powers had not yet appeared).[64] The story "I, Magneto" (1978) is important in this sense. Here, the powerful mutant heads to South America to hunt down the Nazi criminals who evaded Nuremberg.[65] We are shown that in this case Magneto acts as an agent of justice and not for personal revenge, given that, even when he could easily kill a criminal who has caused his people so much suffering, Magneto restricts himself to capturing him and sending him to be tried in Israel.

Magneto, a Holocaust survivor, captures the Nazi criminals who had escaped Nuremberg in South America. His decision to hand them over to the authorities instead of killing them demonstrates a desire for justice, not revenge. © Marvel

Later on, Magneto encounters some mysterious Western agents who kill his girlfriend and accuse him of having caught Nazis who were involved in their secret service, suggesting that in the future he act with more diplomacy and capture only criminals who work for the Soviet Union (this is during the Cold War). It is at this point that Magneto bursts into violence, killing the agents and vowing to dominate humanity because it has become shortsighted and corrupt. If anyone were to suggest that the character Magneto described the Jews as power-hungry

THE MYTH OF THE SUPERHERO

The Thing in one of his first appearances, when he resembled
a giant made of living clay. © Marvel

villains, this story shows that Jewish culture and the experience of the
Holocaust transformed Magneto into an idealist who wanted justice, not
a criminal. Instead, it was the most ruthless fringes of the secret services
that led Magneto to his career of crime and violence.

Another notable example of Jewishization through retroactive continuity is found in the revision of Ben Grimm (the Thing in the Fantastic
Four) as a Jew in a 2002 story entitled "Remembrance of Things Past."[66]
I should also say right off that if there's one superhero who truly seems
like a golem, it is undoubtedly Ben Grimm, who is literally a living mass of
rock; especially in his first incarnation back in the early sixties, where he
is drawn in thick, rough lines, that make him resemble the ancient clay
giant even more.[67]

The story "Remembrance of Things Past" has two parallel levels of
time: the present, in which Ben revisits the street where he grew up and
finds himself defending Sheckerberg, a Jewish pawnshop owner, from a
criminal racket; and the past, in which we see the young Ben hanging
around with a group of local thugs and robbing the same Sheckerberg of
his most prized possession: a Star of David pendant. At the end of the
story, Ben defeats the criminals who are tormenting Sheckerberg, but
the old man gets wounded in the struggle and lies in the doorway, perhaps on the threshold of death, in front of the hero. The same superstrength that enabled the Thing to defeat his enemies has become an ob-
stacle that hinders him from performing CPR without killing Sheckerberg.

The Thing rediscovers a connection to his Jewish roots as he says
a prayer for his old neighbor Sheckerberg. © Marvel

When matter fails, the last hope becomes faith, a faith that emerges in
Ben as a prayer with near-forgotten words (with an "uhm" of uncertainty
right in the middle of the recitation).

Whether the effect of the prayer or a stroke of luck, Sheckerberg
comes to and engages Ben in a dialogue in which the two discuss the hero's
Judaism, that is, an element that, as we are now being told, has always been
present in the world of the Fantastic Four but had never been addressed in
the stories published in the previous decades. In fact, Sheckerberg com-
ments: "All these years in the news, they never mention you're Jewish. I
thought maybe you were ashamed of it a little." "Nah, that ain't it," the
Thing replies. "I don't talk it up is all. Figure there's enough trouble in this
world without people thinkin' Jews are all monsters like me."

The rewriting of Ben Grimm's identity, therefore, is cleverly and co-
herently combined with the new stories, furnishing a plausible reason for
the failure to mention such an important element. This is reinforced by
the fact that Ben is here described to us as a longtime nonpracticing Jew
who, in abandoning the old ways and becoming a famous hero, left behind his own original culture, similar to many Jews who had been forced
by social pressure to change their names to be more easily accepted. This

THE MYTH OF THE SUPERHERO

adds depth to the character and also makes the Jewishization of Ben Grimm acceptable to fans, allowing it to stand up to the scrutiny of the avid followers who, as is their right, like to test the compatibility of any serial development with its earlier stories. For fans, episodes of the Fantastic Four from previous decades where Ben Grimm breaks the Sabbath or gorges himself on pork would not serve to contradict what is said in "Remembrance of Things Past." On the contrary, seeing these apparent contradictions would reinforce the idea of the Jew who had lost himself, who had left his roots behind.

At the end of the story, Ben tries to give Sheckerberg back the Star of David that had been stolen from him, but the old man suggests that Ben keep it, and Ben places it in a compartment of his belt. In this way, his reconciliation with Judaism is masterfully combined with the exigencies of the serial form. That Star of David that Ben will carry with him unseen, that faith he will keep inside that isn't necessarily demonstrated in religious practice, will certainly belong to the identity of the character from now on. In spite of this, as if remaining behind the scenes, knowing that the Thing is a Jew will not limit possible future events in the series. In other words, even if Martians attack Earth on a Saturday, Ben Grimm could still be on the front lines.

The Gospel According to Superheroes

If Judaism has left an important mark on the superhero genre, the contribution of Christianity has been equally extensive and pervasive and, being the religion that the majority of readers identify with, also presents particular problems of representation. It is unlikely that there are legions of the devotees today of Olympic or Norse gods who would take offense at a representation of Hercules or Thor in comics. The same cannot be said of the average reader seeing superhero versions of Jesus, Mary, or the saints springing into action.

Note, that if the idea of Jesus as a superhero seems unacceptable, this comes from a purely cultural prohibition and not from characteristics intrinsic to the superhero genre or scriptural material (seen from a strictly narrative standpoint), as the rare cases that this prohibition is broken demonstrate. Thus, in the film *Jesus Christ Vampire Hunter* (Lee Demarbre, Canada 2001), Jesus Christ returns to Earth to fight monsters and mad scientists, thereby completely fulfilling the function of the superhero.[68] When Jesus, for example, is attacked by a mob of vampires, not having water anywhere nearby, he blesses a beer and uses it against his enemies; later on, Jesus doubles himself to fight two enemies at the same time, and to the bad guy who asks him how it was possible, he replies: "I'm everywhere." And at the end of the film, inevitably, Jesus brings a dead person back to life.

Even though these events can seem jarring, if we investigate their narrative function, we can note that the film does not make up new powers for the protagonist but simply projects the individual traits of the religious tradition onto the plane of adventure and fantasy, using Christianity in the same way that Marvel and DC typically use the pantheons of pagan traditions. Conversely, the same powers attributed to Jesus in the film are also represented with complete naturalness in the superhero universes of the major comics—just think of the fact that the mutant Gambit can transform everyday objects into weapons by charging them with energy (similar to the case of the holy beer); Jamie Madrox, the Multiple Man, can create copies of himself, while DC's Solomon Grundy and Marvel's ninja group the Hand have the ability to revive the dead. The only thing missing in these comics is the explicit connection of these superpowers with the Christian sacred.[69]

Consequently, Christianity is both present and absent in superhero comics. It is ambiguously referenced, as in the cases I have cited of the Watcher or Thor, which pay homage to a very vague divine One, so that any reader looking for the Christian God can find him, but the discourse is not further developed in a clear and organic way. In short, a certain plausible deniability is maintained, as when a government authorizes a particular operation only if, in case of failure, it would be possible to deny any connection with it.

Superheroes who belong to faiths such as Catholicism or Islam—minority faiths in the United States compared with all the Protestant faiths combined—are clearly represented in superhero stories to confer dignity on to the minorities that these religions represent.[70] However, the religious practices of the majority of superheroes are purposely left vague. One gets the impression that almost all the heroes adhere to some sort of Protestant creed that they do not actually practice, or only practice behind the scenes, perhaps going to church between one narrative sequence and the next. In the rare cases in which superheroes are seen with a member of the clergy it is usually for weddings or funerals, occasions that are too interesting dramatically to be eliminated from the

THE MYTH OF THE SUPERHERO

narrative world, and furthermore, that are in no way compromising, since attending a friend's funeral or wedding in a holy building does not automatically mean a person is of the same religion.

Attempts to insert any explicitly Christian supernatural elements have been rare and have had little publishing success—a reader who is punctilious with regard to faith could resent it, whereas Christian readers of lesser conviction might prefer their catechism in church or on religious occasions rather than during their enjoyment of adventure movies or comics. It is thus no surprise that Marvel's *Illuminator* series only lasted a few issues, with a protagonist who receives his powers directly from God ("like a nuke from Heaven") and acts like a true "hero who keeps the faith."[71] Regarding the DC Universe, one must also mention a secondary character, the angel Zauriel,[72] introduced by Grant Morrison primarily because the publishers had forbidden him to use the character of Hawkman, thus pushing Morrison to see angels more as simple human figures with wings (and therefore good doubles for Hawkman) than as elements of faith or theology.[73] At that point the best thing to do with the angel Zauriel was to transform him into a DC Thor, with the Judeo-Christian tradition substituted by the Norse.[74] The promise is kept and in fact Zauriel appeared at the center of battles between Heaven and Earth that unfolded in the same way as such events did in several similar stories with protagonists from pagan myth[75]— such as for example the Amazon invasion of Earth in the DC miniseries *Amazons Attack*. This development reveals yet another problem related to the introduction of the dominant religion within the pagan-inclined superhero world, represented by the loss of the privileged condition of Christianity as opposed to other traditions. Put to the test within the narrative conventions of the superhero genre, the angels aren't all that distinguishable from the rowdy Scandinavian divinities or the alluring Amazons: in fact, in the former case they risk losing us for being less entertaining, in the latter for being less sexy.

The issue is different for the representation of demons from the Christian tradition, which can provide a rich arsenal of supercriminals for our heroes to fight, as long as they are used with a certain degree of tact. In the Marvel Universe, for example, there's an extremely powerful creature who lives underground, loves to tempt mortals, and is called Mephisto, but who the publisher's official guides specify is *not* the devil of the Christian tradition. This is Marvel's official position on Mephisto, published in 2005:

Mephisto rules a fiery nether realm that he refers to as Hell or Hades, though it is neither the Biblical Hell nor Pluto's Olympian Hades [...]. Mephisto delights in impersonating the Biblical Satan. Empowered by the souls of the damned, he often strikes deceptive bargains with the living. Mephisto takes particular interest in the souls of extremely powerful or exceptionally pure beings.[76]

In short, Mephisto might seem like the Christian devil, but he isn't; he may call Hell his home if he so desires, but it remains merely his opinion. In short, the reader who doesn't worry about these things finds in Marvel comics the story of a Mephisto that, let's admit it, really *is* that devil, whereas the concerned censor is reminded that he is just a double. The same 2005 guide explains that the Marvel Universe contains other extradimensional entities similar to Mephisto and that these creatures have exploited our belief that there is only one true source of evil in the universe to pretend to be the *real* Satan and to call "Hell" their realms.[77]

Thanks to this game of mirrors conducted by countless demons in disguise, authors find themselves in the condition of being able to represent all the infernal powers they want, having shrewdly made it impossible to demonstrate that this or that Satan is the "official" Christian one even when he seems to appear in person (as in many Ghost Rider stories).[78] Or rather, they construct the impression that the real devil never appears, that he remains concealed at an even lower and more evil level than his various doubles in a sort of reflection of that sky in where, above the great Thor, there must still be an entity above him. And if these devices seem terribly forced on the part of comics writers, it only goes to show that the underlying issue is rather serious and must be addressed in one way or another.

The issue is also different with Christian symbols, especially Christological ones that may appear in superhero comics. For the majority of religious readers, certain similarities between the superhero world and the Christian tradition ultimately create a sense of familiarity, of recognition. If writers can avoid clichés in the visual and narrative fabric of the stories the comics will not have the tone of a pedantic sermon and will instead draw the reader into the pleasurable game of deciphering a code that he already knows. For example, take the cover of the renowned graphic novel *The Death of Captain Marvel* by Jim Starlin,[79] in which the galactic hero, who dies of cancer over the course of the story, is lying in the arms of Death in a pose that undeniably refers to Michelangelo's *Pietà*. The connection between the superhero and the sacrifice of Jesus is here sanctioned by the fact that Captain Marvel *literally* takes the place of the dead Christ in a cultural reference familiar to everyone. At the same time the recognition of the visual source and the construction of the message are left up to (and not imposed on) the reader, who in fact is free to choose how far to go with it—that is, whether to stop at the artistic reference, as a graphic-compositional device and postmodern wink or whether to go further to consider the religious implications offered by the subject of the *Pietà*.

The reference to Michelangelo's masterpiece—with its static and corpulent monumentality accented by heavy, thick lines—thus creates a significant contrast to the figures of the heroes in the background. They

Captain Marvel's dead body unmistakably recalls Jesus in Michelangelo's *Pietà*. © Marvel

appear to be caught in a haphazard rescue attempt, suspended in the distance of an undefined empty space and even more two-dimensional and surreal. Their effort is visually rendered as powerless and compared to an unavoidable and "unshakeable" fate. The illustration, therefore, doesn't just translate Captain Marvel into the dead Jesus, but it also describes death as a necessary event that comes from a realm out of reach for human beings and shows it as the most absolute reality of what happens in the chaotic and transient realm of earthly life.

The Crucifixion of Peter Parker

In the wake of Starlin's inspired image of Captain Marvel, it is possible to trace significant Christian implications in the figure of the superhero in general. Jesus' paradoxical double nature, both human and divine, equal to all others yet singular and special, seems to somehow respond to the idea of the dual identity of the superhero, who blends in with the common people and then is "transfigured" by his costume and performs "miracles" to save the community. The superhero, after all, in the most basic definition, is a person with exceptional powers who voluntarily sacrifices himself (causing harm to his own private life, risking death, and sometimes actually dying) to use those powers to serve others and the common good.

In this sense, worthy of note are the Christological markers found in the film *Spider-Man 2* (Sam Raimi, 2004). The entire film develops a reflection on the concept of ethical choice, introducing the idea that it is possible for Peter Parker to give up his own superpowers and therefore his identity as Spider-Man. The protagonist, therefore, is no longer forced to act because of an unexpected, unintentional accident with a genetically modified spider (radioactive in the original comic) but rather can choose whether to remain a superhero and fight for the common good (according to the criterion that "from great power comes great responsibility") or become a young man like any other, who can attend college and have a relationship with Mary Jane. In his decision to embrace the heroic life, Peter Parker consciously sacrifices a good part of that private life and consequently reaches greater maturity. Exploits like defeating criminals are the same in the comic and the first film in the series, but here they take on a different meaning, insofar as they are the products of a voluntary decision and therefore only now can be seen as fully ethical. Indeed, without the possibility of choice, ethics could not logically be a factor.

Just as there's no "good will" in the slot machine that lets me win or in the traffic light that lets me pass through without harm, a character for whom heroism is an absolute obligation could not truly be heroic. And, as it is a fundamental point of Christian doctrine that Jesus sacrificed himself voluntarily in order to redeem humanity (otherwise, again, it would not be a real question of sacrifice), it is precisely in *Spider-Man 2* that the representation of the process of choice seems to establish a stronger parallel between the superhero and Jesus, as is clearly symbolized in the subway scene.

Doctor Octopus, to distract Spider-Man during a battle, cuts the brakes on a subway train, which then barrels toward the end of the line. Faced with such a situation, Spider-Man puts his role as protector over that of avenger and lets Octopus escape so he can focus on saving the passengers in the train. Spider-Man leaps in front of the first car and tries to stop the train with his superstrength by planting his feet on the track, which results only in injuring his knee. Then Spider-Man shoots webs onto the walls on both sides of the train, trying to anchor himself to the surrounding buildings. In doing so, he necessarily stretches out his arms and assumes the position of Christ on the cross, the tears in his costume from his fight with Octopus now appearing as a reference to the wound in Jesus' side.[80]

The web seems to work and the train slows down, but, between the train pushing forward and the spiderwebs holding Spider-Man, the pressure on the hero's body is immense. His costume rips, giving the impression of his body being slashed from the inside out. Tobey Maguire's face is contorted with pain and strain, and now it seems clear that the screenwriters

The superhero's symbolic crucifixion on a subway train in the movie
Spider-Man 2. © Columbia Pictures

had him remove his mask prior to this segment precisely to show the torment of the situation more clearly. For Spider-Man, saving the passengers is no longer a matter of intelligence, agility, or skill in battle but only endurance and suffering, with the hope (the faith?) that this horrible pain won't be in vain (Spider-Man doesn't know whether he will really be able to stop the train in time). Note that if Spider-Man chose his own good over that of others, he could stop the torment at any moment: indeed, he would only have to let go of the webs on one side to be thrown to the other, abandoning the train and its passengers to certain disaster. This parallel with Jesus' crucifixion, therefore, is not a just a cliché visual reference but a profound, well-conceived metaphor, in which the elements and significance of the biblical event are effectively transposed onto the cinematic medium and the superhero culture.

As if for greater emphasis, or perhaps for consistency in tone and theme, the reference to the crucifixion goes on for a short time in the following part of the sequence. Spider-Man succeeds in stopping the train—of course at the last possible moment—and faints from stress and relief. To keep him from falling, two passengers hold him up under the arms, visually mimicking one of the many representations of the deposition of Christ's body so common in artistic tradition. The body is brought inside the crowded car and passed over the passengers' heads. The narrative motive is practical, since Spider-Man has to be moved to a place where he can be laid down, but the high camera angle again emphasizes Maguire's pose with his arms open in the form of a cross, thus creating the symbolic image of a resurrected Jesus gliding above a humanity who has been saved by and is grateful to their savior.[81]

The "deposition" of the superhero in *Spider-Man 2*. © Columbia Pictures

THE MYTH OF THE SUPERHERO

The "resurrection" of the superhero in *Spider-Man 2*. © Columbia Pictures

Our Superman, Who Art in Heaven

As I mentioned earlier, the commonalities between Christian and Jewish cultures enable writers to recodify the profound Jewish roots of the superhero comic, at times making Superman, perhaps born as Moses or a golem, into a Christian angel or even a sort of crypto-Jesus.[82] The simple fact that Superman comes down to Earth as an infant who will become the protector and savior of humanity is more than enough to encourage a reading or rereading of the character from a Christological perspective, a reading that the director and screenwriters of *Superman: The Movie* (Richard Donner, 1978) insisted on sometimes to the point of preachiness.

Even in the film's beginning sequences, the representation of Kryptonians in clothing shining with light gives them the appearance of angels or at least of superhuman, semidivine beings, so that Superman's appearance on Earth later seems symbolically like a fall from Paradise. At the beginning we also discover that Jor-El, father of the future Superman, had been entrusted with the thankless task of judging three criminals (dressed in black, of course), whose leader, the rebel Zod, tempts Jor-El by promising him enormous power if he would join their uprising against the planet's government. As it becomes clear that Jor-El won't give in, Zod shouts to him menacingly that one day he will have to bow before him, before Zod is flung into the Phantom Zone. In accordance with a completely transparent symbolism and an intense work of semantic compression, Jor-El then comes to incarnate both God and Jesus at the same time—the first, when he relegates the rebel Zod/Satan to the Phantom Zone / Hell; the second, when he resists a proposal that cannot

The trial against Zod and his accomplices, where Zod (*center*) tempts Superman's father, Jor-El (*left*), by inviting him to join his rebellion from *Superman: The Movie*. © Warner Bros.

but recall Jesus' third temptation in the desert: "Again, the devil took him up on an exceedingly high mountain, and showed him all the kingdoms of the world and their glory. And he said to him, 'All these things I will give you if you will fall down and worship me'" (Matthew 4:8–9).[83]

The roles of Jor-El/God and Kal-El/Christ become clearly defined once the child arrives on Earth. When the Kents find the little one fallen from the sky, Martha confesses: "All these years, as happy as we've been, how I prayed and prayed the good Lord would see fit to give us a child," thus becoming Mary who receives a son directly from God and at the same time defining Kal-El as Jesus.[84] Jonathan Kent, Kal-El's adoptive father, is less fortunate, dying fairly early on in the film from a heart attack[85] to make room for the privileged relationship between Superman/Jesus and the hologram of Jor-El, luminous and immaterial heavenly father who guides Superman on his mission among the mortals. And his teachings have messianic content that requires no particular comment:

> Because even though you've been raised as a human being, you are not one of them. You have great powers, only some of which you have as yet discovered. Live as one of them, Kal-El, to discover where your strength and your power are needed. Always hold in your heart the pride of your special heritage. They can be a great people, Kal-El, they wish to be. They only lack the light to show the way. For this reason above all, their capacity for good, I have sent them you … my only son.[86]

THE MYTH OF THE SUPERHERO

The holographic image of Jor-El resembles a symbolic representation of the Christian God in this scene from *Superman: The Movie.* © Warner Bros.

Add to this the fact that in this film Superman begins his mission at the age of thirty,[87] like Jesus, or that Luthor lives underground like Satan, which has no counterpart in the comic; also add that at the end of the movie Superman brings Lois Lane (Lois Lazarus?) back to life, and you understand how every significant narrative element in the script was planned to construct a coherent image of Superman as a Christ figure. Furthermore, it's not as if it took much effort: adding a phrase here and a short scene there was enough to bend the Superman story and achieve an effective and flawless reinvention of that of Christ. And material differences (budget, production, distribution) aside, the differences in concept between *Superman: The Movie* and a seemingly antithetical film like *Jesus Christ Vampire Hunter* are in truth slight. The biggest, if not the only, difference in their treatment of the hero is that the producers of *Superman* didn't call their protagonist Jesus, and by doing so, were free to put Jesus in a cape and tights not only without offending anybody but instead actually receiving the overwhelming approval of general paying audiences.[88]

Another notable Christian symbol was added to the Superman comics tradition according to a process quite common in the genre, by which certain visual and narrative elements that have emerged by chance during a given character's process of evolution become established in the series because the authors (whether consciously or otherwise) accept them as particularly fitting, in a word, as "right." This seems to be the case for an association that can now be read in many representations of the symbol on Superman's chest. In the character's early stories, the logo with the "S" lacked a clearly defined look and varied in shape and color from one story

In the midst of action, as in this image where
Superman saves innocent people from a collapsing
building, the symbol on his costume takes the shape
of a heart, calling to mind the Sacred Heart of Jesus.
© DC Comics

to the next. In its first appearance, it was a yellow triangle with a yellow
"S." Later on, it was shown in the form of a pentagon or cut diamond
shape resembling a heraldic shield with curved lower borders, with an "S"
sometimes bordered in red, sometimes in yellow. Whether this was due
to thoughtlessness on the part of the authors or, on the contrary, a desire
to experiment before deciding on a definite design, in any case over time
the symbol was established as the version we know today: a pentagon

representing a diamond (a symbol of strength and constancy), with a red "S" in the middle that evokes a serpent (a symbol of prudence), endowed with great graphic dynamism, like a spring ready to be released—perfect, therefore, for expressing the character's extraordinary energy.[89]

To these symbols, noted in various places, at least one more can be added: the heart. It is true that the emblem itself has a simple pentagonal shape, but when Superman lifts his arms to fly or to fight (in other words, precisely when he is acting as a superhero) the top of the symbol bends in the middle, thus forming the graphic shape of the human heart. Considering that the colors of this figure are those traditionally associated with fire, it doesn't seem far-fetched to claim that Superman's crest today vacillates between the cut diamond (with the meanings I have just laid out) and the eminently Catholic symbol of the Sacred Heart of Jesus, also known as the flaming heart.[90] Given that the Sacred Heart represents Jesus' love for humanity, it thus seems particularly appropriate that this is manifested especially when Superman is in action, when, in short, he experiences most intensely his mission of self-sacrifice at the service of humankind.[91]

Silver Surfer and the Sins of the World

The last hero with Christological implications who would be impossible to leave out is Silver Surfer. He was conceptualized in 1966 by Stan Lee and Jack Kirby for a three-part story that presented the first clash between the Fantastic Four and the entity Galactus, a near-omnipotent cosmic being who feeds on energy from planets and was preparing to devour Earth.[92] Kirby had thought of adding a herald for Galactus to the story and presented Lee with a drawing of a mysterious silver-colored surfer. Lee was struck by the figure's noble, spiritual look, like a "space-born apostle [. . .] of almost religious purity,"[93] as he later wrote, and he decided to develop the potential symbolism expressed by that image to make Silver Surfer something like the Christ of Marvel.

This role can already be read within the original Galactus trilogy. Here, Silver Surfer comes to Earth because of Galactus, but thanks to the Thing's girlfriend, Alicia Masters, comes to know the qualities of the human race and courageously decides to rebel against his master and as punishment is imprisoned on Earth. Even if in a slightly vague and altered way, due to the story's narrative demands, the idea is that Silver Surfer acts as a mediator between human beings and a destructive divinity who can only be appeased through the sacrifice of the mediator himself—who thereby fulfills the role of Christ in the passage from the Old to the New Testament. Moreover, with Silver Surfer Jesus' dual human and divine nature is profoundly reflected in a figure in which the physiological-human component, shown in the character's nudity,[94] and the spiritual-divine component, rendered through the shining and impenetrable silver skin, seem inextricably fused.

The Christ-like nature of Silver Surfer is most evident in 1968 when he becomes the hero of his own monthly comic with text by Stan Lee and drawings by John Buscema Sr. In the opening of the first issue, we see a space pod in flames plummeting through the atmosphere (like a bitter reminder, by contrast, to the protagonist's earthly prison) and Silver Surfer diving to save the unfortunate pilot. After coming to his rescue, Silver Surfer leads him to an American aircraft carrier where he is able to receive medical care, but the army, suspicious of the mysterious apparition, sends two war planes to attack the alien.[95] A few seconds later, the misunderstood hero is surfing over Moscow and Beijing, but even there he is met by missiles launched against him by the local military. These scenes immediately introduce what will be a fundamental theme in the stories of this run: that is, the inextricable mix of hate and fear humans have for their own benefactor, here Silver Surfer, whose interventions to assist humanity reach the highest degree of self-abnegation and self-sacrifice.

The same thing happens when we are told about Silver Surfer's past, again centered on the key theme of sacrifice. We learn that Norrin Radd (Surfer's original name) comes from the highly evolved and utopian planet Zenn-La. When Galactus threatened to devour that world, Norrin decided to give up his own liberty (and the woman he loved), offering his services as herald for Galactus in exchange for rescuing the planet. Galactus accepts his offer and gives Norrin the silver covering that protects him from the rigors of space, together with a form of energy known as Power Cosmic that allows him to transform matter at will.

In the superhero tradition, in which characters often acquire their superpowers by birth (X-Men), technology (Iron Man), or uncontrollable accidents (Spider-Man, Daredevil), Silver Surfer stands out: his special gifts are the product of a free choice of self-sacrifice and of renouncing all that his life had been. Thus there is in Silver Surfer the markedly Christian theme of the individual who sacrifices himself for the safety of the world and suffers to save even those who hate him.

In the second story in the series, we witness other brief acts of human hostility against Silver Surfer and another big test for the hero.[96] When

THE MYTH OF THE SUPERHERO

the alien race Badoon attacks Earth, Silver Surfer doesn't hesitate to defend it for a second, countering the rockets and monsters of the invaders with blasts of Power Cosmic. There is one small problem: everything that is Badoon is invisible to the human eye, and because of this the witnesses of the battle from Earth only see big explosions and Silver Surfer rushing back and forth between them. So they end up believing that it was the hero himself who attacked the planet. And once again his prize for saving human lives is a blast of missiles from the army. A few stories later, a descendent of the famous Dr. Frankenstein creates a double of Silver Surfer, and when this double attacks a European village, obviously everyone believes that our hero is the guilty party.[97]

Reading these Silver Surfer stories from the late sixties strongly brings to mind the Sermon on the Mount: "Blessed are the peacemakers, for they shall be called sons of God. Blessed are those who are persecuted for righteousness' sake, for theirs is the kingdom of heaven" (Matthew 5:9–10). The biblical reference seems all the more justified if one notes that in one of these stories the villain is none other than Mephisto, offended by Silver Surfer's goodness and purity of heart and worried about the positive changes he could bring to Earth were the humans to cease pursuing him.[98] Thus Mephisto brings the Surfer to Hell and offers him three temptations: enormous wealth, beautiful women, or a galactic empire he could rule—only if, obviously, he decides to accept Mephisto as his lord. Silver Surfer's predictable rejection is followed by a battle with hellish monsters unleashed by Mephisto for revenge. Without a doubt, the religious framework is there and is quite strong, but it is well balanced with more typical superheroic elements of adventure and action, enabling the series to avoid turning off its potential audience with too moralistic of a message.[99]

The messianic tones that inform the figure of the Silver Surfer reach their peak in the miniseries *Requiem* (2007), which, as the title suggests, tells the story of the hero's death.[100] As happened with Captain Marvel, Silver Surfer also ends his days not in a pyrotechnic battle against the forces of evil but with a long and intractable illness, which provides him with the occasion for personal reflection and meditation on the meaning of his experience. Having returned to Zenn-La to spend his final days there, the dying Silver Surfer becomes the object of a true pilgrimage that takes on the forms of a religious ritual. The Zenn-Lavians want to see the hero who sacrificed himself for their planet; they want to thank him and be inspired by him. Those who go to see Silver Surfer receive,

Mephisto, offended by Silver Surfer's moral purity, tries to bribe him by offering him enormous wealth. © Marvel

like a kind of Eucharist, what is called the "mark of Norrin," a small spot of light on the palm that in difficult moments will instill in them some of the Silver Surfer's calm and compassion. In this way, the saga of Norrin Radd comes to a narrative and symbolic conclusion, describing the most natural outcome of the coming of any prophet and redeemer—that is, sharing a message, developing an idea into a religion, and replacing the lone individual with a vast community of believers that are "marked" by the effects of the original message.

The above are cases in which the presence of a messianic superhero seems to create a single message of hope in the ultimate redemption of the human race—a redemption that Mephisto feared possible in the sixties and that Silver Surfer had essentially achieved on Zenn-La in the

THE MYTH OF THE SUPERHERO

The "mark of Norrin" brings inner peace to those who receive it from the dying surfer. © Marvel

early 2000s. However, there are also interesting cases in which the same points of departure are interpreted differently by writers who make reference to allegories from other religious orientations. The most important example is the Silver Surfer miniseries *In Thy Name*,[101] published a few months after the hero's death in *Requiem* but technically set in a previous time. Here, Silver Surfer comes into contact with two different space cultures: the Ama, aristocratic and long-limbed admirers of reason who have created a seemingly perfect society, and the Brekk, who are instead ugly, short, poor, impulsive, and devout followers of a religion based on the second coming of a mysterious messenger from the sky. It goes without saying that the Brekk will see Silver Surfer in this role. But

Myth and Religion

not so fast—there's a catch. In reality, the Ama, who intend to wage war against the Brekk but want to seem like the victims, have arranged events to make Silver Surfer look like the Brekk's long-awaited messiah, hoping that this will instill such self-confidence in them that the Brekk will finally declare a war that had been in the air for a long time. To this end, once the Brekk have begun worshipping Silver Surfer, the Ama try to provoke a violent reaction from them by kidnapping their supposed messiah and crucifying (!) him, complete with galactic surfboard at the top of the cross to match the spot where, according to the Gospel, the words "This is the king of the Jews" were inscribed.

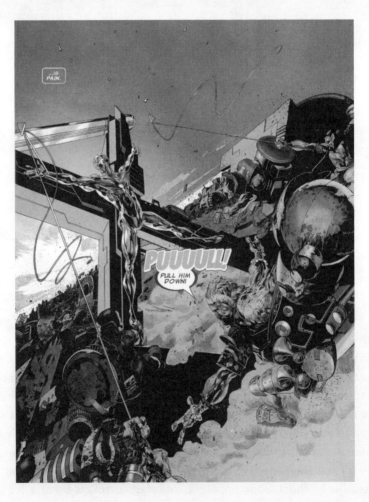

The Brekk free Silver Surfer, who was crucified by the Ama.
© Marvel

THE MYTH OF THE SUPERHERO

In the end, all the intrigues having been revealed, Silver Surfer uses a threat to force the leaders of the two cultures to meet and try to reconcile, but all they agree on is to save appearances by declaring war on each other at the exact same instant, then accusing each other in front of their respective populations. The story ends bitterly, with Silver Surfer far off in space contemplating the explosions from the conflict he was unable to avert.

The traditional elements of the messianic Silver Surfer are pretty much all there, but something has gone wrong; the mechanism no longer works. The hero's purity and unshakeable ethics are now manipulated by political maneuvers that are much more diabolical than Mephisto's ineffectual temptations; the Christological symbols are void of any intrinsic value and are actually used for purposes of death and oppression; the sacrifice occurs, complete with a crucifixion, but it serves to deceive and not to free. Perhaps even more significant is the fact that Silver Surfer, whom the superhero comics expert knows well as a redemptive figure, is here unable to redeem or save a thing, neither as a messiah nor as a diplomat. *In Thy Name* presents a vision of religion and devotion that is much more cynical and pessimistic than the one presented in *Requiem*. In fact, the two texts act almost as complements to each other, with the first showing the redemptive potential of a peacefully shared faith and the second presenting the risks that derive from the collision of politics and religion, with the latter becoming corrupted into a cold instrument of mass control.

The addition of this dark perspective on such a traditionally stable and in his own way reassuring character is perhaps just a sign of the times when *In Thy Name* was published, an early 2008 marked everywhere in the United States by a heavy recession, low morale over the ongoing war in Iraq and the elusive Osama Bin Laden, and a frustration with the Bush administration that by that point had taken over the whole country, including many Republicans. Perhaps *Requiem* described things as the audience might have wished them to be, but *In Thy Name* concentrated unflinchingly on how things seemed to really be at the time.

Because of the similarity in content, I can't help but mention a minor *Legion of Monsters* story from 1976, which is truly of no artistic relevance, but which was strangely reprinted twice in 2007,[102] thus in the same period and climate as *In Thy Name*. The story recounts the coming to Earth of Starseed, a superhuman creature with completely gold skin (an obvious

A dying Starseed shows the Marvel monsters the salvation he could have given them had they not let themselves be dominated by their instincts. © Marvel

reference to Surfer's silver body), who, as fate has it, is met on arrival only by some of the most disturbing creatures in the Marvel Universe: the Werewolf, Morbius the Living Vampire, Man-Thing (a monster made out of semi-sentient mud), and the spirit of vengeance Ghost Rider. Starseed is unfazed by the strangeness of this welcoming committee and

THE MYTH OF THE SUPERHERO

tells his story as the last representative of an ancient race who, after millennia of space travel, has acquired superior knowledge and culture. But fate plotted against Starseed and his intentions to share his gifts with humankind.

Man-Thing, Morbius, and Werewolf are unable to overcome their ferocious instincts and attack the alien virtually without provocation. Ghost Rider tries to stop them, but the monsters' attacks are too much even for him, and Starseed is soon defeated. On the ground, dying, the failed messiah says: "I am not home, I know that now! This is a place of pain . . . of imperfection . . . I could have made it otherwise . . . could have given you hope!" With his last bit of energy, Starseed shows the four evil earthlings how he could have cured them of their imperfect condition, reintegrating them into full humanity; but he doesn't have the strength, and the four protagonists go back to being the unfortunate (but also irresponsible) monsters they were. As with *In Thy Name*, the coming of a messiah here doesn't automatically result in salvation. The story explores the rather disturbing hypothesis that the corruption of humanity is so "monstrous" that, even if a redeemer were to come down from the heavens, we maybe wouldn't recognize or accept him as such and would end up destroying him not in a necessary sacrifice but in simple and inexcusable sacrilege.

In conclusion, Christian symbolism, which seems to be used in the superhero genre primarily to please readers, can also enable the construction of rather ambiguous, unsettling messages that invite us to reject the facile escapism of someone who would want to leave the task of resolving all conflict up to the messiah-hero. The issue can be seen as a secular allegory (human beings have to save themselves on their own) and political warning (be wary of anyone who promises happiness in exchange for complete devotion). It can also be interpreted through a completely religious discourse, with the aim of reminding us that it is not enough for the savior to come, we also have to be ready for him, be a people worthy of a messiah.

Polytheism and Multiculturalism

We have seen that the decisions that led to the formation of Marvel and DC superhero pantheons in the first place had two editorial motivations: (1) to create symbolically elaborate but indirect references to today's widely practiced religions to avoid offending adherents of that religion or making others feel excluded and (2) to feed the ever-hungry publishing machine with new and interesting ideas, a task for which traditional mythologies revealed themselves to be a wonderful source of narrative resources to draw from.

The intentions at the root of this formula can be explained in exclusively commercial terms: selling comics to everyone and selling comics in the long run. Nevertheless, the presence of these strategies on decades of series produced in multiple incarnations and time periods and contributions from the most diverse authors has not occurred without an effect on the genre. Such narrative elements have actually determined the formation of a universe with a specific profile that was perhaps not foreseen at the beginning and that is characterized by the coexistence of cultural frameworks unlike those of any other genre, where Norse gods are placed alongside Mediterranean ones, Valkyries with paladins of medieval epics, shamans with golems, Amazons with angels and devils. That is to say, this is a lively, playful polytheistic universe, enormously inclusive, and thus not exempt from paradox.

For example, when the god Thor claims there is One greater and more powerful than him, only apparently should that reassure the most intransigent monotheist. For there to be absolute Christianity or Judaism it isn't enough for the God of the Bible to be present—he must also be the only divinity. The operation that Thor undertakes is instead to insert that One into the Many, or rather to graft the God of the Judeo-Christian tradition onto a wide, tolerant panorama of religious positions that are alternatives to one another yet miraculously exist together. Perhaps these mythical and religious figures won't always get along, but they present the fantastic yet well-defined model of an irreducibly multicultural and multireligious reality, in which all beliefs and points of view on the supernatural possess the same dignity and truth. That is, it doesn't make sense, in the Marvel Universe, for a priest or a rabbi to go and tell Thor he doesn't exist; instead, they will have to find their own ways to live together with the Other without losing their own identities, and this, precisely, is the key concept of any multiculturalism.

In the superhero world, this tolerant coexistence of all religious positions leads to a complete separation of "church" and "state," based on a secularism that is completely respectful of every religion, a secularism that in fact makes it possible to protect faith from political distortions and exploitation (see *In Thy Name*) according to that warning that, as any Christian

THE MYTH OF THE SUPERHERO

Captain America, under the Goddess's influence,
tries to kill the "infidel" Beast. © Marvel

knows, is already in the Gospel: "Give to Caesar what is Caesar's, and to God what is God's" (Matthew 22:21). This non-oppositional parallelism between the religious and the civil spheres makes it possible for the heroes to contribute to the common good also in ways based on their faith (due to which, for example, Christian heroes are sure to be earning their place in Heaven), but this only in the measure to which these beliefs express values that can be shared by everyone and that are not imposed through coercion of others.[103]

Intentionally or not, then, the voluntary limitation of religious practice in the private sphere in the superhero world has impeded the formation of an official point of view that could be applied to all the characters or at least a basis on which the characters could be judged. At the same time, in the Marvel and the DC worlds, overly aggressive forms of proselytizing are regularly represented as evil and always as the work of criminals. Prime examples of this are the graphic novel *X-Men: God Loves, Man Kills*,[104] in which the Reverend Stryker incites hatred for the mutants, calling for a sort of religious crusade, or the *X-Men* stories that feature the Church of Humanity, a Christian terrorist group who kills mutants because they are supposedly not made "in God's image."[105] In this sense, the superhero genre is an "equal opportunity offender," insofar as it is equally opposed to every type of violent religious fundamentalism, whether generated by the abuse of Islam, Christianity, or any other creed.

The most appropriate example to conclude this chapter, therefore, is perhaps Marvel's crossover saga *Infinity Crusade*,[106] in which an entity called the Goddess literally brainwashes a group of superheroes with deep religious (Daredevil) or moral (Captain America) beliefs, turning them into minions who will help her in her plan to eradicate *all* the evil in the universe—an objective that, since evil is everywhere, the Goddess thinks she will obtain only through the destruction of the universe itself. In this saga, the frequent battles between hero-fanatics and heroes who try to stop the "great crusade" clarify and emblematize that underlying message that, in more "diluted" forms elsewhere, lies beneath the entire Marvel and DC universes. That message is this: It doesn't matter how heroic the characters have been in the past and how convinced they are of serving a noble cause. Once they start to call those who think differently "blasphemers," "infidels," or "sinners," once all mediation is refused and they convince themselves that the Divinity is unquestionably and exclusively on their side, they unfailingly end up becoming the worst of villains.

THE MYTH OF THE SUPERHERO

⚡ 2 ⚡

ETHICS and SOCIETY

Why the United States?

Superhero comics are read and appreciated in numerous countries in the world (as are Hollywood films), but no country has produced them in an amount even remotely on par with the United States. Japanese manga and animation and European adventure heroes are too different from the American superhero to permit anything but a superficial comparison. There have been significant contributions to the superhero genre from the United Kingdom, yet in most cases, they come from authors who work with publishers in New York. Thus, even when they present a thoroughly original point of view, it is still within the framework of American production and audiences. In short, superhero comics can be translated and sold anywhere, but their primary feature is their reflection of the anxieties and desires of the American public.

How did such a strong and, perhaps most important, exclusive relationship develop? Why was it American authors who created the figure of the superhero? Why is it that even today the superhero "doesn't work" when it derives from traditions other than the American, as demonstrated by the fact that an Italian superhero operating in Italy, or a Bulgarian in Bulgaria, can only be considered parodies?

"Truth, Justice, and the American Way"

While one could point out that material means and financial resources might be less abundant in other countries as an explanation for the U.S.-based proliferation of spectacular Hollywood films, it only requires paper, pencil, and ink—tools accessible to anyone—to create superhero comics. The reasons, therefore, must run deeper.

First, three elements constitute the typical superhero profile that, although quite general and to varying degrees also found in other places, prove to be deeply rooted in the culture of the United States. These are

1. optimism, or faith in the practical possibility of improving conditions for oneself and others;
2. pragmatism, which involves identifying the necessary steps for obtaining goals and finding the best way of following these steps; and
3. individualism, understood not as a synonym of "egotism" but as the defense of the irreducible value of the individual personality, in a state of openness in which each individual works for the collective in his or her own way and according to his or her own beliefs and abilities.

Even at a basic level, these three components are reflected in the most common situations in superhero comics. If Magneto attacks the X-Men, the heroes start off with the optimistic assumption that they will be able to win the battle (regardless of whether it seems improbable or impossible), pragmatically use their training to act in a way most likely to lead them to victory, and coordinate their diverse individual powers into one combined operation. Of course, the heroes work together and their team is something more than the sum of its elements, yet these elements are never negated but rather validated and emphasized by their use within the group. This concept is clearly demonstrated in a Justice League story from 1969, in which the villain is the mysterious John Dough, defined as the "most ordinary man in America," who plans to destroy the superheroes because, with their special powers and wild costumes, they present a threat to the bourgeois "normalcy" that he wants to impose on all the people.[1] Faced with such a prospect, Green Arrow, traditionally a hero with a strong political conscience, replies:

Dough's glorification of the average is sheer nonsense! The "world's work" gets done because of what's different in individuals. Each person has a skill, a thing he does better than his fellows! Take enough of those talents, put them together, and you build a civilization! Deny them and you cancel everything that makes us human!

THE MYTH OF THE SUPERHERO

Indeed, masks and costumes are also visual statements through which the characters express what makes each of them irreproducible, unmistakable, and uniquely gifted (for example, the lightning bolt for Flash's speed and the stars and stripes for Captain America's patriotism). The superhero world is therefore the ultimate realm for free individual expression, another fundamental value of American culture, in a powerful intensification of one of the mechanisms by which we define our public image, choosing the clothes we wear or the idea of ourselves we want to project in a particular context. In this world, all costumes, even the most bizarre, can potentially be accepted by others insofar as they tend to be judged in terms of their faithfulness to the individual rather than their conformity to general norms. Thus, while in our trend-dominated world there will be a debate as to whether we should be wearing gray or blue in a certain year, in the superhero world it is understood that gray and blue are a perfect fit for a dark character like Batman, the colors of the flag for Captain America, and so on. In superhero comics, then, the amplified eccentricity and variety of costumes is based on parameters of cultural freedom, tolerance, and acceptance of diversity that are in keeping with the foundations of American culture, according to which all modes of self-expression are to be considered equally valid.[2]

Land of (Superhero) Immigrants

Questions of identity related to the particular social makeup of the United States can be found in the father and archetype of all superheroes, Superman, whom Gary Engle's now-classic study defined as a narrative reflection of the American myth of the successful immigrant.[3] As Engle reminds us, apart from the few survivors of native cultures, American society is composed entirely of immigrants and their descendants, individuals whose personal or family memory preserves the history of the world they came from, the difficult challenge of integrating into an unfamiliar and competitive system, the complex mediation between the values they left behind and those of their host country, and the difficulty of starting from the bottom and with "alien" status.

When Superman first appeared in 1938, the hero's status as an orphan from Krypton in many ways reflected the analogous situation of the millions of immigrants at the turn of the twentieth century. His original name, Kal-El, was Americanized as the vaguely similar-sounding Clark Kent,[4] just as many immigrants saw their names changed, accidentally or intentionally, by the clerks who admitted them at Ellis Island. His original world was as unreachable as the homeland of those who spent their entire savings to pay for passage. It was then up to them alone—to Superman as to the immigrant—to make their way in a new world filled with promise but also with uncertainty. Within a similar context of mass immigration, the story of the actual alien-alien from Krypton took on a highly optimistic and positive tone as well as, in a certain sense, a strong exemplifying function. Indeed, Kal/Clark showed how it was possible to combine the specific elements from one's place of origin (in his case, Kryptonian superstrength)[5] with the culture and values of one's new country (transmitted to him by the Kent family), thus becoming a completely integrated member of his new society, indistinguishable from the others yet also (as the crowning touch to the myth of success) able to obtain a prestigious position as a journalist. Clark Kent's career therefore also reflected the fundamental American myth of internal immigration in which someone faces the above-mentioned challenges on a smaller scale, leaving the small town (Smallville) to make it in the big city (Metropolis). The generic names of Clark's points of departure and arrival allow the reader to identify with any "Smallville" or "Metropolis" in the United States. Furthermore, in the character's double experience of immigration, his culture of origin is not erased but simply restricted to the private sphere, where Kal-El can present himself as an extraterrestrial without creating fear or confusion—as within his family (like with his Kryptonian cousin Kara Zor-El) or in the small community of allied superheroes who know Clark's secret.

Seen in this light, and apart from its elements of fantasy and superpowers, Superman's double identity isn't so different from that of many immigrants who on any given day speak in their native language with friends and relatives, telling jokes and making cultural references only understandable within that group, and then speak in English, discussing *American Idol* and Dr. Phil with their coworkers at the office or when they go to the post office or the supermarket. On a larger scale, this is the experience of the (many) people in the United States who identify with the nation as a political entity, while also maintaining their specific cultural roots. These roots are expressed primarily within their own group and are contained within bipartite designations like African-American, Italian-American, Latino-American, Asian-American, Irish-American, and so on, just as the pseudonym "Superman" combines the Kryptonian (Super) and the terrestrial (Man). In other words, from his very beginnings, Superman has posed

THE MYTH OF THE SUPERHERO

a challenge to the narrow image of the Caucasian community as the only positive model for the American nation. The struggles of the Kryptonian-American, the alien-American, can remind the reader who considers himself a "pure-blooded" American that the "hyphenated" groups' contribution to the development and well-being of the country is fundamental and, in its own way, heroic.[6]

Geoff Johns and Gary Frank's recent miniseries, *Superman and the Legion of Super-Heroes*, further testifies to this implication of the Superman character. Set in the thirty-first century, this narrative tells the reader that Earth has become a profoundly xenophobic planet, closed to other planets' civilizations and perennially afraid of a possible "alien invasion." To support their repressive politics, members of the government of the future fabricated a revisionist history of Superman's life, and thus history teachers tell their students that the twentieth-century hero was

> born Clark Kent in Smallville, Kansas, [...] the only son to Jonathan and Martha Kent. When Clark Kent was a teenager, he was chosen by Mother Earth and given great powers. And he became humanity's protector against extraterrestrial threats.[7]

Thus, if the original Superman has to be redefined as an anti-alien from Earth in order to become a tool for racists, by contrast the immigrant Superman who contributes to his adopted society more forcefully advocates a decentralized and egalitarian vision of coexistence between different civilizations. However, one could also argue that this model actually contains another discriminatory idea: that the necessity of concealing one's original identity in order to be accepted within a society implies a concept of that identity as inferior to the official public identity. Here, the stereotypical image of the upwardly mobile white male from the Midwest becomes institutionalized as the most (or only) desirable identity. In this view, the figure of Clark Kent could be seen as depriving members of other groups equal legitimacy, implicitly asserting that "if you want to be in the majority, you can't be like your forebears," and perhaps even reinforcing the "dictatorship of the normalcy" aspired to by the criminal John Dough.

Undoubtedly, this interpretation has been legitimated in different ways at various points in the series, such as in the forties when the Superman stories reflected, at least to some extent, an official culture that placed enormous pressure on cultural minorities, forcing them to choose between assimilation at the price of complete repudiation of their roots and isolation in micro-communities at a serious disadvantage in terms of opportunity.[8] Even with these limitations, which seem by no means ideal to us today, Superman's positive Kryptonian-American dual identity nonetheless represented a step forward compared with the standards of the time. Most of all, it established a potential basis for more complex and multifaceted developments in the idea of the superhero as symbol of immigrant multiculturalism.[9]

A prime example of this would be when, after a hiatus, the authors of the X-Men decided to focus on the idea of the supergroup as a multiethnic and multicultural society and relaunched the series in 1975. The first story opens with Professor Xavier traveling all over the world to recruit mutants of different origins to his cause. In a justly famous panel, we discover that, in addition to the American Cyclops, the team now includes the Russian Colossus, the Kenyan Storm, the Native American Thunderbird, the German Nightcrawler, the Irish Banshee, the Japanese Sunfire, and the Canadian Wolverine.[10] A caption informs us that Xavier has given everyone a telepathic course in English to enable communication between members of the group, but the very fact that such a course is necessary is symptomatic of the novelty of the situation and the cultural issues it presents. Subsequently, when Xavier forms the New Mutants group seven years later, it includes the American Cannonball, the Brazilian Sunspot, the Vietnamese Karma, the Scot Wolfsbane, and the Native American Moonstar.[11]

Xavier requires heroes in both groups to participate based on their allegiance to common ideals and the joint action of the various members, but neither of the two formations has a specific or defined cultural model that members must conform to in terms of either their heroic or their personal identities. Storm, from Kenya, and Colossus, from Russia, don't have to assimilate to American culture like Clark Kent did. Once the superheroes reach an agreement on the shared values they want to pursue, they work in harmony with their cultures of origin, in a dialogical compromise between past and present.

Thus it is notable that the majority of superhero groups don't have one single uniform, as if, besides being less visually appealing, it would limit the superheroes' individuality when they work as a team. In fact, in the few cases in which an official uniform is adopted, as with the Fantastic Four or New Mutants, what stands out is that, even when a group wears a common uniform, the members each express their individuality. The superhero uniform always maintains a quality of instability (the Fantastic

THE MYTH OF THE SUPERHERO

This group scene of the X-Men from the 1970s demonstrates the great ethnic and cultural diversity of the new collective. © Marvel

Four's costumes are literally made of "unstable molecules") that adapts to the qualities of each character, becoming invisible when Sue Richards uses her powers, growing or shrinking for the flexible Mister Fantastic, or disappearing altogether when Sunspot or the werewolf Wolfsbane activate their powers. Components of the uniform can also take on cultural value, as is demonstrated by the New Mutants' Moonstar, who adds

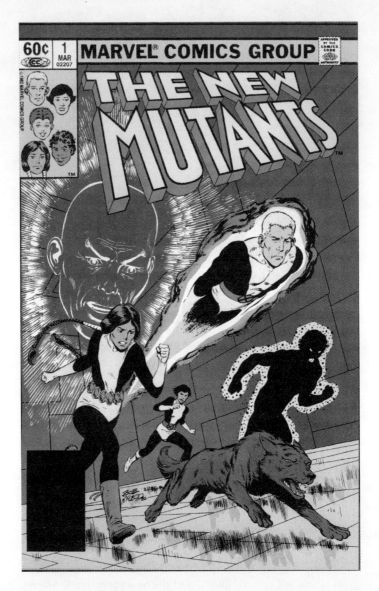

Another group of notable ethnic and cultural variety, the New Mutants, introduced in 1982. © Marvel

the traditional belt from Cheyenne culture to the team's official costume to signal her allegiance to both groups (the public-collective-superheroic vs. the private-individual-familial).

In all these cases, a unified identifying mark such as an official costume design seems not so much to validate but to critique that concept of uniformity that even linguistically lies at the root of every uniform. In superhero comics, it is the general standards of a particular group, at times symbolically represented by the requirement of wearing a common uniform, that must be adjusted to conform to the needs and personal history of the individual, and not vice versa. These marks symbolically signal the acceptance of multiculturalism within the collective superhero system as well as within the characters themselves, due to which in recent decades being a "hyphenated" American is seen as a resource and not a limitation.

Fascists, Vigilantes, and Conservatives

These considerations on what superheroes represent with regard to American society lead us to ask what functions these characters have within that society, or rather, how they can be assessed in terms of ethics and civic responsibility.[12] On such matters, one frequently encounters the following accusations against superhero comics:

- conservatism: the heroes fight not for the betterment of society but only to reinforce the status quo, defeating the criminals who threaten it;
- vigilantism: insofar as the heroes place themselves above the law and resolve conflicts with violence;
- fascism: the superhero sustains the ideal of the exceptional individual who authoritatively imposes his own will on others, which endangers the development and preservation of democratic ideals in the reader; and
- escapism: the superhero, by resolving a series of conflicts in fictional form, leads the reader to social passivity and apathy, creating the unrealistic expectation that someone else will solve our problems for us.

This last point seems weak even at first glance, because it implies that a reader who is exposed to a story in which a particular victory is obtained is discouraged from pursuing similar results. But if that were true, it would also mean that Russian films from the twenties and thirties, which concluded in the triumph of the people, would actually be antirevolutionary because the characters carry out the revolution for the spectator; it would mean that the moral exemplars of Christian tradition, with the virtuous going to Heaven, would lead us to sin and sloth because the character fulfills our moral imperatives in our stead, and so on.

Rather, my impression is that narrative, even where most patently escapist, carries out an exemplifying function as a rule, concretely inviting thought and action in the direction taken by positive characters and discouraging the emulation of negative characters (which is true even when the bad guys win, because it can elicit anger or sadness from the reader).[13] This is a trivial point that I would exclude from my argument if the contrary opinion weren't so widely in circulation. After all, it is simple good sense that tells us that a protagonist facing adversities who is represented in a positive light proposes his own values as desirable to the audience and his own aims as attainable through deeds analogous to the ones found in the story. Anyone who reads an episode in which Superman goes through great struggle and pain to defend his loved ones from a supercriminal can admire a certain moral temperament and the values of sacrifice and familial devotion that the reader may subsequently attempt to apply on a minor scale (without superpowers or supercriminals) in his own everyday life. A prime example: Barack Obama has always been a fan of Spider-Man but certainly the time spent reading his adventures has not led Obama to expect that some superhero would take over for him as president.[14]

With regard to the other charges, these can undoubtedly be considered correct in specific comics published in the past, but applying them to the entire superhero universe fails to acknowledge the fact that many other comics have conveyed completely different perspectives, which make such statements generalizations, perhaps based more on an abstract, overly superficial stance than on a genuine investigation of the genre's complexity. Thus it is not a matter of substituting the widespread notion that all superheroes are "conservative" with the idea that they are all "progressive," but rather of revealing how their fictional world offers a remarkable plurality of approaches and therefore a profoundly democratic scenario, one that welcomes the coexistence of all positions within the political spectrum as a natural component of every authentically free society.

And, if the actions of superheroes seem closer to certain ideological concepts than others, one must remember that, on the concrete level, their mission is basically apolitical. Their attitude toward all innocent people, whether they voted for Obama or McCain in 2008, affiliates superheroes not so much with any particular political group as with the civic and constitutionally nonpartisan institutions whose primary duty is

THE MYTH OF THE SUPERHERO

to save and protect. They are closer, therefore, not to presidential candidates but to nurses, police officers, and fire fighters. A story in which Superman saves a child from a burning building and flies him to the hospital can certainly be interpreted as a practical, individual, heroic action. While it is true that these characteristics of a heroic code of ethics are also part of the fascist imaginary, going from that to seeing such a sequence as necessarily and exclusively fascist seems like quite a leap. If all fascist cultures have emphasized the cult of heroism, it still doesn't mean that all heroism is by definition fascist.

As for the issues of violence and conservatism, a constructive way to address them is reading the superhero figure as a protector of the law, a science-fictional police officer and not some super-politician.[15] It is a well-known and proven fact that many countries' police forces are in fact influenced by specific political groups and that, consequently, their actions, generally speaking, represent the direct expression of that vision. However, it is equally true that this attitude constitutes a transgression of the police's mission in a democratic country. Stories about superheroes, who are equally at the service of all citizens and who equally defend the liberty of all people, are simply positive role models (a utopian ideal, perhaps, but not amoral) of how law enforcement should work in a reasonably fair democracy.

I also want to emphasize that the law enforcement in any given society can only be defined as "conservative" if it defends a conservative society; if it defends a revolutionary or progressive society, it in turn contributes to its revolutionary or progressive efforts. All organized societies in the world have delegated a limited number of their representatives with a series of special powers (such as carrying certain weapons or being able to make arrests) with the aim of defending the rights and responsibilities of the community. This is as true in North Korea as it is in Canada or Hawaii. The same American police who in recent years have acted as enforcers of the laws issued by the current political administration will continue to do the same work with a set of laws that will in all likelihood be modified by a future new government. This to say that the police officer expresses his personal opinions at home, but when he operates within the sphere of law enforcement his actions must conform to the society in which he operates. Superheroes act in a similar way (though not identical, as we will see further on), acting as a sort of ideal superpolice, morally above all sides, who defend values that in the United States are common to all political stances, such as equality, freedom, and justice, with periodic fluctuations in the political barometer depending on the country's general mood.

This is a theme that I will return to. For now, I will simply note that this taken-for-granted, typical stance toward all "good guys" in fiction, when analyzed in detail, actually enables us to understand certain traits superheroes have that are truly unique compared with other types of characters in mass culture. Let us explore the matter more closely.

A Code of Superethics

The Uses of Violence

Superheroes fight supervillains. This fact obviously lends itself to various critiques, for example from complete pacifists who claim that reacting with violence is unacceptable in any case or circumstance, even for self-defense, even at the cost of one's own life, even if it were a matter of choosing between punching someone or getting killed.

One case I take issue with is the thesis argued in Robert Jewett and John Shelton Lawrence's two texts, *The Myth of the American Superhero* and *Captain America and the Crusade against Evil*,[16] which discuss American cultural products like the Western, *Star Wars*, *Star Trek*, violent videogames, and Steven Seagal's public image in the attempt to demonstrate that narrative forms focusing on individual heroism and violent conflict resolution tend to discourage their audiences from exercising democratic values and functions.

While leaving it up to the reader to judge the accuracy of this hypothesis, I just want to note that at a certain point the authors explain how a democratic narrative model might be based on the actions of the passengers of Flight 93, who on September 11, 2001, decided as a group to attack the hijackers and prevent the plane from reaching its target.[17] If this is the desirable example, Jewett and Lawrence's problem with hero stories shouldn't be violence, given that the Flight 93 passengers chose to physically attack the terrorists and not to convince them with friendliness and common sense. This episode also reminds us that, aside from the few complete pacifists I referred to above, the vast majority of those who uphold democratic views agree that in certain cases a violent reaction constitutes the only option for attaining a desired outcome and that, according to very restricted and specific guidelines, a violent reaction is justifiable (as is the case for those who support war as a method

THE MYTH OF THE SUPERHERO

of defense or agree that police officers have the right to physically react against violence aimed at them).

As for using the least possible violence being the core of the moral code of the Marvel and DC superhero, innumerable examples attest to this. Rather than choosing examples arbitrarily, I would prefer to underscore this idea in light of the relative rarity and anomalousness of the cases in which this code is not followed. *Watchmen*, Alan Moore and Dave Gibbons's 1986 graphic novel that redefined the previous conception of the superhero, introduces the figure of the violent and merciless vigilante in the character of Rorschach, who thinks in absolute categories of Good and Evil and tortures criminals without batting an eye. Rorschach corresponds perfectly to the stereotype of the cruel, bloodthirsty protagonist that, according to Moore, superheroes can potentially become. However, what Moore presented in Rorschach was an intentional exaggeration for the sake of example and not intended to be representative of the general state of things. When Frank Miller's *The Dark Knight Returns* came out that same year with an ultraviolent version of Batman, the story caused an uproar precisely because of its novelty and originality, that is, because Batman was never really like that to begin with.

In the nineties, new publishing houses like Image put more violence into their comics, actually eliminating urban settings and social realities in order to present senseless sequences of battles as ends in themselves.[18] The immediate (if short term) economic success of such stories exerted a measure of influence on the "majors," who saw themselves compelled to keep up with the new trend, as in Marvel's *Heroes Reborn* story arc, whose plot unfolds as a mere series of opportunities for the characters to flex muscles that defy all anatomical realism and fire weapons that look like portable cannons.

In this dark climate of comics in the nineties, we find a more interesting response from DC, when Bruce Wayne ends up in a wheelchair after a fight with the villain Bane and the superhero Azrael takes over Batman's mask and cape. He is soon revealed to be a semi-psychopath who beats up villains far beyond what is strictly necessary. In one episode, for example, this new Batman tears a hammer out of an enemy's hand. Although the enemy is now powerless, the "hero" turns the weapon against him and threatens to massacre him (fortunately, Robin intervenes to save the villain).[19] Substituting the man behind Batman's mask allowed DC to have it both ways: the reader got to read a markedly violent story cycle as was in vogue at the time, yet the publisher did not entirely betray their

A typical image from the 1990s series *Cable*, with superhuman muscle mass and gigantic weapons on display. © Marvel

standards for themselves or for the character, with such actions not being performed by the real Batman but instead by an imposter whose actions were not endorsed by the other main characters in the series. This phase in the Batman saga enables us to better grasp the original hero's moral rigor, showing the enormous difference between the real Batman

THE MYTH OF THE SUPERHERO

Azrael, shown wearing Batman's costume, is incapable of controlling his violent impulses and threatens to kill a criminal who has been rendered harmless. Such an action would have been totally against the code of the real Batman. © DC Comics

character as he has always been and the distorted model imparted by other new publishers.

In any case, the idea of employing the least possible violence also fits in with the interpretation of superheroes as superpolice, in the majority of cases without implying incompetence on the part of actual police forces. At the start of his career (the thirties and forties), Superman mostly fought muggers, gangsters, blackmailers, kidnappers—that is, criminals who in reality should have been dealt with by the police. If we look at the hard-boiled fiction and film noir from the same period, we can see that the skeptical representation of the police as corrupt and incompetent was actually a sign of the times and not exclusive to superhero comics. The subsequent establishment of the supervillain figure led the imaginary world of superheroes to a division of labor in which, apart from "filler" events where the hero happens upon a mugging and intervenes, his priority is to combat the superdangers that are beyond the abilities of the regular police and resolvable by him alone. And although the superhero's superior strength does not necessarily imply a criticism of regular law enforcement (who, relative to their abilities, face risks equivalent to those posed by Galactus to Silver Surfer), the superhero's moral commitment can nonetheless function as a point of comparison in the reader's mind between the ideal embodied by the character and the concrete reality that exists outside the comic, in the real world. Or rather, if the superhero's excellence doesn't automatically suggest ineptitude on the part of the police force, neither does it act as apologia or propaganda for it.

First: Thou Shalt Not Kill

A fundamental component of the superhero code of ethics is that they may never kill, for any reason or under any circumstances, not even for legitimate defense, by failure to rescue, or "for the greater good." In this the superhero is distinguished from the image of the superpolice officer insofar as actual law enforcement is permitted to respond to deadly force with deadly force.

This no-kill rule was not in force at the genre's beginnings, during which the earlier undefined freedom of superhero stories, unrest over World War II, and tough-guy image propagated by noir and hard-boiled fiction converged to create rugged protagonists who weren't so worried about the lives and deaths of others. In the first Batman story from 1939, the Caped Crusader lets a criminal fall into a vat of acid and die, remarking that this was the end he deserved.[20] In June 1940, the first Flash story concludes with the hero posing triumphantly before a wrecked car in which the criminal has just been crushed to death, also without having attempted to save the victim and in a scene permeated by the general impression that

THE MYTH OF THE SUPERHERO

"justice has been served."[21] Captain America has the same attitude at the end of his debut story from March 1941 after a criminal gets zapped to death by an experimental machine,[22] while in another story in the same issue he impassively witnesses Red Skull commit suicide by lethal injection. In April 1941, in what by then had almost become a common theme, Starman watches a villain fall into a crevice, presumably to his death, although he could have easily saved him with his "magnetic wand" (that can lift objects).[23] And we should recall that these were times when Superman also committed homicide during paramilitary operations, for example destroying weapons factories full of civilian workers.[24]

The no-kill rule seems to become established in the fifties, in part a consequence of the Comics Code, instituted in 1954, which limited the representation of violence in comics. Thereafter, superhero stories such as those of Batman and Superman were obliged to take on a more fantastic-comic tone, as pure entertainment, with the consequent disappearance of macabre themes. Starting in the late sixties, the no-kill policy became an even more serious issue, going from a restriction to an openly represented and debated topic, as it is today for the vast majority of Marvel and DC heroes (with the relatively rare exception of psychopathic characters like the Punisher, who freely kills his enemies and who is therefore disdained by true superheroes, or of characters whose moral compass has been damaged by various type of influence, such as brainwashing, indoctrination, mental control, demonic possession, genetic manipulation, and other such events). At most, in the array of possible battle situations, for superheroes only the killing of wild animals or nonhuman monsters (for example, Wonder Woman decapitating Medusa) is acceptable, and even then only if absolutely necessary. There is even a story in which Captain America finds himself in mortal combat with Baron Blood, a Nazi vampire (!), and although the enemy is twisted and technically already dead, the decision to kill him weighs on Captain America and leaves the superhero profoundly bitter. His only comment: "it is a victory, to be sure … but it is not a clean victory."[25]

In short, for one reason or another, most superheroes of the past fifty years have considered human life to be absolutely sacred; all life, their own as much as that of the lives of innocent people or even criminals. When faced with the option of averting a threat by killing the enemy, the traditional hero will do whatever it takes (no matter how impossible it seems) to protect himself and disarm the enemy without killing him.

In this comic from the 1940s, Starman witnesses a criminal falling
into a crevice without bothering to intervene. © DC Comics

If forced to choose between stopping an enemy and saving civilians,
the real superhero will always leap to the civilians' rescue (as with the
subway sequence in *Spider-Man 2*), even if letting the criminal go would
potentially endanger a greater number of people later. A classic case is the
story arc *The Death of Superman*, in which the protagonist has to choose
between saving a family trapped in a burning house and fighting the ultrapowerful villain Doomsday, who is rapidly heading for Metropolis, where
he could create a real massacre. Superman chooses to put Doomsday off
by trapping him in the mud at the bottom of a lake, then flies off to save
the family, and finally returns to fight Doomsday.[26]

If Superman had only focused on Doomsday, it would have meant
certain death for the family, but his chosen course of action optimisti-
cally entails at least the possibility of being able to save everyone: first
the family and then the residents of Metropolis as well. The superhero's
respect for life refutes the rational calculus of utilitarian thought (according to which sacrificing two people is preferable to sacrificing a
million) and demands alternative solutions aimed at saving every life at
stake, dealing with the different conflicts one at a time. The issues
raised by this conception of the superheroic mission are the focus of a
Justice League storyline called *Pain of the Gods*, which goes into great
detail in describing the personal suffering and complex consequences
that heroes go through when they are unable to save the innocent despite their best efforts.[27]

THE MYTH OF THE SUPERHERO

Superman tries to stall Doomsday by putting his adversary at the bottom of a lake so the superhero can save the innocent people placed at risk by the battle. © DC Comics

Batman's dilemma: whether to allow Joker to plummet to the ground, thus preventing his future crimes, or to remain faithful to his principle of defending life and let loose a homicidal madman. © DC Comics

For superheroes, then, respect for life is an absolute value, unrelated to individual actions. The hero's task is to save the murderer or the perpetrator of genocide just as much as it is to save the innocent child, one no more or less deserving of life than the other. In the miniseries *Lovers and Madmen*, the Joker has no qualms about putting this conviction to the test in Batman. Believing that the hero's claim that "all life counts" is only hypocrisy, the Joker jumps off the roof of a skyscraper. The scene is magisterially played out in an alternation of color-saturated panels with the Joker shrinking to show his increasing distance and panels with somber shapes and colors where Batman's mask appears to grow as we come closer to it, as if the author and the reader were trying to scrutinize the character's insides through his mask. The two parts are connected by captions with the hero's thoughts, scattered across the page in a zigzagging line that visually mirrors Batman's torment.[28]

In this scene one can sense that Batman is tempted to let the Joker die. It is this very temptation that makes the character more human and his choice more agonizing and dramatic. Batman can violate his beliefs and rid himself of an enormous problem, or he can save a mass homicide and condemn himself to continue fighting the Joker's crimes. But after a moment's hesitation, on the next page, Batman's choice is completely clear: "Life matters. By my hand or not . . . murder is a violation of my very soul. *No matter how good it would feel*" (my italics). And with an acrobatic leap, endangering his own life, Batman catches the Joker and sets him on the ground without a scratch, ready for the Arkham Asylum and not the cemetery.

On the basis of this same mentality, superheroes refuse to euthanize anyone, even when it is requested from someone enduring atrocious suffering and is presented as the only possible solution. In two different Marvel stories, a scientist whose consciousness is trapped inside a computer asks a superhero to turn off the machine and bring his pseudo-life to an end. One of them is Machinesmith, who tries to convince Captain America to destroy the host computer without telling him that it contains his consciousness, knowing full well that the hero would never consent otherwise;[29] the other is Mendell Stromm, who directly asks Spider-Man to destroy the computer he is imprisoned in. After much reflection, Spider-Man develops an electronic virus that puts Stromm's consciousness into a coma, sparing him any further suffering until a way of reintegrating him into a human form is found.[30]

The superhero code of conduct is actually so well known in the fictional universe of the genre that on occasion the villains try to take advantage of it. Speaking of humans and machines, in an episode of *Iron Man* a sentient supercomputer connects part of its circuits to the brain of a human being held hostage, trusting that the hero won't destroy the system so as not to kill its human component.[31] And, in fact, Iron Man is forced to find another way to resolve the situation.

Mendell Stromm begs Spider-Man to euthanize him by unplugging the computer that keeps him prisoner. © Marvel

A fundamental corollary to the refusal to kill is also the complete moral separation of superheroes and criminals. Like critics and readers, at times superheroes themselves wonder about the legitimacy of their fight against crime, pursued with means that are outside if not against the law and sometimes based on disturbing motives not unlike those of the criminals.

THE MYTH OF THE SUPERHERO

Does Batman not act on a pathological desire to avenge his parents' death, the same way revenge leads so many villains to the path of crime? In this gray zone, the imperative not to kill, which supervillains almost never follow, represents the clearest, most reassuring line between the heroes' world and the criminal world, assuring us, even in the darkest, most ambiguous instances, that the hero has not sunk to the criminal's level. In some cases, this position can have surprising effects.

In a collection of comics commemorating the tragedy of September 11, when the understandable anger and frustration in American public opinion easily gave rise to the demonization of the enemy, we find a story in which the superhero Static and a friend are discussing the international situation.[32] The friend is completely upset. Like many people at the time, she just wants the United States to react, to attack someone, hardly caring whom, as long as it is the people responsible or even just someone somehow connected to them. Static asks if she would even agree with attacking innocent people, and she (as we have all heard someone say before) replies that the others, the terrorists, haven't paid the least attention to harming the innocent. Static replies: "And these are the people whose example you want to follow?" If he knew where to find the real culprits, Static continues, he would take care of them without hesitation, but what would happen if, in order to get to them, he ended up harming some innocent in the criminals' family? Or someone who just happens to live in the vicinity? The point that Static carries across, in the end, is that superheroes (and citizens alike) should never treat evil actions committed by others as an excuse to commit evil in return.[33]

Note that for almost the entire story Static is wearing regular clothes, sitting in a restaurant having a soda, and exchanging ideas like any other young person, thus underscoring the idea that it is not just the costume or the superpowers that make the hero, but also (if not primarily) temperament and moral clarity, strength of spirit, control over one's most visceral and destructive passions. Mentally going back to the first months of 2002 (when the story was originally released), to that desperate climate of "us vs. them," we see that the above statements were no trivial matter. They required the courage to go against the expectations of many readers, to deny the audience a feel-good solution, and to provoke thought at a time when nearly everybody just wanted to give in to rage.

With decades of narrative developments involving hundreds of characters and multiple authors, it would be unrealistic to expect that even the
most ironclad ethical norms would always be respected. Violations can
occur simply due to publication errors, to achieve dramatic variation, or
to show the superhero as a more human and complex figure. In superhero comics, however, ethical transgressions are described as extremely
serious violations of conduct loaded with consequences for the hero
who gets embroiled in them. This is just as it is in the real world, where
the fact that homicide occurs doesn't mean society condones it or that
laws against it are not in place.[34]

We must recall that, as in the examples of superheroes going over-
board with the use of violence, occasional exceptions to the rule can
serve to underscore the rule itself without subverting it. Once again, Captain America offers a good example precisely because the moral fortitude
traditionally attributed to him gives his rare departures from his moral
code a huge significance. And, if no rule is more rigid than the prohibition
of killing and if no hero is more respectful of the rules than Captain America, one can clearly see how his committing a murder would represent one
of the most problematic situations in the Marvel Universe.

In one 1986 story, Captain America successfully infiltrates an organization of international terrorists, but unfortunately, one of the terrorists
turns a machine gun on a group of innocent hostages, destroying one life
per second. The writers deny Cap the usual alternative routes for saving
everyone (including the criminal) and force our hero to choose between
killing a criminal or letting many civilians be killed. Forced to react in
brutally utilitarian terms, without much time to think, Captain America
grabs a machine gun and kills the terrorist, committing what he declares
to be his first homicide.[35] Even here, Captain America is no Rambo, and
so throughout the following episode he continues fighting the terrorists
in a state of terrible remorse, rejecting the consolations of reason: "The
image of that man being smashed through a stained glass window by the
impact of my bullets haunts me. Under the circumstances *perhaps* I had
no choice. It was one life...his...against the many hostages he could
have killed. Still I curse myself for not planning better...for not *preventing* such a situation from arising" (my italics).[36]

Still lost in thought, Captain America finds himself facing Flag-Smasher,
the head of the terrorist organization, in a battle where the chromatic

Captain America and Flag-Smasher fight in a stark,
snowy landscape while the hero is tormented by
remorse for having killed a terrorist. © Marvel

elements of the panels serve to emphasize the moral significance of the
events. The enemy's costume is black and white, the snow-covered landscape where the fight takes place is white, with just a few black rocks
poking out and an indistinct gray sky in the background. The scene takes
on the symbolic connotations of Manichean contrast, of the archetypal
opposition between light/white/good and shadow/black/evil as two
forces that alternate and intertwine without becoming combined. It is
almost as if Captain America, with his refusal to accept the homicide he
has committed, is also fighting the reductive, strictly defined ethical
view of those who always claim to know where good ends and evil begins—a view that he too has succumbed to at least once, momentarily
turning himself into an executioner and the terrorist into a condemned
man. Captain America's colorful costume thus comes to indicate the hero's awareness of the complexities within the range of ethical possibilities

Captain America rescues Flag-Smasher, who was wounded in the previous battle, and warms him with his own body. © Marvel

and his desire to adapt and reconcile differences before they become irremediable conflicts.

Further on in the story, Captain America is presented with the opportunity to return to his deepest convictions. After Flag-Smasher accidentally falls into a crevice, Cap courageously goes down to save him, splinting the terrorist's broken leg and digging a hole in the snow where the two wait for help, keeping each other warm. The elongated shape of the panels recalls the analogous frames that depicted the struggle that just ended, but the similarity of the panels serves more than anything else to emphasize the difference in content. Where it was rigid visual and narrative contrast before, here Captain America collaborates with the enemy for the survival of both, while in the shadows, the cloth Flag-Smasher is wrapped in and the red of the eyes of his mask merge with the same colors in Captain America's costume. Thus heroism is seen not only during

THE MYTH OF THE SUPERHERO

the fight but also when the hero is able to overcome the barrier separating him from even his most terrible enemies, from those who have forced him to pervert his own fundamental convictions and become a killer. Once Flag-Smasher recovers, he returns the favor by trying to shoot Captain America with a revolver, but it hardly matters: Captain America has won a crucial personal battle, proving to himself that the hero's task is to protect, not to destroy, and confirming the moral difference between himself and his enemies (a goal for which even Flag-Smasher's ingratitude turns out to be advantageous).

In more recent years, a similar case happens with Wonder Woman having to kill Maxwell Lord, who had created a form of telepathic control over Superman and was using DC's most powerful hero for his own criminal interests.[37] After tying up the criminal with the lasso of truth, Wonder Woman discovers that Lord's mental control over Superman is irreversible and that the only possible choice appears to be killing Lord or leaving him in control of a potential weapon of planetary destruction (which, among other things, would render any attempt to try or incarcerate Lord futile, given that Lord could always use Superman to free himself).

Faced with these alternatives, Wonder Woman breaks Lord's neck, literally without batting an eye. We don't see Wonder Woman's inner torment from up close as we do with Captain America. This makes sense given that she is an Amazon, a mythical warrior whose strong code of honor doesn't allow displays of emotion in matters of battle. She also seems to show the influence of the enormously popular television series 24, which in recent years has popularized the theme of necessary, fully, and absolutely utilitarian sacrifice, with the government agent Jack Bauer always ready to kill or be killed if it serves the good of the country.

Although Wonder Woman looks as tough as Jack Bauer when she kills Lord, homicide in the superhero world constitutes a devastating drama unlike anything in contemporary television or film. Whereas the characters surrounding Jack Bauer always end up condoning even his most extreme actions, Batman and Superman lose all faith in Wonder Woman, convinced, in accordance with the formula of the superhero genre, that she should have found another solution at any cost, even if it was against all odds. As if that weren't enough, the computer Brother Eye transmits images of Lord's homicide all over the world without explaining the circumstances of the event, thereby creating a wave of anti-superhero sentiment throughout the planet, causing a domino effect with worse and worse consequences.

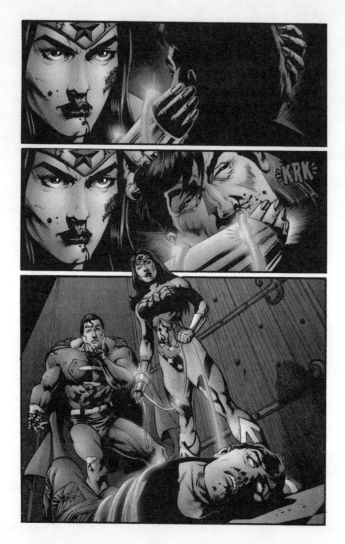

Wonder Woman kills Maxwell Lord to prevent the
destruction he might have caused using his control
over Superman's mind. © DC Comics

To redeem herself, Wonder Woman takes on more positive tones in
the series that follows, *Infinite Crisis*, where she assists the reconciliation
of two Supermen from different dimensions and convinces Batman not
to kill a villain. Still, at the end of the saga Wonder Woman hangs up her
superheroine costume and retires to meditate on her actions for a year.[38]
In short, the way back is long and tortuous and clearly demonstrates the
high price superheroes must pay for defying their most sacred rule.

THE MYTH OF THE SUPERHERO

Further, these stories show how an apparently superficial genre such as that of superhero comics, ostensibly not very introspective and based on the main characters' concrete actions, actually entails an ongoing ethical discourse behind the motives and the significance of those actions, a discourse that readers, as witnesses to morally complex choices, are asked to formulate opinions and judgments about, developing their own awareness. A refined novel or auteur film can make us consider profound, big questions about art, poetry, beauty, knowledge, the role of the intellectual, the meaning of things, the mystery of living, but the explosive genre of the superhero comic at least trains us to think about the questions that most often come up in reading news or opinion pieces, such as: Was this or that decision the right one? Is it really true that there was no alternative to a certain course of action? When, how, and to what extent are certain responses to provocation legitimate? Up to what point can we use the enemy's means before we become the enemy? How much can we compromise our values in order to defend ourselves before becoming unworthy of defense?

Killing in the Movies

The strict no-kill ethical code is something completely unique to the superhero comic, which in this aspect is much more restrained than the thriller novel (where the hero—or antihero—isn't so tortured if he ends up killing the bad guy in a fight) and is definitely more pacifist than any Hollywood film. Anyone who has seen a number of Hollywood action or adventure movies will have noticed that the final face-off often corresponds to two contrasting yet complementary situations: (1) the bad guy has to die so that the spectator has the unequivocal impression that "justice has been served" and (2) the good guy cannot kill the bad guy lest he also seem like a killer and lose the audience's sympathy. In the majority of cases, the solution to this dilemma goes through three stages:

1. The hero defeats the bad guy and prepares to turn him over to the law;
2. The bad guy rebels, betraying the hero's trust, and tries to attack him again; and
3. The hero is forced to kill the bad guy out of legitimate self-defense; or alternatively, during their second fight an accident occurs and the bad guy is, unfortunately, killed; or the bad guy

commits suicide and the hero is unable to stop him. The hero is not particularly upset by the event, which in reality is depicted like some sort of divine retribution.

I am sure that every reader could think of numerous examples that would verify the commonness of the above scenario. Now, what happens when Hollywood transfers the much more rigid schema of the superhero comic on the screen? What system of conduct will have to adapt to the other? It is simple: to maximize the production's financial investment, the film will have to meet the expectations and familiar formulas of viewers, not necessarily those of the more limited number of comic book readers.

An important sequence in Sam Raimi's film *Spider-Man* (2002), for example, follows precisely the above chain of events: (1) Peter immobilizes his Uncle Ben's killer, but when he realizes it is the same criminal he previously let go, he slackens his grip in surprise; (2) the criminal takes advantage of this to point a gun in Peter's face; (3) Peter again defeats the criminal, who accidentally trips and falls out a window. Peter stands there watching him fall, with a disturbed expression on his face, sure, but the scene still gives us the impression that the uncle's death has been avenged (which is what the director wants the spectator to believe).

Unfortunately, this is all wrong! Peter Parker has just learned that with great power comes great responsibility and then watches a pickpocket die as if it were no big deal, without intervening? His uncle just died because he didn't act for the common good, and now Peter fails to save someone a second time? Any reader of superhero comics immediately senses that the "right" decision (morally, and in terms of the character's history) would be Batman's, who jumped to rescue Joker from falling to his death. Primarily, any reader senses that behind the superhero mask, the protagonist of this film is a different sort. In fact, in the original story from 1962, Spider-Man turned his uncle's killer in to the police.[39] In a recent comic book retelling of that same story, Spider-Man, almost mad with pain and feelings of guilt, dangles the killer off the top of a building as if he were going to kill him but, after scaring and humiliating him this way, says: "You killed a good man tonight. What do you think I should do? I ought to kill you right now. But I have a responsibility. Even to you."[40] Indeed, in the subsequent panel, the criminal is being delivered to the police, unharmed. This episode demonstrates that the failure (or unwillingness) to rescue the criminal in the *Spider-Man* film is not a matter

THE MYTH OF THE SUPERHERO

Even in recent origin stories, the comic book version of
Spider-Man refuses to give in to the desire for revenge
and spares the life of his uncle's killer. © Marvel

of the movie's having been made in a contemporary and more cynical era,
but of pure conventions of their respective media. The superheroes in
comics, now as in the sixties, prefer to fight to prevent anyone's death,
even of the people they hate. In this respect, superheroes show a greater
ethical depth than action movie protagonists, even when the film portrays the very same superhero.

Things get even worse with *Daredevil* (2003), by Mark Steven Johnson. Here, by the end of a fight the current bad guy, Bullseye, has been rendered completely harmless; he is literally on his knees begging for mercy, but the film's hero cannot resist the temptation to avenge Elektra's murder and thus kills him by throwing him out a window. And note that this happens *in a church*—not only the criminal but also the Christian precept of turning the other cheek literally goes out the window. Then in the final battle, Daredevil decides not to kill Kingpin when he has the opportunity and smugly explains his choice by declaring "I am not the bad guy." This brief moment tries to demonstrate that Daredevil is a true hero and that he has understood the limits that must never be surpassed, but it seems difficult to shake the impression that this is just a false redemption, or that in any case the superhero guilty of murder has been let off the hook a little too easily. If we take this flash of insight after killing Bullseye for pure personal satisfaction and compare it with Captain America's tortured remorse over having had to kill solely for the purpose of saving human lives, the difference between the ethical code of screen and page superheroes becomes evident.

Superman II (1980), by Richard Lester, represents a slightly different case, where in the end the Man of Steel takes away the villain Zod's powers, and then, without any plot-driven reason, breaks his hand and throws him into a crevice, presumably killing him. Here, the Christian symbolism permeating the film series (Zod/Satan, Superman/Jesus/God, as we have seen) prevails over the character's ethical and psychological continuity within the comics canon, thus obliging the script to reproduce the traditional scene of Lucifer's banishment to Hell, without considering the fact that the killing of a defenseless victim constitutes the greatest possible distortion of Superman's ethical profile.

Among the many supervillain film deaths, however, the most weakly constructed takes place in the otherwise excellent *Batman Begins* (Christopher Nolan, 2005), where in the final battle Batman leaves Ra's al Ghul on a train speeding toward certain disaster. The hero's single, sophistic explanation is: "I don't have to save you." Whereas superheroes in comics constantly, seriously, and profoundly reflect on their obligation to save all people (as in the analogous situation in *Lovers and Madmen*), the screen Batman gets by with what is almost a play on words, as if this willful, self-satisfied failure to rescue a human life didn't amount to homicide, as if it didn't mean that the screen Batman has become trapped in that very cycle of hate, resentment, and revenge that should be the province of villains alone.[41]

THE MYTH OF THE SUPERHERO

Returning to Static, who in 2002 called an infuriated nation to prudence, and to Captain America, who risked freezing to death to save Flag-Smasher, we realize that loving their friends and hating their enemies as Hollywood heroes do, is actually something anyone is capable of, whereas putting oneself on the line to come to an enemy's aid is truly something special and highly admirable. And, even if loving one's enemies is a high ideal, unattainable for most people, it is at least a goal better than many others; it offers a direction, even if one may ultimately fall short of that moral code. In any case, the tendency is that film adaptations may use superhero masks and powers, but seldom do they include those inner qualities so fundamental to the comics superhero and that truly make these characters "super."

For or Against the Government

Building on Campbell's definition of the classic monomyth, Jewett and Lawrence develop the description of a plot that they call the "American monomyth" that, according to their interpretation, forms the basis of many products of American fiction:

> A community in a harmonious paradise is threatened by evil; normal institutions fail to contend with this threat; a selfless superhero emerges to renounce temptations and carry out the redemptive task; aided by fate, his decisive victory restores the community to its paradisiacal condition; the superhero then recedes into obscurity.[42]

This description of superheroes might have had some validity when they were created and might apply to certain stereotypes about superheroes that have been popularized by repetition in the media. But it doesn't truly reflect the way the comics themselves have been for quite some time. The first problem is that in reality the community the superheroes are fighting for is often far from paradisiacal, especially in recent decades. An example of this point can be seen in a famous Green Arrow and Green Lantern story cycle from the early seventies in which the two heroes travel throughout the United States and encounter all-too-real problems like racism, drugs, the expropriation of native lands, pollution, and worker exploitation, in which the fantastic component of the stories functions primarily as an allegory of the real.[43]

In this regard, the question of superhero patriotism is highly complex, especially in the case of characters who represent their country in an official manner, such as Captain America or even Uncle Sam, a character who originated in nineteenth-century political comics as a representation of the United States and is brought into the superhero world as a living embodiment of the American spirit. In periods of strong nationalistic sentiment, like during World War II, when the Captain America and "super" Uncle Sam comics first appeared, these characters were easily made into positive, reassuring symbols, intervening in a conflict where the line between good and evil seemed to neatly coincide with nationality (Americans good, Axis bad). At the same time, the close connection with the political system requires the most patriotic heroes to continually monitor the governing bodies and to implicitly or explicitly judge their actions. The spider on Spider-Man's costume is always a spider (even if at times a radioactive spider and at others a shamanistic one, as we have seen), but the stars and stripes on Captain America's costume mean very different things depending on whether it's the early forties, the Vietnam War era, or the period following September 11.

This is important because the patriotism of Captain America and of many other superheroes doesn't remotely correspond to the myopic nationalism that involves the facile and unquestioned support of a given country's culture and a certain government's actions. Rather, Captain America represents a very different type of patriotism widespread among Americans, in which above and beyond the government, citizens identify with certain fundamental values such as equality, liberty, and justice, and determine the best ways to pursue them and the political figures who can guarantee them as they occur.[44] When Superman, at least starting in the fifties, claims to fight for "truth, justice, and the American way of life," it must be recalled that this "American way" does not mean passive acceptance of the political reality, but, as Patrick Eagan says, a "government by consent of the governed. It is human rights protected by the government. It is the right to rebel when our rights are chronically violated."[45]

In short, this kind of patriotism requires its citizens to actively monitor and potentially critique their government's actions. As Batman unambiguously states in a story from March 2008, when no one can see what a government is doing, what that government is doing becomes an abuse.[46] Nor is this a democratic credo only applicable to American society, but rather it is a transnational ideal, a desirable objective for other countries as well. As I write these words, I receive an e-mail message with a request to sign an appeal against the Italian government from philosopher Norberto Bobbio that says:

THE MYTH OF THE SUPERHERO

The path to democracy is not an easy journey. So we must be constantly vigilant, not resign ourselves to the worst, nor give in to a complacent faith in the fatefully "progressive" destiny of humankind.... The difference between my generation and that of our fathers' is that they were optimistic democrats. *We are, we must always be, democrats on the alert.* (emphasis in the original)[47]

Captain America would sign without hesitation. This is in fact the same as his ethical framework, according to which one must always work to defend certain fundamental values (including pride in democratic institutions) but only support the government's actions when they correspond to that perspective. In this regard, Captain America and (the majority of) other superheroes like him differ from the aforementioned "supercop," whose duty is to represent the authorities and current laws in every instance, even if they conflict with his personal opinions. If Captain America or Superman usually support the government, therefore, it is the result of voluntary choice and on a case by case basis, not in accordance with abstract and static positions, and always with a full awareness of the "right to rebel when one's rights are chronically violated."

When the Watergate scandal hit the United States and caused a profound crisis of faith in institutions, Captain America was the superhero most compelled to tackle the discrepancy between a cynical and corrupt reality and the ideals of the nation. During this time, Captain America became the victim of a plot hatched by the Secret Empire, whose aim was to take control of the country and replace the inconvenient "Cap" with a fake hero (their agent) whose image was completely constructed by the media. These were the years of the Cold War, and yet the criminal association didn't follow the typical representation of a communist conspiracy, since the political and publicity methods used by the Secret Empire were infused with a version of a very Western capitalism that is distorted, unconventional, and power-hungry. Even the hood the coconspirators wore evoked the homegrown blight of the Ku Klux Klan more than yet another Soviet caricature. Discredited and wanted for a murder he didn't commit, in the end Captain America succeeds in bringing down the Secret Empire, but only at the cost of a terrible discovery. The hero in fact tracks down the head of the organization as he is trying to flee into the White House, and when he finally pulls off his mask, he discovers that the criminal is an eminent politician, who explains: "High political office didn't satisfy me! My power was still

Captain America takes down the head of the organization Secret Empire
that is operating inside the White House—corruption has penetrated
the top of the American system. © Marvel

too constrained by legalities!"[48] The story does not tell us exactly who
he is, but even so the reference to the politics of the time (and particularly to president Richard Nixon) is unmistakable.

The subsequent episode in the series is particularly devoid of action
and shows Captain America meditating on recent events and his role as a
symbolic representation of the nation.[49] In the end, feeling that he cannot be associated with what his country has become, the hero decides to
abandon his patriotic identity, yet since he still has his superpowers and
therefore the responsibility to use them for the common good, he makes
himself a costume free of symbols and goes back to fighting crime under
the name "Nomad," the man without a country.[50]

The years 2006 and 2007 saw a similar instance in which the Marvel
Universe developed a story arc entitled *Civil War*. It started with a cata-
strophic accident caused by a group of young, inexperienced superheroes,
in which hundreds of civilians died. Because of this event, the government
decides to regulate superhuman activity with the Superhuman Registration Act, which requires all superpower-endowed beings to reveal their
identities to the police force and complete paramilitary training, after
which they become official heroes in service of the state. Many heroes
considered the requirement to register with the government, however, to
be against the principles of individual freedom granted by the U.S. Constitution. This leads to the breakout of a huge civil war between rebel heroes

THE MYTH OF THE SUPERHERO

and registered heroes, with the surprising participation of several super-villains who have been employed by the government to track down unregistered heroes. The effect is disorienting, disturbing: changing a single law is enough to turn an entire narrative universe upside down, with the good guys as outlaws and the villains as national heroes.

More important, however, is the fact that in this new situation, where it is a matter of deciding whether to go along with the government or with the country's founding values, Captain America chooses to be independent from official authorities and even becomes the leader of the renegade organization that fights against the Registration Act.[51] And, even if the writers were evasive and claimed that the story was purely fictional (the typical denial), few readers could fail to notice that the Superhuman Registration Act was an obvious reflection of the U.S. Patriot Act signed into law in 2001 and renewed in 2005 and again in 2011. This act was intended to aid the fight against terrorism by granting the authorities the power to monitor citizens' telephone calls and e-mails without a court order— which was felt by many to be a serious infringement of personal freedoms and privacy. Captain America clearly agreed and fought on the larger scale of superhero fiction the same battle that many American citizens were fighting in the real world.

Far from acting as a simple "yes man," Captain America has historically proven to be a sort of commentator on political fluctuations: optimistic, trusting, and conditionally open to authorities, as citizens who trust their government should be, but he is also able to retract his support drastically should moral constancy demand it.

Something similar could be said, somewhat surprisingly, for Uncle Sam, who as an incarnation of the American spirit doesn't always act in accordance with the government or the majority but instead has occasionally provided critical commentary on the country's situation. In a 1997 Uncle Sam miniseries by Steve Darnall and Alex Ross,[52] we find our hero reduced to vagrancy, tormented by visions of past errors in American history like the war against the natives, slavery, and lynching. This is an Uncle Sam who, at the dawn of the new millennium, wants to look at his situation and make sense of his own past. He is disheartened by the gap between the loftiness of the ideals he has strived for and the actual results that have been achieved.

Meanwhile, Uncle Sam notices the rise of a new type of American spirit (represented by an Uncle Sam double with a costume made of television screens), one that is more cynical, ruthless, and only interested in acquiring power; a spirit that the authors clearly identified with the Republican party, as is demonstrated by the fact that the double introduces himself as a supporter at a rally for a politician with the face of Rush Limbaugh. At the end of the story, the two Uncle Sams face off by the Capitol building. The traditional Uncle Sam comes to a clearer vision of his identity, admitting the terrible errors that were committed in the past yet also acknowledging the slow and painful progress that has been made, especially considering his own general attitude as healthier than the alternative proposed by his adversary:

> I won't deny that mistakes were made . . . even if history textbooks do. But I won't pretend that mistakes never happened. And once in a while . . . sometimes very slowly . . . we made some progress. I tried my best to make people take pride in facing the problems. You're telling them to to take pride in ignoring problems. What you've got here, son . . . it's all vanity. It's a big advertisement for a product that doesn't exist. You are the spirit of a nation. But it's not America.

It is also significant that the new Uncle Sam accuses the old one of humiliating the United States with all his complaining, which shows that this is also a conflict between two different visions of patriotism: that of the traditional Uncle Sam, Captain America, and many other superheroes, which calls for active participation and the continual exercise of one's faculty of judgment on the government's actions; the other, that of the new Uncle Sam and other various fringes of public opinion, to whom protesting against any of the government's decisions *in itself* means betraying one's own country and being anti-American.

In 2006, in the same period as Marvel's *Civil War*, Uncle Sam made a comeback in the miniseries *Uncle Sam and the Freedom Fighters*, this time fighting an android who had secretly replaced a presidential candidate.[53] The android's strategy is clear and simple: it consists of manipulating religious fundamentalist groups to his own advantage, making Hollywood produce films contrary to his enemies, and organizing terrorist attacks that he can later blame on his adversaries. Or, in the villain's words: "I want every American's attention focused on these desperate times. When their president takes drastic patriotic action against our domestic and foreign enemies, they will stamp 'yes' on any bill I put before Congress."

Uncle Sam and the Freedom Fighters may not excel in subtlety but undoubtedly achieves the goal of accurately reflecting to a certain extent

Uncle Sam battles his cynical and materialistic alter ego at the
U.S. Capitol building. The face-off will determine which of
them will be the dominant social and political spirit in today's
United States. © DC Comics

the sentiment of suspicion that many Americans must have felt around
that time. The weapons of mass destruction could not be found and
even those who had seen the Iraq War as an act of preventive defense
had begun to fear there was a more sinister plan afoot—to fear that the

government they had elected and trusted in could really have been replaced with something else.

"Fanta-chronicles" of the Present

In an essay first published in Italy fifty years ago, Umberto Eco argued
that Superman's primary concern was the defense of private property,
with a consequent tendency toward small-scale interventions, in the
form of "charity," and a general lack of interest in problems of a broader
scope like tyrannical governments or world hunger. This led Eco to wonder why Superman didn't free the Chinese from Mao's control or help
the economy of poor countries.[54]

Eco's essay, which has enjoyed enormous success over the course
of the decades, at several points suffers from the extension of one of
Superman's various iterations to an overly one-dimensional concept of
the superhero, which he then applies to all the manifestations of the character. For example, the claim that for Superman "the only visible form
that evil assumes is an attempt on private property"[55] is accurate in reference to the fifties, when the restrictive norms of the Comics Code made
it so that superheroes could devote themselves to only the least problematic endeavors, like stopping common burglars or attending charity benefits. If the stories from the thirties and forties are taken into account (as
would be necessary if one wants to discuss Superman overall), one finds
that the hero's actions got to the heart of a society suffused with disturbing elements of darkness. These were the years when Superman
fought entrepreneurs who scrimped on the safety of their workers or orphanage directors who exploited children; he went against husbands who
beat their wives, he brightened the situation of the hopeless on the verge
of suicide or the imprisoned who suffered unusual cruelty; he kept the
innocent from being sentenced to death by mistake and even stopped a
war after forcing the commanders of the two armies to debate.[56] In short,
even by the early sixties, when Eco's essay was published, the mechanism
of seriality had already produced diverse versions of Superman that manifested themselves differently throughout the publications, making it necessary to consider the character's chronology as a whole in forming judgments of him.

As for the idea that Superman and superheroes are usually occupied
with avenging or preventing local crime rather than changing the overall situation, Eco's claim revealed what was and would have been an

THE MYTH OF THE SUPERHERO

illuminating narrative approach. The reason for this limitation can likely be found in the way series are constructed (rather than in ideology, as Eco proposed), and therefore in the influence that mode of publication exercises on the formation of content.

But let's take a step back. Superman's initial exploits into the fabric of American society had quickly developed what could be called (surprisingly) a realistic norm, or at least semi-realistic, according to which the superhero genre portrayed the adventures of characters who were equipped with extraordinary powers in a world largely based on the reality actually experienced by the reader. Superheroes, aside from adventures nonetheless important in the context of fantasy and sci-fi, usually operated and still operate within a semi-fantastic transfiguration of current events, often at the same time as those events develop.

During World War II, the heroes boldly leapt to fight Nazi spies; during the Cold War, the Fantastic Four were hit with cosmic rays during an attempt to beat the Soviets in the Space Race;[57] while the Metal Men incited rebellion of a robot people on a distant planet under the power of a giant robot who clearly represented the Soviet Union.[58] In 2002, as we have seen, Static reflects on September 11, and not many years later Spider-Man attends Barack Obama's inauguration.[59] If this event doesn't seem *that strange*, or at least not equally as strange as Gandalf or Luke Skywalker being at the same ceremony, this is because the conventions of the genre have trained readers to accept the free intermingling of present realities and superheroes in tights.

This close connection with the social and political context of the moment is one of the factors that seriously limit the stories' narrative possibilities, prohibiting superheroes from changing the course of primary events without the narrative slipping into the kindred yet different genre of the alternative history. The cover of the first two issues of Captain America showed the hero throwing a punch in Hitler's face. Such an action, so effective for a cover illustration, couldn't have been shown in the stories in the album before the Allies had actually won the war. If Captain America had defeated Hitler in 1941, or if the Metal Men had led the Russian people to overturn the Communist regime in 1964 (instead of undertaking a similar endeavor with alien robots), subsequent publications of both series would have presented a jarring contrast between the everyday worry and uncertainty the reader was going through and the stories of peace and triumph that would have immediately seemed senseless and out of place.[60] This is where seriality comes

At Barack Obama's inauguration, the newly elected president meets Spider-Man and admits to being a big fan. © Marvel

into play: in an individual, self-contained story there would be no problem with veering into fantasy history. With a publication that bases itself on continuing only as long as audiences support it, it is necessary to keep in touch with the actual reality that the reader is immersed in. Seen in this light, the heroes' choice not to step into the larger political picture loses its particular ideological connotations and becomes an expedient common to every era and used to secure the satisfaction of patrons. Just as the poets of the past littered their works with references to the princes who protected them, so the Marvel and DC comics artists move with current events to establish an enduring relationship with their readers, who buy each new issue and like to see their own reality (and therefore, indirectly, themselves) reflected in the work.

As a result, superhero comics typically represent the major events of the present in two ways: (1) addition, or the fantastic story nested within the real telling us that *beyond* the events that we know of, others have also taken place, orchestrated by our heroes[61] and (2) substitution, that is,

THE MYTH OF THE SUPERHERO

some of the events we know about happened for other reasons than the official ones, thanks to the superheroes' contribution. For example, Spider-Man can be inserted into Obama's presidential inauguration, with Spider-Man guarding the event and the villain Chameleon trying to stop it (addition); while in the real world Obama is simply sworn in, in the Marvel world this happens only because Spider-Man is able to avert the Chameleon's sabotage attempt (substitution). In neither case, however, can the superhero comic modify the main event, for example, exchanging Obama's inauguration into one in which McCain becomes the new president.[62]

Always because of adhering to the serial format and not promoting conservatism, superheroes are often obligated to concentrate on smaller matters and to right individual wrongs. If they used their powers to re-solve the world's larger problems, they would create a narrative situation that lacked a pretext for telling new stories and thus justifying new is-sues of a title. An irrevocably perfect world, without enemies or prob-lems, would be a world without narrative, or at least, conflict-based nar-ratives such as those found in superhero stories.

This sort of hypothetical world was courageously explored by comic writer J. Michael Straczynski in the series *Rising Stars*, which tells the story of a group of human beings who attain superpowers from a mysterious celestial energy.[63] After various adventures, the heroes realize that these powers must have been given to them for a specific reason, and so they decide to use them to resolve all humankind's problems—hunger, war, and so on. Obviously, there are forces opposing the creation of Heaven on Earth (such as fanatic soldiers in the army who don't want to lose their jobs), but in the end the protagonists succeed in their goal of making the world perfect and at that point, inevitably, the series concludes. Col-lected in a single volume, *Rising Stars* can be read today as a long and highly innovative graphic novel, but just as that—a graphic novel that is self-contained and not a proper serial of the Superman or Batman sort.[64] A series can even be sustained by the battles necessary to construct a perfect world but not by the perfect world that ensues after all the bat-tles are won.

If I hesitate to label the superheroes' disinterest in large-scale change as political, considering it instead primarily the result of mere exigencies of production, this does not detract from the cultural implications and the signifying effects that the mechanisms of comic books determine in the stories. This issue has been dealt with at certain points by the writers themselves, choosing to make the reader aware of the reasons behind the small scale of the stories and offering justifications from within the superhero narrative universe.

In one *Superman* episode from 1974, the question of the limits on superheroic intervention is still mentioned in generic terms. Superman finds himself battling a wizard who is fully devoted to the good of humanity (for example, building underwater cities to offset the problem of overpopulation) but who takes no heed of the negative consequences, which quickly begin to cause accidents. And when Superman tries to reason with him, the wizard is already too consumed with power to listen to reason.[65]

This theme is treated in greater depth in a 1986 Booster Gold story with the promising title "The Lesson."[66] Here, a group of aliens asks Booster and Superman to help them take down Galeb, the tyrant who rules their planet. Booster enthusiastically accepts but is surprised when Superman says he wants to think it over first.

BOOSTER: How can you say that? These people need us!

SUPERMAN: Political affairs are never cut-and-dried, Booster... and this is a totally alien situation.

BOOSTER: But we have powers, Superman! It's our responsibility to help the oppressed!

SUPERMAN: In this case, we must step aside. As on Earth, we must allow people to govern themselves, to determine their own course.

BOOSTER: No! Galeb is evil, right? And we fight for justice, right? So, what's the problem?[67]

The confrontation of the two characters reveals that it is precisely the one who considers himself a true hero (but is not) who automatically thinks he is in the right, claims the authority to label others as evil, and takes action based on his first impulse. The story's subsequent developments go on to show that Galeb was not a tyrannical ruler as Superman and Booster had been led to believe and that the group of rebels was actually led by Galeb's brother and were seeking power for themselves. If the heroes had listened to the impetuous Booster, they would have ended up supporting an unjust rebellion against a legitimate government. Thus Superman's lesson, at the end of the day, is that the responsibility of those with great power also includes restraining oneself from acting on assumptions and delineating things too neatly when it comes to complex political matters, even when acting with the best intentions.

Another notable example can be found in *No Man's Land*, a story arc that involved all the titles related to the Batman world from March to November 1999. During this period, the authors told of a huge earthquake that had reduced Gotham City to a pile of rubble torn between the ferocity of the criminal gangs and the courage of the survivors trying to restore a functioning society. For the narrative to develop, Gotham must obviously be kept from recovering too quickly. So, the authors must explain why powerful beings like Superman don't just rebuild the city overnight.

The episode "The Visitor" takes measures toward making this failure to act plausible. Superman arrives in Gotham convinced he can easily fix the situation.[68] At the beginning of his visit, Superman is disturbed to see that the citizens of Gotham, worn out from hardship and social breakdown, have chosen to rely on criminal bosses who are practically worshipped as idols. Superman, with the help of an engineer, begins to rebuild a power plant that could restore light to Gotham, making the streets safer and obviously giving them a tangible sign of hope (light triumphing over darkness). But virtually before Superman has even finished repairing the plant, long lines of survivors come to pay homage and bring gifts to the engineer, who has become, to his dismay, the local leader. Superman tries to explain to the crowd that there is no need for this sort of idolatry, but he quickly realizes his words fall on deaf ears. The city's regeneration, Superman realizes, won't coincide with the simple reconstruction of its buildings. Instead it awaits the populace's return to a state of trust in themselves and the authorities. They must recover their dignity and a communal spirit that can't be imposed suddenly from above but must form gradually in the minds of the people. "They aren't ready yet," Superman remarks bitterly at the end of the story, as he takes his leave of Batman and Gotham without having managed to resolve anything.

Also in 1999, in the self-contained story "Peace on Earth," Superman finally decides to face the problem of world hunger, bringing the surplus crops from wealthy countries to the populations of poor countries.[69] It seems to go well, except that in several countries the undertaking is met by hostility and distrust from the people, who see the hero as an agitator, demagogue, or dangerous usurper, just as with real politics when nations refuse foreign aid, considering it an implicit criticism and insult. At the end of "Peace on Earth," Superman understands the absurdity and even arrogance of forcing others to accept charity, no matter whether in good faith and with the best intentions. On the final page we see Clark Kent (not Superman) doing volunteer work with a group of children planting crops in a field. "Patiently and gently," Clark explains, "I share with others the way to scatter the seeds a few at a time, evenly between the rows so that each one will have enough space." These are key words: gentleness and patience rather than abrupt intervention, collaboration instead of imposition, and the sharing of skills and knowledge instead of mere material goods (thus not just the seeds but also how to plant them).

In the 2001 story arc *Spirit of Truth*, Wonder Woman travels to a part of the Middle East where the civilians are being used as human shields in military operations. Seeing herself as a goddess on Earth and having the moral certitude of being in the right, Wonder Woman goes to investigate the matter in a small village but is unexpectedly attacked by the mob of villagers. Like Superman at the beginning of "Peace on Earth," Wonder Woman had thought of herself in terms of absolute heroism without taking into account the cultural relativity of such a concept, the complexity of the people's possible reactions (for example, perhaps not appreciating this outsider sticking her nose into their politics), and the different traditions of those she aims to help. It has to come to the point of Wonder Woman getting pelted with stones by Muslim women before she realizes that her sexy Amazon costume, so effective in the Western world, is profoundly offensive in a country with a different culture. At this point, Wonder Woman changes into local dress to infiltrate a prison camp and save several hostages. At the end of the story, a certain wariness toward the foreign heroine remains in the local population, but it is partly mitigated by Wonder Woman's attempt to understand the host culture, to work alongside its members and not above them.

In 2004, Superman finds himself in a similarly awkward situation. Having gone to the Middle East to investigate a paranormal phenomenon (i.e., on a fully superheroic pretense), Superman is moved to anger and pity by the local conflicts he witnesses. Choosing to act as the people's protector, Superman seizes and destroys every weapon in the region. This only brings about the unintended effect of making both sides hate him and obliging them to wage war with rocks.[70] Superman is reminded that political interventions must incorporate collective forces rooted in the people's culture, that a man or a superman alone can only fight some of the symptoms of the turmoil but cannot effect changes on a deeper level.

A little later, Superman comes up against General Nox, a local dictator the hero had considered deposing, but who, rightly or not, is being cheered by the crowd. And the hero, who doesn't want to overturn a government against the will of its people, is left with no other option

"THOUGH I'M USED TO MY TRADITIONAL ATTIRE, IT ONLY MADE THE CLASH OF OUR CULTURES MORE PAINFULLY EVIDENT. I COULD NOT BLAME THEM FOR LASHING OUT."

"I HAD COME SEEKING TRUTH, AND THEY GAVE ME THEIRS BY THE HANDFUL."

"I LEFT, HUMBLED AND HEARTBROKEN."

Wonder Woman, who had tried to save a group of Middle-Eastern women, is attacked as a foreigner with suspicious conduct and offensive clothing. © DC Comics

than to assist the long process of reconstruction. Also, given his experience in *No Man's Land*, Superman seems to remember that deposing a dictator without eliminating the causes that brought him to power only paves the way for an identical substitute. By helping to rebuild schools, offices, and infrastructure, at least Superman alleviates the state of indigence and isolation that may have pushed the people toward a dictatorship that promised fast major solutions. From then on, it will be up to the

Deprived of more sophisticated weapons by Superman, warring
populations instantly move on to fighting with rocks. © DC Comics

people themselves (whom Superman wants to lead only by example, not
by force) to develop their own awareness and determine their own relationship with the government.[71]

At various points in history, public opinion in the United States and
abroad has considered the nature of the country's military interventions,

THE MYTH OF THE SUPERHERO

which are sometimes seen as humanitarian aid and sometimes as ruthless imperialist force. In the early years of the twenty-first century, much of the discussion has revolved around the question of Iraq and the legitimacy of the occupation of a foreign country and an outsider-led transition to a democratic model. If the 2004 Superman story is reread in this light (as was obvious when it was originally published), one can see that the underlying message isn't exactly "conservative" (in the sense of "let's just leave things as they are"), but a cautionary tale that does not console the reader but provokes him with questions like: "Does it make sense to force peace on people who don't want it, only treating the symptoms but not the cause?" or "If a leader we see as a tyrant is accepted by his people (like Nox), do we have the right to remove him from power?" Against the simplification and naïveté of the optimism of those who think they can apply their own values and methods of intervention with equal success to all cultures, these stories instill doubt, spark discussion, and push us to see the limits of direct unilateral intervention in the face of complex geopolitics. It is true that these stories demonstrate how superheroes sometimes stumble in reacting to matters of gradual, profound social change. But these stumbles provide occasions when the heroes are shown as reaching moral awareness and overcoming an overly self-centered worldview in favor of embracing a more open and tolerant network of egalitarian reciprocal relationships.

In short, if superheroes prefer not to use their powers to change the world that doesn't necessarily mean that they revere reality as it stands or that they are oblivious to the need to improve it. Rather, the heroes have the awareness that it is neither their right nor their mission to decide the fate of humanity and extend their own worldview to everyone: advocate it, yes, by sacrifice and example, but not impose it. Here we have come to the crux of the matter: what superheroes defend is not the status quo but rather the conditions of freedom that allow citizens to decide for themselves whether to maintain that status quo or whether and in what way to change it.

In 2008, this theme reemerged as the focus of the miniseries *JLA: That Was Now, This Is Then*, which tells the story of two battles ten years apart between the Justice League and the ultrapowerful alien Titus, who came to Earth to proclaim himself its sovereign and divine protector. During one of the battles, Titus congratulates the heroes on their great courage and offers them enormous power in exchange for their complete submission. In particular, Titus tells Superman that under his rule Superman will be able to convince mankind to cease war on a global scale and finally start living in complete, absolute peace. Note that Titus's proposition does not involve personal gain but the power to help others and, thus, has a just aim. Yet, this is unacceptable to the heroes, because it involves the loss of their liberty and the coercion of others. As in the majority of superhero comics, the end does not justify the means, and the true hero is the one who defends the people's right to dissent (even from the hero himself).

In the last page of this story, we see the protagonists drawing conclusions from their experiences. In the section set in the nineties, shown in the two top frames, the heroes are on Earth, and Martian Manhunter is giving a heartfelt but fairly paternalistic speech on the value of humanity and the pride he feels in serving it. The protagonists look at the sea and the moon and see the infinite, the sublime, and the universal, still simple ideals, in some sense naïve, that the heroes subscribe to. In the section taking place in the present, shown in the two bottom panels, however, there are no longer such comforting certainties. Martian Manhunter looks more worried, and the heroes, now on the moon, have stopped looking at the sky and decide to concentrate on Earth, on reality, on the people. They realize that this is the moment to go back among the others.[72]

Can we read this story, set in 1998 and 2008, as representative of a shift in the view of American public opinion? Does signal this change in focus the end of the magnanimous (albeit simplistic) desire of being able to take on the role of the planet's protector—an idea that was still credible in the previous decade but bitterly contrasted by the seemingly interminable war in Iraq and the controversial use of resources for going after Bin Laden? If this is the underlying message, what the end of the story proposes is not anti-Americanism but a sign of that conscientious patriotism John F. Kennedy discussed in one of his most famous speeches:

[This] is the most important topic on Earth: peace. What kind of peace do I mean and what kind of a peace do we seek? Not a Pax Americana enforced on the world by American weapons of war. Not the peace of the grave or the security of the slave. I am talking about genuine peace, the kind of peace that makes life on Earth worth living, and the kind that enables men and nations to grow, and to hope, and build a better life for their children—not merely peace for Americans but peace for all men and women, not merely peace in our time but peace in all time.[73]

In conclusion, serial narration and the conventions of the genre oblige superheroes to act within a sphere of intervention that is separate from

THE MYTH OF THE SUPERHERO

The heroes of the JLA shown in 1998 (*above*) and 2008 (*below*) reflect on their role as protectors of humanity. In the more recent scene, they decide to reduce the physical and symbolic distance that separates them from the rest of humanity. © DC Comics

the political evolution of a country. Resourceful writers can mask this structural limitation by endowing it with plausible motives within the plot. In some cases they can even use the situation to their benefit. Stories such as the above do much more than reinforce the tacit norms of the superhero genre. Rather they construct a specific line of discourse. This evolution is fundamentally gradual: first, the limited scope of superheroic actions is purely a *fact*, which emerges as a consequence of serial format, perhaps without the writers even noticing it, simply because these sorts of stories seem "right," "appropriate" to the selected form. Over time, critics and authors themselves have noted this characteristic and started treating it as a *theme* that they make sure to justify on the narrative plan (as in *No Man's Land*). Finally, with changes in historical context, the now thematized idea lends itself to a deeper, more complex recodification, and writers seize the opportunity to make it a true *message* to the reader.

Yet this idea, which has taken on such force in recent years, can be found more sporadically in previous eras as well, when it took the more generic form of a debate against the hoarding of power in the hands of a single entity. Essentially, quite often it is the supervillain who holds or purports to hold enough power to control the world and chooses to act precisely to that end. In a Justice League story from 1979, a villain takes control of Superman's body, but Green Arrow notices the change immediately because the "hero" is acting like the supergroup's boss instead of a *primus inter pares*—first among equals—so profound is the incompatibility of authoritarianism with the figure of Superman.[74] In a story from the sixties (very campy, but delightful in its way), the figure of Composite Superman is created, who contains all the powers of the Legion of Super-Heroes and whose appearance is at once both ridiculous and monstrous. Of course, the excess of power quickly turns into thirst for world domination and Composite Superman becomes a frightening foe for the heroes themselves.[75]

We can also trace this theme all the way back to the "prehistoric" origin of the superhero genre, the 1930 science-fiction novel *Gladiator* by Philip Wylie, which greatly influenced the creation of Superman and, indirectly, all superheroes after him. The protagonist of *Gladiator*, Hugo Danner, is a superstrong, invulnerable human being, truly a proto-Superman (the first "man of steel"),[76] who over the course of the novel tries to find his place in society, but sometimes is rejected by human beings for fear of his strength or is disillusioned by the cynicism and pettiness of the world around him. At the end of the story, Hugo reveals his powers to an archeologist, who responds by explaining to him what his destiny should be:

> Don't you see it, Hugo? *You are not the reformer of the old world. You are the beginning of the new.* We begin with a thousand of you. Living by yourselves

THE MYTH OF THE SUPERHERO

Composite Superman absorbs the power of all the members
of the Legion of Super-Heroes. © DC Comics

and multiplying, you produce your own arts and industries and ideas. The
new Titans! Then—slowly—you dominate the world.[77] (my italics)

Hugo is initially tempted by the offer but soon starts to have serious
doubts about the morality of such a project and wonders whether pos-
sessing enormous powers necessarily implies the right to use them on
others as well. Tormented by uncertainty, Hugo climbs a mountain and in
a fit of desperation goes so far as to challenge God. At that point, a lightning bolt comes down from the sky and incinerates the superman, putting
an end to his dilemma.

While this is certainly a contrived and clumsy ending, the message has made an enduring impression on the superhero code of ethics. Sometimes superheroes are tempted to remake the world in their own image and likeness. Yet, they resist that temptation to grandeur and content themselves with reforming the old world a bit at a time, along with the other inhabitants of Earth. These heroes, in adhering to the American way of life, have learned the fundamental lesson that the government of a free country is based on the consent of the governed, not on the decision of the strongest.

⚡ 3 ⚡
EPIC and NEOBAROQUE

Superheroes and the Epic

The parallels between superheroes and mythical heroes, which I discussed in chapter 1, now lead us to consider the relationship between the narrative genre of the superhero comic and the literary genre where mythical heroes have featured with particular prominence: the epic. We shall see whether these two narrative forms share significant correspondences in scope, content, and structure.

Epic Definition

For the sake of concision and clarity in defining a subject as complex as the epic, we will draw on the definition formulated by Sergio Zatti in his meticulous profile of the genre. Three excerpts from his study *Il modo epico*, translated in English as *The Quest for Epic: From Ariosto to Tasso*, are of particular interest here. I will enumerate the most relevant points and then explore them in greater detail. The first set of Zatti's points provides a more theoretical outline of the basic concept of epic:

> An event is "epic" when it [1] establishes some sort of specific relationship to the sublimity of archetypes and models of the past; [2] more or less explicitly connects its contingent determinations to ancient values; [3] is infused with a heroic vision of the world; and [4] forms part of the historical memory of a collective.[1]

Another useful definition concerns the structure and aims of the epic genre, which consists of

[5] a narrative poem of significant length that [6] depicts a single heroic figure or community in high language, and [7] deals with a historical event—a war or conquest, or [8] another kind of heroic quest, or [9] some other significant mythical or legendary endeavor.[2]

And further, Zatti explains that the epic work is

[10] typically long and elaborate in narrative design, [11] episodic in sequence. [. . .] It would be difficult not to grant the status of "epic" to a story that includes at least a partial combination of the following: [12] a council of gods, [13] a catalogue of warriors, [14] katabasis, or descent into the underworld, [15] prophetic dreams, [16] ekphrastic digression on magnificently forged weapons, [17] the representation of sacrifice or other religious rituals. Other recurring narrative traits include [18] battles between armies and duels between heroes, [19] descriptions of games and contests, [20] accounts of fantastic adventures, sometimes of superhuman dimensions, that feature the presence of superior forces and powers.[3]

Now let us explore how these definitions apply to the superhero genre. I also encourage the reader to consider the points in the following list in relation to other genres he or she is familiar with and decide whether they correspond with the three citations above. My basic thesis is not simply that are there parallels between superhero comics and epic as it is classically understood. Rather, it is my contention that the epic has a closer (if not an exclusive) affinity to superhero comics than it does to any other contemporary narrative genre; or rather, that no contemporary genre exhibits the specific qualities of epic as much as the superhero comic does.[4] Whether this suggests that superhero comics are the heirs to classical epic and continue its traditions will be addressed further on in the chapter. For now, let us proceed with our comparison.

1. *A specific relationship to the sublimity of archetypes and models of the past.* The superhero universe, so charged in tone and action, fosters the possibility of seeing the struggle between the basic forces of the human soul behind its stories, whether in terms of archetypes in the psychological sense or, more broadly, in the sense of narrative form. We can think of narrative archetypes that hinge on the dialectics of life/death, war/peace, good/evil, which are at the heart of nearly all superhero stories. These are often accompanied by the concept of hubris that compels a superpowerful character to defy rules and restrictions or by archetypes that, although

THE MYTH OF THE SUPERHERO

universal, also happen to be particularly entrenched in American society, such as the voyage, the hero as the maximum fulfillment of one's potential, the frontier (terrestrial or intergalactic), honor, and duty.

2. *A more or less explicit connection to ancient values.* As we saw in the previous chapter, the superhero is directly related to the traditional values of American society, such as freedom, independence, initiative, courage ("the home of the brave," as the national anthem goes), which constitute the oldest moral foundations of the nation.

3. *A heroic vision of the world.* This aspect is self-explanatory: right down to the name, the entire genre expresses the idea that heroes walk among us on Earth and that human fate unfolds with actions dictated by courage and strength of spirit.

4. *The historical memory of a collective.* The superheroes of today, following after the revolutionaries of the American War of Independence and the men of the frontier, are living representatives of the national values mentioned in point 2. The long duration of the publication of superhero comics also allows the genre to act as a bridge between past and present, as if to testify to the contemporary endurance of the founding values of the past. The original Captain America, Steve Rogers, fought the Nazis in the forties, was frozen in icy waters toward the end of the Second World War and brought back to life in the sixties, and continues to fight for justice and freedom up to the present day. Because of this, he represented the spirit of resistance and sacrifice of that battle for decades, though in very different ways, as I discussed in the previous chapter. Heroes like Superman and Wonder Woman, who have been on the scene since the thirties and forties, are the upholders of the same proactive and determined approach to resolving problems, which over time has been applied to the Great Depression, World War II, the Cold War, and later crises, up through September 11 and the present day. Their history parallels modern U.S. history and to some extent that of other countries as well.

5. *Of significant length.* As I stated in the introduction, the narrative universes of Marvel and DC are the expressions of editorial projects that aim to continually build on previous material in a logical manner and possibly without contradictions, a new chapter for every episode. Therefore, these narrative universes present us with what is probably the largest and most complex metatext in all of human history—it is doubtful that anyone could name another example of a collective narrative that dozens of authors have worked on every day for seventy-five years, coordinating thousands of characters and amassing millions of pages.

6. *A single heroic figure or community.* The superhero genre alternates stories of characters who act alone with the adventures of various super-teams.

7. *A historical event—a war or conquest.* As we have seen, the superhero genre often enters the stage of collective events, which may be rendered literally (World War II, the Cold War), through allegorical transposition (instead of the conflict between capitalism and communism, a war between earthlings and alien invaders), or a hybrid of the two (Captain America becomes Nomad after the historic Watergate scandal *and* the conspiracy of the fictional organization Secret Empire).

8. *A heroic quest.* The quest is a very common model in the superhero genre, where the superhero must often come into possession of an elusive object that will enable him to save himself / someone else / a community / the world / the universe / the multiverse from imminent danger.

9. *A significant mythical or legendary endeavor.* As we saw in chapter 1, many superheroes are modern versions of ancient myths, and their endeavors parallel or reimagine the tradition. Thus the debut story of Wonder Woman begins with the background of the ancient war between Hercules and the Amazons,[5] while the Thor title contains nothing less than a retelling of the Ragnarök, or Twilight of the Gods, the apocalypse story from Norse mythology.[6]

10. *Typically long and elaborate in narrative design.* In point 5, I mention the length of the superhero opus taken as a whole. Yet, even if we limit ourselves to smaller sections, each issue of a superhero comic builds on the continual interweaving of characters and plots gradually built through each story arc. This is a true return to plot technique, which is intensified by the multiplicity of interrelated events and the often masterful use of the cliffhanger.

11. *Episodic sequence.* Individual issues of superhero comics present a narrative nucleus with its own internal sense and structure, which is centered on a few key characters (as in single-hero titles like *Spider-Man*) or divided into several subplots (especially with supergroups like the Avengers or the X-Men). Each of these narrative nuclei adds a piece to the whole but never completes it, concluding plotlines that were introduced in previous issues and beginning new stories that are developed over the following months or even years.

12. *A council of the gods.* This element can be found in many superhero comics, sometimes represented literally (as in the Thor series when the gods of Asgard convene) or sometimes with transparent symbolism. If

THE MYTH OF THE SUPERHERO

The principal superheroes of DC hold council
at their lunar base. © DC Comics

superheroes are directly or indirectly based on ancient divinities, every time superteams meet to decide on a course of action, the theme of the council of the gods may be evoked.

The Justice League of America provides a prime example of the assembly of superheroes as divine council during several periods: first from 1970 to 1984, when the group's base was a satellite orbiting the Earth,[7] then from 1994 to 2005, when the base was transferred to the moon,[8] and again from 2007 on, when the heroes have bases both in Washington, D.C., and on a new satellite.[9] And when Superman, Batman, Wonder Woman, and other heroes meet at a location thousands of miles above the Earth to make decisions that may determine the very fate of humanity, it is difficult to not read such a scene as the most direct modern derivation of the ancient heavenly council.

13. *A catalogue of warriors.* All superheroes are warriors by definition. In the war poem just as in the superhero genre, the reader must be introduced to the warriors involved in the story, which is all the more crucial here insofar as the number of characters in each narrative universe is enormous, and the rosters of the supergroups often change. All it takes is missing one or two issues of a particular title and you may find yourself reading stories about characters you have never encountered before but who are now central to some new development. To mitigate the sense of confusion new or occasional readers may face, authors of superhero comics will often place a large illustration over one or two panels at the beginning of a story with captions providing the heroes' names and in some cases a brief summary of their origins and powers as well.

In the first panel of the series *The Mighty Avengers,* the characters' identities are made explicit in an image in which the heroes are shown springing into action against a threat that is only represented on the following page.[10] This enables new readers to encounter all the characters at the start. For expert readers this has a reinforcing effect, facilitating an emotional connection between the new story and the ones they have already read. And while the catalogue of armies in epics constitutes one of the least interesting elements for today's reader, the presentation of heroes in a comic can be integrated into an action sequence like this one, which will be slowed down but not interrupted by the reader examining the characters' names. Scanning the names scattered over the image doesn't take away from the story but actually heightens the suspense by delaying the reading of the page and to some extent deferring the resolution of the mystery ("What or whom are the heroes fighting?").

In other cases, the function of the catalogue of heroes takes the form of large scenes featuring a crowd of primary and secondary superheroes, in this case without labels. The reasons for such absence are partly visual, since an overly dense composition of figures and written names could be incomprehensible. At the same time, this solution fulfills the essential function of strengthening the bond of "complicity" between publishers and devoted readers. With this type of scene, it is never necessary to know exactly who each character is. Thus new or casual readers can follow the unfolding of the plot undisturbed, reading the image generically as a "large gathering of heroes" (which always implies a very serious situation). Yet the fan who looks at this image will use his knowledge from previous readings, identifying even the most obscure characters and thus experiencing the pleasure of recognizing the reference (which requires

THE MYTH OF THE SUPERHERO

The names of the Avengers are presented in an action scene in which the heroes respond to an emergency. © Marvel

specific knowledge of the genre as a whole), the coded message that the expert reader knows was created especially for him. Furthermore, in this way, providing a large visual catalogue of heroes provides a sense of unity to the immense mass of characters that have accumulated over decades of serial narration and consequently achieves what the insertion of genealogies

A gathering of superheroes from different parallel
dimensions in *Crisis on Infinite Earths* by Marv Wolfman
and George Pérez from 1985–1986. © DC Comics

accomplished in the epic poem. Like in that form of narration, the catalogue of superheroes, as Zatti writes, "binds the present of the action to
a historical continuum, seeks to integrate it into an uninterrupted flow
of time."[11]

14. *Katabasis, or descent into the underworld.* This is another theme
that recurs in superhero comics more than in any other contemporary

THE MYTH OF THE SUPERHERO

genre, taking two forms. The first is explicit, when at some point during an adventure, the hero goes down into one of the many possible underworlds to defeat a supernatural creature (as in the myth of Hercules and Cerberus) or to save someone who is being unjustly held there (as in the story of Orpheus and Eurydice). This can be tied to the superhero genre in a particularly interesting way by looking at a 2007 *New X-Men* story in which a group of students at the Xavier Institute are trapped in a hellish dimension called Limbo. The young age of the protagonists imbues their adventure with the significance of a rite of passage, a final test before transitioning to adulthood—and, sure enough, this event concludes a saga entitled *Childhood's End.*[12] Another example from the Marvel Universe is the unusual but significant case of a story arc published between 2007 and 2008, in which Wolverine comes back to life after having been killed, because he fought and defeated the Angel of Death in Purgatory.[13]

The second type of katabasis is implicit and occurs when characters miraculously return from the world of the dead after an only vaguely described trip there. This device originates in the specific characteristics of serial narrative, where the character who dies and comes back to life provides a way to represent the powerful, tragic event of the death of the hero, but then to resume the series again shortly thereafter, a potentially infinite number of times. But if this tendency to return from Hades is the consequence of a publishing strategy, that is not all there is to it. For a resurrected hero, whatever the reasons behind his resurrection, symbolically represents something altogether different from a hero who has not undergone this profound experience.

15. *Prophetic dreams.* Prophecy is a common theme in the superhero genre, but it plays a different role from that in the epic, where it serves to ensure the correspondence between human actions and the necessary, providential plan willed by divine beings. In the superhero world, which is centered on the secular concept of the freedom of the individual to pursue his own destiny, prophecies of a future predetermined by greater forces and external to individual will often take on a negative, ominous, and suffocating tone. Therefore, compared with the classical model, the superheroic attitude does not consist of the tortured yet accepting resignation to the inevitable (as with the pious Aeneas who must abandon his beloved Dido by the decree of Olympus), so much as the affirmation of one's own self-vision, within a framework where the more overwhelming the eventuality decreed by the prophecy, the more noble

the choice to go against it becomes. To name just one example, in the saga *Camelot Falls*, the magician Arion appears before Superman and prophesies that if he continues with the heroic work he believes in, he will condemn the entire human species to extinction. Yet, if he steps back and lets certain catastrophes take place, that will "only" destroy most of humanity and enough survivors will be left to start the cycle of civilization over again.[14] In accordance with the antiutilitarian optimism we previously examined—where a superhero deciding whether to save one person here or two people there usually prefers to break the rules and try to save all three—Superman chooses to defy the prophecy and to fight both present evils and future cataclysms. As a consequence, he immediately encounters trouble in an attack from Arion, who had hoped for the hero to complacently retire.[15] The idea of the prophecy not as herald of the inevitable but only as an apparently insurmountable (and thus more heroic) challenge is fully represented in this case.

16. *Ekphrastic digression on magnificently forged weapons.* Even on an obvious level, ekphrasis, or the evocative verbal description of an object or work of art, finds correlations with superheroes derived from traditional pantheons. Thor's hammer or Wonder Woman's lasso, created in divine realms and celebrated for their inimitable qualities (the former's majestic power, the latter's ability to penetrate the human soul) closely correspond to the magnificent and precious arms of the epic (think of Arthur's Excalibur, for example). However, one can only speak of a corresponding form of ekphrasis in comics when a visual representation does not fulfill a purely functional role in the story, as in a battle where Thor's hammer is simply part of the action. Rather, a properly ekphrastic representation of the precious object occurs when it is not being used and is presented as a subject for admiration and wonder. The object is then depicted according to a specific visual and rhetorical treatment that offers that object *in itself* to the contemplation of the reader.

On a 1983 cover of *The Mighty Thor*, the famous hammer does not serve as a weapon or a tool but is rather displayed in order to be admired.[16] The firm grip of Thor and Beta Ray Bill fighting to take control of it, their opposing forces cancelling one another out, the lines of the hammer exactly perpendicular to the edges of the page, without any diagonals, give the impression of a still object, wedged into a rock, on which our eyes are free to linger. The sense of the artifact's importance is accentuated by the lines that converge at it and that are not kinetic—they do not indicate movement but rather draw our eye to the hammer from

THE MYTH OF THE SUPERHERO

Thor and Beta Ray Bill battle for the right to wield the
Mjolnir hammer. The composition of the image
emphasizes the importance of the hammer as
the conceptual focus of the action. © Marvel

every point on the page.[17] We can read the inscription on the hammer,
which clearly is there also during action sequences but that is not always
shown in the stories because of distance or so as not to distract the
reader from the action.

In stories with science-fictional elements, the same principle applies to
high-tech tools and weapons. The superhero comic has the ability to use

The futuristic cannon being built by the Fantastic Four is
presented as the real protagonist of the panel. © Marvel

many strategies to create a sense of the extraordinary sublime uniqueness
of a machine, as a rule devised by exceptional minds like Tony Stark, Reed
Richards, or Doctor Doom. This celebratory rhetoric is traditionally found
in the series *The Fantastic Four*, where it is normal to expect the supreme
genius Reed Richards to invent some device that will inspire reverential
awe in the reader. Notable examples can already be found in the first years
of the series, with graphic renderings by Jack Kirby that emphasize the
power and exceptionality of the device, as we can see with a supercannon
from 1962, triumphant in the center of the image, dramatically pointed toward the outside of the page, directly at the reader, and placed in extreme

THE MYTH OF THE SUPERHERO

foreshortening with the hefty Ben Grimm in the background, made tiny to accentuate the magnificence of the weapon.[18]

17. *The representation of sacrifice and other religious rituals.* For the reasons discussed in chapter 1, various types of rituals are often ascribed to villains who want to conjure evil forces for their own benefit. Exceptions include some good characters, such as Doctor Strange, the supreme magician of the Marvel Universe, whose rituals are always for a just cause and constitute an adequate fantastic transfer of pagan content.

18. *Battles between armies and duels between heroes.* Examples are so abundant that one wouldn't know where to begin. The entire genre revolves around the concept of combat, which can vary in scale from a duel between a hero and a villain to a battle involving supergroups of various sizes, to wars between actual armies, as in the aforementioned *Civil War* or the story *Wonder Woman: Diana Prince*, where Ares's troops fight Amazons, Valkyries, and paladins of Roland.[19]

19. *Descriptions of games and contests.* This is a theme that has enjoyed success throughout the entire history of the genre, though inflected in different ways depending on the period. In the fifties and sixties, when

Muhammad Ali defeats a powerless Superman in the ring.
© DC Comics

our characters were involved in more carefree matters compared with during World War II and today, it was not unusual for superheroes to take breaks from the fight against crime to take part in charity benefits[20] or athletic competitions against one another.[21] We can also recall the vaguely surreal stories of superheroes who find themselves in the ring with real athletes, as in the fight between Superman and the Italian-Argentine wrestler Antonino Rocca[22] or the famous boxing match between Muhammad Ali and, again, Superman (who, temporarily deprived of his powers, takes a sound beating).[23]

In more recent decades, the atmosphere of the stories tends to be more uniformly adventurous and dramatic, with little space for particularly playful digressions. Consequently, the organized battles (in the guise of contests) also tend to have a more serious tone and are integrated into the continuity as events of great importance. See for example *Contest of Champions* (1982), the first miniseries published by Marvel, in which two cosmic entities decide to resolve a conflict by each kidnapping twelve superheroes to form two teams who are to compete in a kind of treasure hunt, searching for the pieces of a mysterious artifact.[24] A few years later, this idea is elaborated in one of the most acclaimed series of all time, *Secret Wars* (1984–1985), where the ultrapowerful alien Beyonder transports superheroes and supervillains to a planet created specifically to host a major "ontological-sociological" experiment: having the two sides fight to see whether evil prevails over good or the opposite.[25] We must recall the maxiseries from the nineties entitled *Marvel Versus DC*, in which two cosmic entities representing the narrative universes of each publisher face off by pitting their own champions against one other, with Batman against Captain America, Superman against Hulk, Wonder Woman against Storm, and so on.[26] In the twenty-first century, we have the saga *World War Hulk*, where Hulk is placed in New York's Madison Square Garden and goes up against the principal heroes from Marvel in a series of pseudo-gladiatorial fights.[27] In short, the theme of the contest has changed over time, with the stakes raised to planetary and cosmic proportions, but nonetheless it remains recognizable and relatively common.

20. *Accounts of fantastic adventures, sometimes of superhuman dimensions, that feature the presence of superior powers and forces.* All it takes is removing the "sometimes" and this *is* the superhero comic, in its purest and most unadulterated essence.

At the conclusion of this comparison between the epic and the world of the superhero, it seems clear that the similarities between them are

THE MYTH OF THE SUPERHERO

Wonder Woman and Storm fight to establish the supremacy of
their respective narrative universes of origin. © Marvel/DC Comics

certainly too strong and numerous to ignore. Although the authors may
often not be conscious of these correspondences, the fact remains that
reading a superhero saga stirs the reader to responses that are remarkably
analogous to those activated with an epic poem.

To cite Zatti's study once again, I want to recall that "epic's power to fascinate" the reader lies in its "ability to transform chronicle into myth,"[28] as happens in book VIII of the *Odyssey*, where Ulysses, upon reaching his hometown of Ithaca, hears a bard singing the adventures he has just returned from—"the chronicle of a past so recent that its protagonists are still experiencing its effects yet that has already crystallized in public consciousness as history."[29] Therefore, if at one point epic was chronicle, or regardless, if epic can be *experienced* as fixed chronicle, is temporal distance from the narrated events truly necessary to decide whether a particular narrative belongs to the genre? Besides the fact that throughout literary history there have been occasional experiments in the "heroic-civic" poem, that is, epic based on political events contemporary to the author,[30] if we remain within the canon, one is made to wonder: Were Ulysses' adventures recounted just a few years after their occurrence "less epic" than the same story later told by Homer? Wouldn't Melville's *Moby-Dick* perhaps also deserve the title of "epic," even though it narrates events that are set only a few years before the book's composition?

If we consider the possibility of a present narrated in epic form, it is my belief that—also keeping in mind my considerations in the previous chapter—the superhero genre can be understood not only as a present epic but also as the epic of the present. Just as the Homeric bard used the Trojan War, the superhero genre incorporates the events that have the most relevance for the society addressed in the work (in this case, the Western readers faced with the Great Depression, World War II, the Cold War, September 11...) and refines such events, shedding their most isolated and ephemeral details, to project its figures into the heroic realm of myth and the absolute, of great forces and clear-cut conflicts. Just as the multiplicity of events in the Trojan War were concentrated by Homer into a selection of pivotal episodes (like the duel between Achilles and Hector or the scheme of the Trojan horse), in the 1940s, the endless battles of World War II were condensed into the duel between Captain America and Red Skull, while the anxieties of many Americans about technological modernization were reflected in the clash between Superman (super, but man) and the monstrous machines of Lex Luthor.

This idea of an epic in constant formation, of epic as chronicle of the contemporary world, also constitutes a profound response to the cult of the present that is deeply rooted in American culture. Once the founding values of the Constitution are taken as a solid base to build on, American culture tends to project itself toward the present and the future with a social and geographic mobility that is difficult to imagine for someone who has not experienced it, which allows—and in a certain way invites—constant self-reaffirmation, redefining oneself in terms of goals that should not be overly constrained by the past. The basic right to the opportunity to improve one's condition, the flexible economic and social fabric that enables the search for or the creation of such opportunity, the mass culture that emphasizes the figure of the hard worker who can create his own success (the "self-made" man)—these are all factors that inevitably promote the acceptance of change as a way of increasing one's own happiness. A fairly common life story in the United States could be someone growing up in Florida, attending college in Boston, relocating to California for work, at thirty-five resigning to pursue another degree in Texas, and starting a new career in Michigan. Pragmatic as well as cultural factors, in contrast, would make it much harder for a European to follow a path of comparable variety in the Old World. In this sense, superheroes' extraordinary powers of mobility, from the ability to fly to teleportation, can be seen as amplified references to the typically American geographical and social mobility that the lives of many citizens revolve around.

Nor should we underestimate the psychological import of these geographical moves within a vast nation like the United States—vast enough to truly offer its citizens the opportunity to found a new identity for themselves, to the extent that some people, when they arrive at their new residence, decide to change their names to increase the psychological distance from their past self. In short, in the United States, the optimistic motto "today is the first day of the rest of your life" resounds deeply (certainly more deeply than in many other parts of the world) and is seen as a privilege of freedom and choice to keep closely guarded. This, in superhero comics, is reflected in three principal ways:

1. Characters evolve over a continuous arc, which makes it possible to avoid redundancy and at the same time keeps the character recognizable to the devoted reader issue after issue. Due to gradual development over time, for example, heroes' costumes may vary in design (Spider-Man in red and blue, then black and white, then yellow and red) or new adventurers may wear old capes (Azrael in Batman's place), but the overall character is

continually reinvented through yet not annihilated by its variations.

2. Characters have multiple identities, with many that alternate between being a regular person and a hero. This narrative device can be perceived a symbolic reflection not only of cultural plurality (as previously discussed) but also of the radically different stages that an individual can go through, especially in a country like the United States, where even the mere geographical vastness facilitates the idea that if someone fails in one place that person can seek opportunities for success and personal redefinition elsewhere.

3. Many of the characters have a superhuman flexibility (like Plastic Man, Elongated Man, Mister Fantastic, the Metal Men) or powers of complete transformation, which DC's Metamorpho and Beast Boy exemplify. In a country where the opportunity to reinvent oneself carries the concomitant, unsettling risk of losing one's identity in the process, the superheroes who change form provide a sort of positive model of the individual who can change in different situations in even the most astonishing ways, but who, deep down, is always true to himself despite any new version.

All this is to say that one should not be surprised if the superhero comic as modern American epic takes the form of the serial celebration of a constantly evolving present, because it is precisely in the intentional act of defining the shape of this fluctuating present that the heroic dimension of the individual is constructed. The decades of superhero stories that have accumulated from 1938 to today have thus created an extraordinary ensemble of "mythical presents," each of which is in a sense absolute, foundational, original, and immutable in its own way, though within an endless sequence of narrative nuclei that are equally foundational and absolute.

Superheroes: The Return of the Baroque?

While the superhero genre constitutes the modern epic for a nation that, in its own way, has conserved a heroic vision of life, the superhero genre also lends itself to interpretation with a rather different, in some ways even opposite, framework. In fact, one can see this type of comic as an expression of some recent tendencies and intellectual orientations that various critics have grouped under the term *neobaroque*, a concept

THE MYTH OF THE SUPERHERO

that defines the contemporary resurgence of those grandiose artistic modes and dynamic forms of sensibility of seventeenth-century baroque culture that supplanted the equilibrium and harmony of the Renaissance worldview.[31]

The neobaroque is not an artistic movement or a particular school but rather a widespread orientation, in late twentieth- and early twenty-first-century society and taste. To Ezio Raimondi, it is manifested in creative works as the "search for forms—and their valorization—in which we witness the loss of wholeness, of globality, of ordered systematicity in favor of instability, polydimensionality, mutability,"[32] or in other words, the "passage from totality to discordant plurality."[33]

The idea of the neobaroque, then, refers to an exchange between art and world, to certain elements from the past that return in recent film, literature, and other media, not necessarily because an author decides to reference seventeenth-century style, but because modern Western life presents a cultural scenario in many ways so similar to that of seventeenth-century Europe that new authors dealing with their *own* questions for their *own* audiences happen to produce works with strong correspondences to those of the previous era. Similar causes, after all, do tend to lead to similar effects. If the world and people of today are neobaroque (as we will see shortly), the works that most resonate with us, that reflect us, will also be neobaroque, which is all the more interesting when seen not only in so-called high culture but also in works of great popular success. This, in fact, will be the ultimate test of whether neobaroque sentiment is a common condition, even if not necessarily termed as such or recognized by those who experience it.[34]

Even in a very general sense, among today's various forms of expression, the superhero comic seems to tend toward certain characteristics of the baroque, such as the penchant for excess, the "pathos, passion, emphasis" in which "the measure of still forms that weigh on the Earth is substituted by movement, rapture, a broad sense of the immense and the sublime."[35] Consider the exaggerated bodies of the superheroes outstretched in flight or fighting convulsively for the fate of the planet, and you will see that this type of figuration has closer ties to the baroque than to any other artistic style of the past.

To see more clearly the parallels between the two styles, let us look at the fundamental characteristics of the baroque and neobaroque as defined by Raimondi in his useful synthesis and discuss the manner in which these play a significant role in the superhero genre.[36]

The 1600s was a century of great upheavals and tensions, materially dev-astated by the Thirty Years' War, by famine and plague, culturally frac-tured by the direct opposition between the Reformation and Counter-Reformation, and shaken up by ethnographic discoveries that led to the threat of relativization of values. This all occurred at the same time as the advance of an astronomical science that "calls all in doubt" (as John Donne wrote), eliminating the Aristotelian celestial spheres and locating the sun (not the Earth) at the center of the universe, thus transforming our planet into a grain of sand floating between unfathomable immensities.

The social and epistemological shifts that resulted from this situation caused many to doubt even the possibility of formulating a satisfactory, all-encompassing system of classification, especially in this world and in this life. If true and certain knowledge belongs to God only, as the official culture of the time often affirmed, it is no surprise that in 1632 Pope Ur-ban VIII wanted Galileo to specify that in his *Dialogue Concerning the Two Chief World Systems,* he did not intend to offer human beings the absolute truth, only a hypothesis.[37] A similar skepticism seems to have resurfaced, albeit through different channels and in different ways, in the second half of the twentieth century,[38] after the failure of "total" projects like the ma-jor totalitarianisms of the early part of the century. The very concept of a single, unified, and all-encompassing ideology has been profoundly under-mined by the alienating proliferation of information, especially after the advent of the contemporary media and social media, the increased possibil-ity of traveling and relocating (and therefore encountering the Other), the plurality of perspectives brought about by increased attention to minorities and far-flung cultures. Along the lines of the present cultural climate, an in-clination toward the fragment and the detail has been transferred from these phenomena to the dynamics of recent art. Such inclinations, however, can often be found in the superhero comic as well, although somewhat unexpectedly and in contrast to the unifying narrative forces at the core of the Marvel and DC universes. Let us explore how.

First, we must note the mechanism of gradual formation of these interlinked (or rather continually interlinking) universes. The authors create one title after another, the stories catch on, characters in the various titles start to appear in others as well, events that take place in one series also have repercussions in others that aren't directly con-nected. The resulting proliferation of narrative elements must be taken into consideration by the authors, who are charged with the task of avoiding contradictions. Thus, for example, if the island nation Genosha is destroyed in the series *X-Men*, when the protagonists of *The Avengers* series go there later it must be shown in ruins.[39] If in one title Thor is shown to be stronger than Armadillo, and Hulk stronger than Thor in another, then in a future battle between Hulk and Armadillo—regardless of which Marvel title it appears in—as long as nothing has changed in the makeup of the characters, Hulk should be able to defeat Armadillo (according to a concept called "hierarchical continuity").[40] Essentially, all the stories in a given narrative universe are inextricably linked, giving us the impression that with every new publication we are looking out a window at a full and vital narrative universe, which "exists" per se and remains coherent even when we are not looking.

Up to this point, we have been dealing with the totality of the epic. Epics sooner or later stop and place the words "the end." But the superhero comic continues to add stories, characters, situations, and details as long as the financial support of readers allows new issues to be produced. The narrative universe thus continues to expand until the cosmos circumscribed by a concluded story explodes into an immense narrative space with such a large number of stories and characters that no one can absorb them all. The reader who adds a narrative thumbtack to his mental map of the Marvel and DC Universes with every issue also feels like he has only mastered a larger or smaller fragment that branches out into a macrotext unknowable in its totality—a totality that exists in the pages of every Marvel or DC issue put together but that none of us can ever truly possess. Similarly, the author trying to connect his own stories with stories from the series' past always knows that he could miss something, that it would only take not knowing or not remembering some minor issue from decades back and the continuity could potentially be broken. Thus, he also knows that every new issue, while it expands the size of the map, also increases the complexity of the system and can create incompatible narrative segments.

The vastness of this macrotext means that, simply due to the number of stories that have amassed, the Marvel and DC narrative universes call into doubt the idea of the objectively analyzable work. Since readers only know portions that, however enormous, are always partial, one could say that every single reader perceives a virtually different Marvel or DC Universe, composed of his own selections. Someone who has mainly read stories from the fifties and sixties would know a more optimistic DC

Universe, whereas someone who has focused on the various subgenres might perceive narrative universes primarily dominated by horror, stories of magic, pure action, inner torment, costumed soap operas, and so on.[41]

The constant rewriting and retroactive variations of heroes' pasts through the development of the series creates just as much of a problem for the entire metatext. One emblematic example: Clark Kent's Earth parents. In the first Superman story, in 1938, the infant alien is found by a passing driver and left at an orphanage; then we see him as an adult, without any mention of a family. So we presume that he grew up in the institution without ever having been adopted.[42] In a 1939 retelling, Mary Kent and her (unnamed) husband adopt the newborn, raise him, and die when Clark is an adult.[43] In later years, Mary Kent's name inexplicably changes to Martha, her husband becomes Jonathan, and in 1963 the two die when Clark is still an adolescent.[44] From 1986 on, they are still alive when Clark is an adult and are major guiding figures who advise him on his superhero career.[45] In 2003, they are younger than they used to be, they resemble the actors who play them in the television show *Smallville*, and they have a more difficult relationship with their adopted son.[46] After the reboot of the entire DC Universe in September 2011, Jonathan and Martha Kent died when Clark was still a child. And this just in the comics, without taking into account the various versions in film, television, radio shows, and cartoons. So who are Superman's Earth parents? The dead ones, the living ones, or the ones who were never even there? If we apply the same criteria we used for the heroes' religious plural symbolism to this continual rewriting of the characters, we can see that Martha Kent is just as *real* as Mary Kent. Even if we can distinguish the most enduring and successful versions of the character, ultimately, all the variations are equal in terms of their degree of reality in the narrative universe that they belong to.

The publishers themselves, when dealing with cases of this sort, try to eliminate contradictions by resorting to the most implausible of plot devices. For example, DC has multiplied the narrative universes in their own titles for decades, saying that if there was a discrepancy between a story from today and one from ten years ago it is because the old stories took place in a parallel universe, almost identical to today's except for precisely those particular variations. The device of this sort of multiverse is by no means trivial and essentially affirms the equivalence of character variations that I mentioned above, according to which Martha and Mary both exist, even if on two different planes. Obviously, as the issues progress and the stories branch out, the parallel universes also begin to proliferate

THE MYTH OF THE SUPERHERO

chaotically, reaching a point where the readers and even the authors can no longer find a way out and the narrative spirals out of control. Publishers respond to this situation in various ways, but all of them are temporary. In 1985, DC introduced a cosmic catastrophe that destroyed all but one of the universes in their multiverse: clear, clean, transparent, unified, and primed for new developments. This is a temporary solution, given that, unless a series ends for good, over the years and decades there will be new generations of readers and inevitable evolutions in taste, and authors can only respond by modifying the present and rewriting the past. The cosmic sweep, for example, did not prevent Clark's parents from getting younger in 2003 or suddenly resembling television actors. This is completely understandable when the choice is between staying idealistically faithful to a dated version of the narrative that the public no longer wants or remaking the tradition in order to maintain a dialogue with readers.

In the superhero comic, the unifying impulse of the epic mode is followed by authors and remains fully effective only up to a certain level of complexity and for a certain amount of time, yet inevitably it comes up against this tendency to disaggregation that suggests a narrative universe transcending all possibility of complete comprehension—a universe that transforms even the most established and enduring elements into constellations of narrative fragments that coexist yet are incompatible. Facts are transformed, as Urban VIII would have liked, into hypotheses.

The Penchant for Citation

The baroque inherited the idea of the artist inspired by art itself instead of nature from the form of expression known as mannerism and combined it with the spirit of the uncertainty of the times, which was marked by a widespread skepticism about whether it was possible to completely master the real and to distinguish truth from illusion. If the world was a theater (as the most common metaphor of the seventeenth century claimed) and if reality was a divine fiction whose ultimate meaning remained unknown, then such condition overturned the traditional hierarchical relationship between nature and art. The former was no longer necessarily preferable to the latter, while the art that was seen as most adequately describing that world had to assume openly artificial and spectacular modes. This can be seen in the evolution from Renaissance painting, with its light-filled landscapes depicting the perfect integration of man and nature, to baroque painting, where figures often emerge from a dark, undefined space, illuminated by dramatic rays of light, caught in emphatic poses and in luxurious costumes. Essentially, painting no longer directly described events but rather created a theatrical representation of those events.

In literature, the concept of art constructed out of other works of art often manifested itself as a massive turn to citations and reworkings of previous texts to the point that the new work could seem almost like a library of citations. Undoubtedly, many literary works of the Renaissance contained frequent allusions to previous traditions, but they were recast and completely absorbed in a new and harmonious whole. However, Giambattista Marino's *Adonis*, the greatest masterpiece of baroque literature, published in 1623, is almost entirely a collage of citations, reworkings, translations, satires, and parodies, all crafted precisely to be perceived as reproduced material. What the reader is thus asked to do is not only follow the story but also to try to discover the sources inserted in the new work and to appreciate the labor of careful re-elaboration and combination that they have been subjected to. The spirit of the work, therefore, tends to be playful, even if it is a very cultured and cerebral playfulness. The overarching tone of the work, which is the expression of an author who openly challenges the reader to recognize his sources, often manifests as a tone of complicity and smug irony.

That this baroque tendency has come back into fashion in recent decades is demonstrated by the novels of Umberto Eco (among countless other examples), which are refined patchworks of materials drawn from elsewhere, or the Indiana Jones movies, which are filled with filmic citations,[47] or the majority of the episodes of *The Simpsons*, or the hit musical *Mamma Mia!*, which constructs a new story by putting old Abba songs into a new context.

This type of phenomenon is prominent (especially in the past twenty years or so) in superhero comics, which have developed a tradition of materials and generic norms that are established enough to make their own background a potential object of citation and discussion. And the comic, being a medium that is a hybrid of word and image, lies at the juncture of at least three distinct traditions that can be cited in an equally direct manner: literature, static visual art (painting, sculpture, photography), and comics themselves.[48] Literature, to which the comic is linked by its verbal component, is evoked anew through dialogues or captions. Citations of this sort are almost always respectful of the original source, and for the uninitiated, and often the aficionados as well, they confer a certain veneer of respectability on the new product, placing it under the protection of

THE MYTH OF THE SUPERHERO

The DC superheroes raise the United Nations flag as a sign
of hope against the alien invasion that has struck Earth.
The reference to the famous photograph of the flag
raising at Iwo Jima is evident. © DC Comics

the canonical masterpiece. A well-known example is the miniseries
Kraven's Last Hunt by J. M. De Matteis and Mike Zeck, in which verses
from William Blake accompany the scene where Kraven buries Spider-
Man, giving a more universal and profound dimension to the scene and
more generally to the conflict between the two protagonists.[49]

Also, the history of visual art, in many respects linked to the comic by
its visual component, can also provide a major source for graphic renderings of the present, as we saw in chapter 1 with Michelangelo's *Pietà*

shown at Captain Marvel's death. In a similar fashion, on the cover for the DC miniseries *Invasion!* the superheroes' courageous teamwork against the alien invaders takes the form of Joe Rosenthal's famous photograph of the flag raising at Iwo Jima.[50]

In the sixties, with the triumph of Pop Art, for a time Marvel wanted to make a direct connection to the artistic movement, appending the label "Marvel Pop Art Productions" to the covers of their comic books. This device served to blur the conventional distinctions between "high" and "low" culture, ideally continuing, in print form, what Andy Warhol and especially Roy Lichtenstein were doing in their works, openly citing comics. While these artists were demonstrating that "high" art could make use of comics, Marvel claimed that the comic was in itself an art adequate to the society of the time.

A notable reference to this period and the artistic potential of the comic medium appeared in a Spider-Man story from May 2008, where our hero is up against Paperdoll, a disturbing two-dimensional girl who crushes her adversaries by enveloping them in her body.[51] The primary battle takes place in an art gallery where a retrospective on Pop Art is being held, with paintings in the Warhol style featuring Captain America and Doctor Strange.[52]

The cover of the issue is also a good example of the continuity between comics and pop painting, with Spider-Man in the foreground, drawn using the conventions of line and shading that call for us to perceive him as animated and three-dimensional. In the background, a Lichtenstein-esque painting, overtly false, flat, still, shows how the visual language of the popular comic—when considered in its iconicity rather than in its dynamic and adventurous components—has at times been considered to reach the status of art. The exchange becomes even more intense when one notices that two of the girl's fingers in the painting are ominously extended in front of Spider-Man's arm and that her thought balloon ("Oh Bobby, they could never love you the way I could . . . Never! Never!!!") refers to the content of the story, in which Paperdoll is pathologically obsessed with actor Bobby Carr. Thus we realize that the image in the background is actually Paperdoll, who has flattened herself against the wall to camouflage herself as a painting and to attack Spider-Man by surprise.

This visual solution demonstrates even more clearly that there is no substantial difference between Pop Art and popular comics other than the presence or absence of an implicit narrative in the images. Here, Paperdoll provides proof that a single image can have both meanings, at one point

THE MYTH OF THE SUPERHERO

Pop Art and the superhero comic (represented by
Spider-Man) are placed side-by-side in a single image.
© Marvel

appearing as a stable and immobile painting, at another as a character in a
comic book. Indeed, once one has noticed the fingers emerging from the
background, the image is completely reinterpreted with comic devices: the
hand becomes animated in a menacing gesture, the tears on her face start
to flow, and even the phrase in the balloon becomes an action in progress,
a thought that is "happening" at the same time that we are reading.

A major source of citations and references of various types is also, as I
suggested earlier, the comic itself. As early as the fifth issue of the *Fantastic Four* (1962), Johnny Storm is shown reading the first issue of *Hulk*,
which at the time had just been released.[53] This simple event is sufficient
to make readers aware of the possibility of a special type of intertextual
play in the Marvel Universe. Within this universe, in fact, we can locate
the Marvel comics themselves, insofar as the superheroes' adventures
that take place in that universe act as the inspiration for comics that are
later published and read on that same plane of reality (just as, in Part 2 of

Johnny Storm of the Fantastic Four is shown reading comics from
the same publishing house that created him. © Marvel

the baroque-era novel *Don Quixote,* the character Don Quixote discusses
the first section of the book).[54]

Sometimes even the authors remind us that the comics referenced
are "historically" accurate within the Marvel Universe, because several
heroes correct the proofs for their own series (!), with the result that
the comics that are hypothetically read by their characters are virtually
identical to the comics read by the external reader. This element is uti-
lized very creatively in a narrative arc where She-Hulk, a lawyer by
profession, is hired by a law office that specializes in cases regarding
superpowers and whose archive is composed of a basement full of
Marvel comics—thus one can see Jenny Walters (She-Hulk's alter ago)
consulting an issue of *She-Hulk* that talks about her past. The originality of this *She-Hulk* story arc lies in the fact that the authors are granting previous comics real legal value within their own narrative universe.
After all, if Marvel comics recount events that actually take place in the
Marvel reality, and if they have even been approved by a federal authority like the Comics Code, then these comics correspond to authen-
ticated historical documents and in fact can legitimately be used in
court! In this situation, the present story opens up not only to include
events from the fictional past of the Marvel Universe, but also the devoted reader, who sees himself reflected in the figures of the various
legal employees who invest time and energy going over old comics to
build their cases, just as the reader continually searches through his
own collection to pick up an interrupted storyline or figure out an

THE MYTH OF THE SUPERHERO

Jenny Walters reads (and critiques) an episode of *She-Hulk* about the adventures of her youth. © Marvel

unclear reference or resolve an apparent contradiction between different points in the series.

Even more interesting are the cases in which the citation reproduces an entire previous narrative passage in a different form. Let us consider the opening page in the first issue of the new Justice League of America series, relaunched in October 2006. The image is structured in four horizontal panels, the first of which introduces the setting for the action (the bat cave) and the subsequent panels showing the chest symbols of Batman, Superman, and Wonder Woman.[55] The up-close framing on the symbols gives the table a certain solemnity, accentuating the core values and mission of justice that the characters embody and that their symbols express, which is a very appropriate opening given that soon it will be those values that motivate the three characters to reform the Justice League. In November 2007, in the opening of the saga *Injustice League*, we have a series of images that is an obvious remake of the one from the previous year, with the setting panel now depicting a secret base and

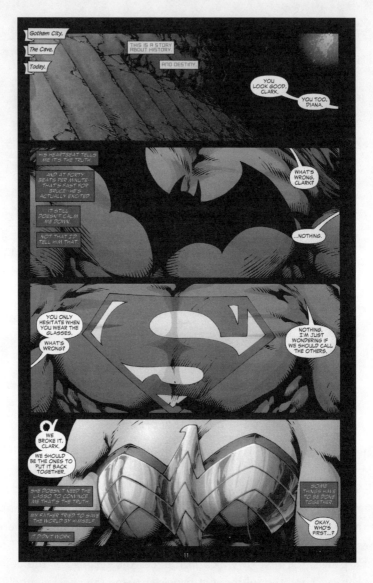

The JLA series launched in 2006 opens with the symbols of the
group's three major superheroes and of the DC Universe.
© DC Comics

then close-up representations of the chests of Joker, Lex Luthor in battle
armor, and Cheetah, the archenemies of Batman, Superman, and Wonder
Woman, respectively.[56] Even for those who miss the connection, the
parallel images still work to provide the basis for the story. For those
who do realize the connection, the citation also creates the pleasure of

THE MYTH OF THE SUPERHERO

The opening panel of the saga *Injustice League* mirrors the debut of the new JLA series but in distorted form, substituting the symbols of the supercriminals for those of the heroes. © DC Comics

recognition and generates a stronger symbolic connection between the two groups, who are truly mirror images of each other.

A particularly impressive visual correspondence of this sort appeared in two Iron Man adventures published a hundred episodes and more than

Two trips back in time taken by Iron Man and Doctor Doom in 1981 (*left*)
and 1989 (*right*) are represented in panels that are compositionally related.
© Marvel

eight years apart.[57] Both stories involve Iron Man and Doctor Doom, two
characters who are similarly covered in high-tech armor, and both develop
the theme of time travel in parallel ways, the first taking place in King
Arthur's Camelot and the second in the year 2093. The visual citation
again rewards the devoted reader, accentuating the play of vertiginous
doubling on which these stories are based, and in an unexpected manner,
almost managing to give us the sense of time travel. As soon as the reader
notices the reference to the earlier comic, he can see the present blending
with the past and finds himself mentally making a chronological leap not
entirely unlike that of the two protagonists, only on a smaller scale.

Whatever the motivations and the successes, in any case this strategy
of citation breaks the continuity of the reading and weakens the emotional impact of the story. There are rare cases of lyrical fusion between
text and image (as with Blake in *Kraven's Last Hunt*). We are trying to
recognize the visual citations and decipher their implications, so our
suspension of disbelief is temporarily put aside and the characters in the
text, no matter how attached to them we may be, appear in all their

THE MYTH OF THE SUPERHERO

fictional nature as conventional signs created for the free play of ideas between the authors and the reader. Again, then, the unity and apparent body of the represented world collapse to reveal a complex, artificial construction, whose varied structures the reader is left to appreciate.

Loss of the Center

As I have already suggested, the enormous number of geographical, ethnographic, and scientific innovations that burst onto the European cultural scene in the seventeenth century brought with them the threat of relativism and an extremely profound sense of disorientation (in addition to the metaphor of the theater, the metaphor of the labyrinth was prevalent), encouraging authors who wanted to take this situation into account to create works with hopelessly complex narrative structures, with any organic coherence absent or almost impossible to find, in which proportion and the hierarchy of the various parts is missing and in which the discourse stutters or keeps obsessively turning back on itself. Giambattista Marino's *Adonis* is one example. Instead of telling a story with a beginning, exposition, and end, it provides a variation on what took place in the first part in the second (and thus the text has either two centers or none),[58] or Emanuele Tesauro's colossal rhetorical treatise *The Aristotelian Telescope* (1653, 1670), where the uneven division of chapters and paragraphs seems purposely designed for the reader to get lost in the text, and the uncontainable stylistic exuberance continuously enacts what the treatise itself prescribes, rendering it, in fact, a self-reflexive text. We might also think of those baroque paintings where the extravagant and copious decorations on the frame attract more attention than the painting inside it, resulting in an unstable, indeterminate work, where the spatial-visual center no longer corresponds to the aesthetic and conceptual center.

In what sense can the superhero comic be seen as a work without a center? By now, the answer should be fairly clear. There is the formal level, where the serial nature of the publications creates a specific perceptual effect. As a result, any story being read is at the center of our attention for that moment and our temporary idea of the Marvel or the DC Universe. Still, this is never really the conceptual center of the entire macrotext, never a keystone that connects everything and holds it together. Even with the stories of cosmic cataclysms, where the entire fictional universe depends, at least for a time, on a specific event, once that event is placed within a developing series, it loses its absolute value. And if readers were asked what they consider to be the most important event in the Marvel and DC Universes, each would have a different response and many would probably consider the question senseless. The entire work, then, can be appropriately conceived of as a baroque labyrinth, with issues that continually branch out into parallel stories where different points of entry and different paths of exploration are equally possible, but the whole never leads to a simple, unitary system.[59]

Another centralizing principle lacking in the superhero comic is the voice of the author. This is not so much or not only because the stories are generally written by one artist and drawn by another—given that this is only a routine matter of multiple authorship that could still result in a thoroughly unified product. Rather, what is unique is that such a vast number of different writers and artists have alternated over the course of the decades to develop a single narrative universe, each adding a different contribution to a metatext that transcends each of its authors and that cannot be considered "by" any one of them. The narrative contradictions that we have discussed at length are essentially nothing more than the result of this polyphony of authorial voices that together construct a collective work without flattening or canceling one another out, each remaining recognizable in the general picture but with no owner of the picture itself.

This is viewed by the publishers themselves as a great resource, as we can see in a self-reflexive story of the *Fantastic Four* where the playwright Roberto Aguirre-Sacasa represents himself at the time when he started as a writer for Marvel. In that occasion, the editor advised him:

> Be true to your voice. Meaning: every writer has a certain voice, a certain personality that makes him or her unique. That sets him or her apart from the Grant Morrisons of the world, the Neil Gaimans of the world, the Garth Ennises of the world. [...] What I am saying, bro, is this: the Fantastic Four chose you to write their comic book because of some...quality X in your voice. Don't stifle that. Don't be afraid to put some of yourself in what you write for Marvel.[60]

The same thing happens with the various graphic approaches that different artists have taken over the course of decades, at times profoundly altering the status of the characters. It is well known, for example, that the longer the ears on Batman's cowl and the more jagged the bat on his chest, the more threatening and "tough" the hero seems (or rather, becomes). Again, the succession of different styles within the same title has

THE MYTH OF THE SUPERHERO

enabled the authors to follow the evolution of the audience and to create an interesting gamut of variations on a single theme, while also contributing to freeing the characters from being the expression of only one voice.

In some cases, it is the comic itself that, through the use of imitation, pays homage to the creative richness that has come from different styles within a single character's history. The Batman miniseries *Two-Face Strikes Twice* from 1993, recounts two parallel stories, one drawn in the style of the 1940s and the other in contemporary style, enabling the juxtaposition of different graphic modes to highlight the constitutional duplicity of the principal villain.[61] In a 2005 Fantastic Four story, we find Sue Richards, the Invisible Woman, telling her friends about an old fling she had with the superhero Black Panther. The flashbacks from the past are appropriately drawn in the classic style of Jack Kirby, the artistic creator of the series.[62]

Even more representative of the possible implications of the change in visual style is a 2005 story in which the imp from the fifth dimension Mister Mxyzptlk, who has the power to alter reality, shows Superman and Lois Lane scenes from a hypothetical future in which they have a daughter. These scenes are drawn in the styles of three acclaimed comics authors: Frank Miller, Bruce Timm, and Bill Watterson.[63] The ironic penchant for imitating the style of another is combined with the idea that using a different style truly corresponds to creating a different reality, that a story drawn by two different artists is no longer the same story but something else.

A perfect representation of the effects of this alternation of authors in a long-lived series can be found in the commemorative episodes of *Superman #400* (October 1984) and *Batman: Legends of the Dark Knight #0* (October 1994). The first issue contains eight stories about the perception that future centuries will have of Superman. At that time, according to the authors, the superhero will have become the subject of myths, legends, and semireligious celebrations, separating him from the texts that have generated him and for all intents and purposes turning him into a figure of folklore. In the second issue, we find a gang of villains talking about Batman as an elusive and multifaceted legend. What is striking is that both sets of stories, in order to show the heroes as figures of the public imagination, choose to focus on the variety of artistic styles. Consequently, the eight stories about Superman are drawn by eight different artists and are also interspersed with twelve additional illustrations by others. The Batman story is drawn by sixteen authors and contains a dizzying variety of tones and interpretations. While two classic heroes are

In a 2005 story, the flirtatious exchanges between Sue Richards and Black Panther are drawn in Jack Kirby's classic style. © Marvel

celebrated by gathering a large group of artists around them, the multiple graphic incarnations in these albums reinforce the concept of the superhero belonging to everyone and no one, of whom anyone could be the author through the creation of a "true" and "accurate" Superman or Batman, even if profoundly different from all the others.

THE MYTH OF THE SUPERHERO

The possible future of Clark Kent's family is shown by Mister Mxyzptlk as a panel from Bill Watterson's *Calvin and Hobbes* to indicate the lively and sassy daughter Lois and Clark could have. © DC Comics

And when I say "anyone" that is literally what I mean. The serial nature of the superhero comic that makes it a work perpetually in progress, always expandable, truly makes every reader a potential author. With this type of publication, the publishers need a constant rotation of collaborators. A fan with ideas and talent and who wants to work hard always has the potential to be able to write or draw stories for Marvel or DC one day. This is then the ultimate proof that in the superhero genre there are many (potentially countless) authors but no true Author.

To all this we could add the other characteristics of superheroes we have discussed previously that contribute to giving the genre an identity that is in its own way centrifugal and that contrasts with the idea of order and unity underlying the epic poem. These characteristics are the plurality of the religious traditions that meet peacefully within the same context, the same supergroup, and even the same character (Superman as Moses/Jesus/shaman), and the acceptance of individuality and the intrinsic value of cultural differences. Thus the Avengers have welcomed into their ranks not only men and women of diverse nationalities and ethnic groups but also science and magic (Iron Man and the Scarlet Witch), the human and the machine (Machine Man), man and animal (Tigra), the gigantic and the tiny (Goliath and Wasp), the rational and the irrational (Hank Pym and Hulk), the human and the divine (Thor or Hercules), the material and the immaterial (the hefty Hulk and the Vision, who can dematerialize, or Pulsar, who transforms into light), the present and the past (Captain America who returns after being cryogenically frozen during World War II).

How, then, is it possible to bring together the two frameworks I have outlined in these discussions of the epic and the neobaroque? How can superhero comics be understood as both epic and neobaroque? The answer, I believe, lies in emphasizing the influence of the epic technique especially (but not only) at the level of themes and narrative modes and the neobaroque foundations especially (but not only) at the level of the general conceptualization and "ideology" of the stories. Broadly speaking, what appears to be neobaroque is first and foremost the increased tolerance in American society today, which perhaps unlike any other places value on the profound richness of a tradition of immigration from all over the world, with the consequent coexistence of cultures, religions, ethnicities, languages, talents, and also limitations, which, however, can ideally be compensated by the strengths of another group.

The United States is also liberating itself from an overly rigid, narrow idea of the "Author" of national history. There is a strong current in the country today of abandoning the white-Protestant-male-centric view and recognizing the contributions of many groups to its development. Nor is it surprising that the United States has expanded the traditional concept of literary canon almost to the point of irrelevance, because people have come to understand, rightly so, that in a culture composed of immigrants from every continent, reading European literature is well and good but not intrinsically "better" or more prestigious or useful than knowing the literature of Sudan or Korea or Peru.

This broadened concept of contributions to society, furthermore, should suffice to demonstrate the groundlessness of certain discriminatory positions that reject exposure to cultural or religious diversity for fear of losing their identity or homogenizing all cultures into a single mass. On the contrary, the United States of today demonstrates that it is precisely through the reciprocal interaction of various groups that each of them has had the opportunity to know themselves better, defining, by contrast and comparison, the characteristics and aims that constitute their most unique identity.

The superhero genre provides an epic form of representation of this neobaroque world, as if placing a magnifying glass over the ideas expressed above. Such a procedure accentuates these ideas in a spectacular, charged manner but also leaves their most recognizable and relevant traits intact. The superhero comic, therefore, lies at the juncture of epic and neobaroque; it is the neobaroque narrated in epic form, or rather, the celebratory epic poem of a neobaroque society that emphasizes the organic integration of all forms of diversity. Thus the superhero epic celebrates not only the triumph of Good over Evil, as appears at first glance but also the superhuman effort of its characters and readers to free themselves from what over the course of history has been one of the most nefarious concepts: the absurd concept of purity.

CONCLUSION

Over the years, Marvel and DC superhero comics have distanced them-selves from the basic "us versus them" formula and the racist or other-wise discriminatory stereotypes that plagued them in their early phase, becoming a collection of stories that, as a general rule, tend to avoid gross generalizations and accept many forms of diversity.

In chapter 1, I illustrated this concept by showing how the superhero comic creates a narrative universe in which different religious cultures can peacefully coexist in society and even within a single person. In chapter 2, we saw how the encounter with otherness does not necessarily lead to moral relativism but instead allows an ethical engagement that lasts as long as the members of different cultural groups can agree on a few very general principles, freeing each person to put those principles into prac-tice in whatever way he or she sees fit. As a result, in contemporary super-hero comics a good or a bad guy alike can be black or white, man or woman, Eastern or Western, young or old, beautiful or deformed, a nerd or a jock, American or foreign, Catholic or Protestant, Christian or Mus-lim, since what defines the traits that constitute a hero or a criminal are solely their individual actions.

Even behind the seemingly monolithic clash between Good and Evil at the core of superhero narratives, what was initially a highly simplistic genre has developed all the nuances of an ethical code based on personal choice. This has also enabled the genre of superhero comics to move away from the facile escapism that was present at its very beginning, re-placing it with often irresolvable or as-yet-unresolved conflicts that prompt the reader to reflection or debate.

Certainly there are also economic motives for this. You have readers thinking about a story, talking about it with friends, sending out e-mails,

blogging, going to conventions. In the end there is a much higher proba-
bility that they will want to read the next issue to get a better understanding of the situation. But the fact remains that other contemporary
mass-produced works, also motivated by commercial interests, rarely
present the kind of complex and provocative narratives found in superhero comics, as is apparent if one compares a story in which Superman
wants to stop a war and gets pelted with rocks with the formulaic Hollywood ending (enemy defeated, hero triumphant) or with any popular
action show or thriller novel.

And I don't think it is an exaggeration to attribute the function of "active" entertainment to a visually compelling and literarily pleasing genre
like the superhero comic, first of all because I don't subscribe to a "mas-
ochistic" ideal of culture, according to which "good" or valuable art and
literature are by definition difficult to approach and understand or, essentially, should not be "too enjoyable" or accessible to mass audiences (but
whether there's a division between entertainment and art, or what constitutes that division, is undoubtedly subjective). Furthermore (more objectively speaking), the superhero plot's focus on a dense sequence of
exceptional actions invites readers to consider the ethical validity of each
one. The complexity of the vast superhero macrotext, loaded as is with
narrative self-contradictions, creates the healthy and nowadays rare experience of being exposed to discourses in which every divergent interpretation has its own legitimacy and is equally composed of both strong and
weak arguments. Therefore, consciously or not, readers of superhero
comics are trained to accept and even appreciate the coexistence of ideas
that seem (and to a certain extent are) irreconcilable.

Theorist Kwame Anthony Appiah has recently written about the historical significance of this kind of mental mechanism. In reference to social changes such as women's liberation or increased openness toward
homosexuality, he notes that many opponents to change have adapted
not so much because they were rationally convinced that these positions
were right, but because repeated exposure to them showed that they
weren't such a big deal after all. In other words, they got used to living with
an idea that was once new and unacceptable. While theory and ideology
seek to create a perfect world for their own adherents (and generally fail
to do so), reciprocal practice and habit have led to a society that is at least
more open and more respectful of other positions than it was before. For
this reason, Appiah urges that "we should learn about people in other
places, take an interest in their civilizations, their arguments, their errors,

their achievements, not because that will bring us to agreement, but because it will help us get used to one another."[1] If this is true, the superhero comics of recent decades fulfill a certain purpose in a frequently chaotic and confused society such as ours.

Behind the dazzling facade of bold colors, spectacular physiques, and intense action sequences, superhero comics familiarize their audiences with a hypothetical model for a multicultural, multiethnic, and multireligious society, one that is averse to the rigidity of fundamentalism and able to defend itself against its enemies without stooping to their level. A society that, even with a thousand problems and contradictions, manages to keep afloat by holding on to a few general values (like freedom and justice) that are flexible enough to be shared by all without stifling the traditions and beliefs of the individuals within it. And the great thing is that superhero comics do not try to preach these ideas: they show them, narrate them, make them seem and feel right, and in this way, in the manner described by Appiah, enable readers to get used to them and become more inclined to at least consider them possible.

THE MYTH OF THE SUPERHERO

Notes

Introduction

1. For more on the history of comics, there are numerous reference books, a complete list of which would be overwhelming for our purposes. On superhero comics in particular, the following books provide a good idea of the history of the genre: Gerard Jones and Will Jacobs, *The Comic Book Heroes* (Roseville, CA: Prima Publishing, 1997); Les Daniels, *DC Comics: Sixty Years of the World's Favorite Comic Book Heroes* (Boston: Bulfinch Press, 1995); Les Daniels, *Marvel: Five Fabulous Decades of the World's Greatest Comics* (New York: Abrams, 1991); Peter Sanderson, *Classic Marvel Superheroes: The Story of Marvel's Mightiest* (New York: Barnes & Noble Books, 2005); Mike Benton, *Superhero Comics of the Golden Age: The Illustrated History* (Dallas: Taylor Publishing Company, 1992); Mike Benton, *Superhero Comics of the Silver Age: The Illustrated History* (Dallas: Taylor Publishing Company, 1991); Trina Robbins, *The Great Women Superheroes* (Northampton, MA: Kitchen Sink Press, 1996); Angela Ndalianis, *The Contemporary Comic Book Superheroes* (London: Routledge, 2009).

2. Some of these superheroes include figures destined for long-term success such as Batman (by Bob Kane and Bill Finger, 1939), Captain America (by Joe Simon and Jack Kirby, 1941), and Wonder Woman (by William Moulton Marston and Harry G. Peter, 1941).

3. Founded by Martin Goodman, Marvel began publishing in October 1939 under the name Timely Publications. Their first publication was *Marvel Comics*, which contained, among others, the first stories of Namor the Sub-Mariner and the original Human Torch. In 1941 Joe Simon and Jack Kirby created one of the most famous superheroes of all time, Captain America, and at the same time, Timely named the young Stan Lee editor-in-chief. In 1951, Goodman changed the name to Atlas and began responding to the steep decline in superhero comics sales by expanding publication to include romances, Westerns, horror, and spy novels. Starting in 1961, with the launch of Stan Lee and Jack Kirby's *Fantastic Four*, the company by then renamed Marvel Comics radically revitalized the genre by introducing the concept of the superhero with super-problems, in other words, a less optimistic or simplistic character. Marvel's most important creations, beyond those mentioned here and in

note 4, include Thor (Stan Lee and Jack Kirby, 1962), Iron Man (Stan Lee, Larry Lieber, and Don Heck, 1963), the Avengers (Stan Lee and Jack Kirby, 1963), Daredevil (Stan Lee and Bill Everett, 1964), Silver Surfer (Stan Lee and Jack Kirby, 1966), Ghost Rider (Roy Thomas, Gary Friedrich, and Mike Ploog, 1972), and Wolverine (Len Wein and John Romita Sr., 1974).

4. Hence the Fantastic Four (Stan Lee and Jack Kirby, 1961), a member of which, Ben Grimm, perceives his superstrong body as a monstrous deformity; Spider-Man (Stan Lee and Steve Ditko, 1962), a hero who unintentionally causes the death of his own uncle; and Hulk (Stan Lee and Jack Kirby, 1962) and the X-Men (Stan Lee and Jack Kirby, 1963), heroes pursued both by the authorities and by civilians.

5. Image was founded in 1992 by a group of artists who were dissatisfied with their previous work with other publishers and wanted to keep creative control over and copyright to their characters. These artists, along with some of their most renowned creations for Image, are Erik Larsen with *Savage Dragon*, Jim Lee with *WildC.A.T.s*, Rob Liefeld with *Youngblood*, Todd McFarlane with *Spawn*, Whilce Portacio with *Wetworks*, Marc Silvestri with *Cyberforce*, and Jim Valentino with *ShadowHawk*.

6. DC, founded by Major Malcolm Wheeler-Nicholson as National Allied Publications, debuted in 1935 with the comics magazine *New Fun*, the first comic book completely dedicated to original strips, initiating the format that the superhero genre is most identified with. In 1937, Wheeler-Nicholson published the magazine *Detective Comics* and renamed the publishing company Detective Comics, Inc., which appeared in abbreviated form as DC on their covers from 1940 on. In *Adventure Comics* #1, which came out in 1938, DC founded the superhero comic genre with the publication of the first Superman story by Siegel and Shuster. They later capitalized on Superman's popularity by creating other superheroes such as Batman, Wonder Woman (see note 2), Green Lantern (Bill Finger and Martin Nodell, 1940), the Flash (Gardner Fox and Harry Lampert, 1940), the Spectre (Jerry Siegel and Bernard Baily, 1940), Hawkman (Gardner Fox, 1940), Aquaman (Mort Weisinger and Paul Norris, 1941), Green Arrow (Mort Weisinger and George Papp, 1941), and the first superhero team, the Justice Society of America (Gardner Fox and Sheldon Mayer, 1940). In 1956, the comeback of the Flash character signaled the reemergence of interest in superheroes during the still difficult period of the 1950s, so much so that people spoke of a new era, a "Silver Age" of comics. The year 1986 marks another milestone for the whole genre with the publication by DC of *The Dark Knight Returns* by Frank Miller, Klaus Janson, and Lynn Varley and the launch of the miniseries *Watchmen* by Alan Moore and Dave Gibbons. These two works took the question of heroism and ethics to such levels of complexity and were so artistically successful that general audiences and critics alike were forced to recognize that the superhero genre has (at least potentially) the ability to compete with more confirmed narrative genres.

7. Dark Horse arose from the initiative of Mike Richardson, who began publishing an anthology of independent comics in 1986 under the title *Dark Horse Presents*. Specializing in series inspired by film and television, Dark Horse has published superhero comics, most notably in the Comics' Greatest World imprint in the nineties.

8. Alan Moore and Dave Gibbons, *Watchmen* (New York: DC Comics, 1987); Frank Miller, Klaus Janson, and Lynn Varley, *The Dark Knight Returns* (New York: DC

Notes to Pages 1–6

Comics, 1986); Kurt Busiek and Alex Ross, *Marvels* (New York: Marvel Comics, 1995). The *Astro City* series, created by Kurt Busiek, began being published in 1995 by Image Comics, thereafter by Homage and DC/Wildstorm. The Vertigo imprint, launched by DC in 1993, publishes comics geared toward older teens and adults that feature controversial themes and often unusual—when not outright experimental—narrative techniques.

9. Art Spiegelman, *Maus: A Survivor's Tale* (New York: Pantheon Books, 1986 and 1991).

10. Douglas Wolk also laments this in his *Reading Comics: How Graphic Novels Work and What They Mean* (Cambridge, MA: Da Capo Press, 2007), 342: "For those of us who've been passionate about comics for ages, it's hard not to resent *Maus* a little for being a lot of other people's sole idea of what art comics are like. It's the equivalent of what Bob Marley is to reggae, the one fine example that too often stands in for the whole and becomes an inappropriate model and reference point. [...] Part of what rankles, of course, is the general perception that *Maus* was a one-of-a-kind work with no historical precedent (and that therefore if you love *Maus* you can still safely ignore the rest of the medium), when in fact Spiegelman is more deeply attached to the whole history of comics than any other cartoonist this side of Chris Ware."

11. John Stuart Mill. *The Spirit of the Age* (New Haven: Yale University Press, 2007), 70.

Chapter 1. Myth and Religion

1. This is the subtitle of Richard Reynolds's study *Superheroes: A Modern Mythology* (Jackson: University of Mississippi Press, 1992), in particular 53–60. On superheroes, religion, and mythology, see Don LoCicero, *Superheroes and Gods: A Comparative Study from Babylonia to Batman* (Jefferson, NC: McFarland & Co., 2008); Greg Garrett, *Holy Superheroes! Exploring the Sacred in Comics, Graphic Novels, and Film* (Louisville, KY: Westminster John Knox Press, 2008); Chris Knowles, *Our Gods Wear Spandex: The Secret History of Comic Books Heroes* (San Francisco: Weiser Books, 2007); edited by B. J. Oropeza, *The Gospel According to Superheroes: Religion and Pop Culture* (New York: Peter Lang, 2005); C. J. Mackie, "Men of Darkness," in *Super/Heroes from Hercules to Superman*, edited by Wendy Haslem, Angela Ndalianis, and Chris Mackie (Washington, DC: New Academia Publishing, 2007), 83–95; Jamie Egolf, "Dreaming Superman: Exploring the Action of the Superhero(ine) in Dreams, Myth, and Culture," in *Super/Heroes from Hercules to Superman*, 139–51; Peter Coogan, *Superhero: The Secret Origin of a Genre* (Austin: Monkey Brain Books, 2006), 116–25; Geoff Klock, *How to Read Superhero Comics and Why* (New York: Continuum, 2002), 39–50.

2. Dennis O'Neil, "The Man of Steel and Me," in *Superman at Fifty! The Persistence of a Legend!*, edited by Dennis Dooley et al. (New York: Macmillan Publishing, 1988), 55.

3. Joseph Campbell, *The Hero with a Thousand Faces* (Novato, CA: New World Libra, 2008), 23. See also Stephen Harper, "Supermyth!," in *The Man from Krypton: A Closer Look at Superman*, edited by Glenn Yeffeth (Dallas: Benbella Books, 2006), 93–100.

4. For a more recent example, see Kurt Busiek and Jesus Merino, *Superman* #673, April 2008, later reprinted in the volume *Shadows Linger* (New York: DC Comics, 2009). At the end of the story, Superman brings some machinery to Earth from the

aliens who had tried to invade the planet. Note that in this story this new technology is called a "boon," the same exact term Campbell uses in the above passage to describe the hero's gifts to the community.

5. O'Neil, "The Man of Steel and Me," 51.

6. Gardner Fox and Harry Lampert, in *Flash Comics* #1, January 1940, reprinted in *The Golden Age Flash Archives*, vol. 1 (New York: DC Comics, 1999). Something of a precedent can be found in Namor, the Sub-Mariner, from 1939, who also has winged feet but is an aquatic creature and isn't presented as a mythological descendant. See Bill Everett, "The Sub-Mariner," in *Motion Picture Funnies Weekly*, April 1939, undistributed, then published in *Marvel Comics* #1, October 1939, available today in the volume *The Golden Age of Marvel Comics* (New York: Marvel Comics, 1997). Also, Quicksilver (the Marvel universe mutant endowed with superhuman speed) has two tufts of hair that evoke Mercury's wings.

7. Bill Parker and C. C. Beck, *Whiz Comics* #2, February 1940, now in *Shazam! The Greatest Stories Ever Told* (New York: DC Comics, 2008). In 1942, Billy's sister, the spinoff character Mary Marvel, is created; for her, "Shazam" confers the power of Selena's grace, Hippolyta's strength, Ariadne's skill, Zephyrus's fleetness, Aurora's beauty, and Minerva's wisdom. See Otto Binder and Marc Swayze, *Captain Marvel Adventures* #18, December 1942.

8. Gardner Fox and Howard Sherman, in *More Fun Comics* #55, May 1940, recently reprinted in *The Golden Age Doctor Fate*, vol. 1 (New York: DC Comics, 2007).

9. Martin A. Burstein and Jack Kirby, "Mercury in the 20th Century," in *Red Raven Comics* #1, August 1940, now in the volume *The Complete Jack Kirby*, vol. 1 (New York: Pure Imagination, 1997).

10. Jack Kirby recycled the same ideas in another story the following year, when he introduced a character who is visually identical to Mercury (with the same wings on his head and feet), who also fights his cousin Pluto, but is called "Hurricane, son of Thor, the god of thunder, and last descendant of the ancient Greek immortals." This Mercury son-of-Thor was clearly a device to use the same character from the previous year in a different periodical and to avoid copyright problems. Yet it would seem that Kirby had a fondness for this fusion of Thor and Mercury, which would explain the winged helmet that the author gave his Thor in 1962 (instead of the more predictable "Viking" helmet with horns). And aren't those Mercury's wings on the mask of Captain America, who appeared for the first time in the same issue with Hurricane?

11. William Moulton Marston and Harry G. Peter, *All Star Comics* #8, December 1941–January 1942, now in *Wonder Woman Archives*, vol. 1 (New York: DC Comics, 1998), 10–11.

12. William Moulton Marston and Harry G. Peter, *Sensation Comics* #1, January 1942, now in *Wonder Woman Archives*, vol. 1, 18.

13. William Moulton Marston and Harry G. Peter, *Wonder Woman* #1, Summer 1942, now in *Wonder Woman Archives*, vol. 1, 151.

14. Dennis O'Neil and Mike Sekowsky, *Wonder Woman* #179, December 1968, now in the volume *Diana Prince: Wonder Woman*, vol. 1 (New York: DC Comics, 2008).

15. Dennis O'Neil and Mike Sekowsky, *Wonder Woman* #183, August 1969, now in *Diana Prince: Wonder Woman*, vol. 1.

16. Greg Rucka and Drew Johnson, *Wonder Woman*, vol. 2, #210, November 2004, reprinted in the collection *Eyes of the Gorgon* (New York: DC Comics, 2005).

17. In fact, in some cases the healing conducted by the shaman includes a component of adventure more like a superhero's journey than a medical story. This happens when the patient's soul has left his body and is trapped in the spirit world. Therefore the shaman has to go into a trance to reach that plane of existence, defeat its guards, and free the sick person's soul. See Joseph Campbell, *The Masks of God: Primitive Mythology* (New York: Viking Press, 1959), 261; Piers Vitebsky, *Shamanism* (Norman: University of Oklahoma Press, 2001), 66–69 and 74–78, and the general discussion in Mircea Eliade, *Shamanism: Archaic Techniques of Ecstasy* (London: Penguin Arkana, 1988). Eliade's text, considered a classic for decades, has been contrasted by Alice Beck Kehoe, *Shamans and Religion: An Anthropological Exploration in Critical Thinking* (Long Grove, IL: Waveland Press, 2000), which I point out so that readers can compare for themselves. For a discussion of neo-shamanism and the impact of shamanistic tradition on contemporary culture, see Roger Walsh, *The World of Shamanism: New Views of an Ancient Tradition* (Woodbury, MN: Llewellyn Publications, 2007).

18. Lucy Wright, "Shamans vs. (Super)heroes," in Haslem, Ndalianis, and Mackie, *Super/Heroes*, 127–37.

19. Still, a significant difference must be noted, which is that the shaman travels in the spirit world in an altered, often drug-induced mental state. This element is absent in superhero comics, if only because the representation of drugs (or their use by the heroes) was long prohibited by the Comics Code—a code of conduct decreed by comics authors in the fifties to reassure parents of the morality of their work. On the Comics Code, see David Hajdu, *The Ten-Cent Plague: The Great Comic-Book Scare and How It Changed America* (New York: Farrar, Straus and Giroux, 2008); Amy Kyste Nyberg, *Seal of Approval: The History of the Comics Code* (Jackson: University of Mississippi Press, 1998).

20. Campbell, *The Masks of God*, 249.

21. Ibid., 231.

22. Eliade, *Shamanism*, 3–32, especially 19 and 28.

23. Campbell, *The Masks of God*, 255. See also Campbell, *The Hero with a Thousand Faces*, 149; Eliade, *Shamanism*, 46–48 and 57.

24. Eliade, *Shamanism*, 156–60. For a more complete discussion, see the entire chapter "Symbolism of the Shaman's Costume and Drum," 145–80.

25. Ibid., 147.

26. Ibid., 179.

27. The juxtaposition of heroes and criminals on this list should not be surprising; the tradition includes shamans who use animal spirits for healing as well as shamans who use those same sources of power for evil aims.

28. Old episodes of the series, including the heroine's origin story, can now be read in Tarpe Mills, *Miss Fury* (New York: Pure Imagination Publishing, 2007).

29. I write "seems" because in the story it isn't clear if Snake Dance really casts these spells or if they are a trick (perhaps achieved through hypnotic suggestion). Yet even this ambiguity isn't outside the province of the traditional shaman figure,

who for some is an authentic agent of the supernatural and for others is a skilled trickster-conjurer.

30. Gary Friedrich and Tom Sutton, *Marvel Spotlight* #8–11, February and August 1973, now in the volume *Essential Ghost Rider*, vol. 1 (New York: Marvel Comics, 2005).

31. Bill Mantlo, George Pérez, and Jack Abel, "An Ending!," in *The Deadly Hands of Kung Fu* #19, December 1975.

32. The first Vixen story came out in 1978, during a time of serious difficulty for DC Comics. It was published in the limited-edition anthology *Cancelled Comic Cavalcade*, vol. 2, edited by Joe Orlando (New York: DC Comics, 1978), which was created primarily to establish DC's copyright on the characters. For Vixen's real editorial debut, see Gerry Conway and Bob Oksner, *Action Comics* #521, July 1981. Recently, Vixen received the honor of her own miniseries, *Return of the Lion* #1–5 (December 2008–April 2009) by G. Willow Wilson and Cafu, where the heroine embarks on an initiation journey similar to that of a traditional shaman.

33. Chris Claremont and John Byrne, *Uncanny X-Men* #120, April 1979, now in *Uncanny X-Men Omnibus*, vol. 1 (New York: Marvel Comics, 2006).

34. Also striking is the fact that Shaman's real name is Michael Twoyoungmen, which represents his dual nature as a medical scientist and mystical healer, as "Canadian" and "native," but that could also allude to that intrinsic duality (as a person who is both common and special) which, as we have seen, shamans and superheroes share.

35. Introduced in, respectively, Mark Gruenwald et al., *Contest of Champions* #1, June 1982, then in an eponymous volume (New York: Marvel Comics, 1999); John Byrne, *Alpha Flight*, vol. 1, #5, December 1983, now in *Alpha Flight Classic*, 1 (New York: Marvel Comics, 2007). In several X-Men stories there is the character Gateway, an Australian shaman who helps the heroes to travel around the world with his powers of teleportation. This character was introduced in Chris Claremont and Mark Silvestri in *Uncanny X-Men* #227, March 1988.

36. Dennis O'Neil and Edward Hannigan, "Shaman," in *Batman: Legends of the Dark Knight* #1–5, November 1989–March 1990, later reprinted in the volume *Batman: Shaman* (New York: DC Comics, 1998).

37. At one point Bruce Wayne, in his Batman mask, even conducts a healing ritual, guided by an old shaman!

38. John Ostrander and Tom Mandrake, *The Kents* #4, November 1997, later reprinted in the volume *The Kents* (New York: DC Comics, 1999). See also Ivan Baio's reading in *Supereroi™. Araldica e simbologia mitka dell'eroismo dai miti classici a Superman e The Authority* [Heraldry and Mythic Symbolism in the Classic Myths of Superman and "The Authority"] (Latina, Italy: Tunué, 2006), 76–80.

39. J. Michael Straczynski and John Romita Jr., *Amazing Spider-Man* #507, July 2004, now in the collection *The Book of Ezekiel* (New York: Marvel Comics, 2004).

40. J. Michael Straczynski and John Romita Jr., *Amazing Spider-Man*, vol. 2, #31, July 2001, now in the collection *Coming Home* (New York: Marvel Comics, 2002).

41. Stan Lee and Jack Kirby, *Fantastic Four*, vol. 1, #72, March 1968. See Oropeza, *The Gospel According to Superheroes*, 3–4.

42. Steve Gerber and Jim Mooney, *Marvel Spotlight: Son of Satan* #17, September 1974, now reprinted in *Essential Marvel Horror*, vol. 1 (New York: Marvel Comics, 2006).

43. John Byrne, *Avengers West Coast* #52, December 1989, reprinted in the volume *Avengers West Coast: Darker than Scarlet* (New York: Marvel Comics, 2008).

44. Dan Jurgens, Eric Larsen, and Klaus Janson, *The Mighty Thor*, vol. 2, #28, October 2000, now in *Across All Worlds* (New York: Marvel Comics, 2001).

45. The same thing happened with DC. In 1940, the Spectre received his powers directly from God, here represented as a simple ray of light and given the generic name "the Voice." See Jerry Siegel and Bernard Baily, *The Spectre* #3, in *More Fun Comics* #54, April 1940, now in *Golden Age Spectre Archives*, vol. 1 (New York: DC Comics, 2003), 42. Some months later, Doctor Fate traveled to the realm of the dead and encountered a being of pure light with the generic epithet "The Wisdom Who Rules the World." See Gardner Fox and Howard Sherman's untitled story in *More Fun Comics* #56, June 1940, now reprinted in *The Golden Age Doctor Fate* (New York: DC Comics, 2007).

46. Simcha Weinstein, *Up, Up, and Oy Vey! How Jewish History, Culture and Values Shaped the Comic Book Superhero* (Baltimore: Leviathan Press, 2006), 16–17. On Judaism and American comics, see also Arie Kaplan, *From Krakow to Krypton: Jews and Comic Books* (Philadelphia: Jewish Publication Society, 2008); Paul Buhle, ed., *Jews and American Comics: An Illustrated History of an American Art Form* (New York: New Press, 2008); Danny Fingeroth, *Disguised as Clark Kent: Jews, Comics, and the Creation of the Superhero* (New York: Continuum, 2007); Estelle Strazdins, "Conqueror of Flood, Wielder of Fire: Noah the Hebrew Superhero," in Haslem, Ndalianis, and Mackie, *Super/Heroes*, 275–87.

47. However, I want to specify that an author's particular ethnic or religious group does not *in itself* necessarily guarantee that this background is actually reflected in the artistic creations of that author. If it seems impossible that the cultural makeup of authors such as the aforementioned would not have somehow influenced the development of the superhero genre, in some cases it may very well be that a Jewish author wrote stories without any Jewish elements, perhaps to appeal to a primarily Christian audience as is found in the United States, or simply because the author had distanced himself from his cultural origins and thus his creative work shows the traces of that separation.

48. This is alluded to ironically in *Superman II*, when a group of tourists sees the hero saving a boy from Niagara Falls and a woman from the group remarks: "What a nice man! Of course he's Jewish!" in *Superman II*, directed by Richard Lester (and Richard Donner, not credited), 1980.

49. Michael Chabon is one of the many to associate the figure of the superhero with the golem, as in his novel *The Amazing Adventures of Kavalier & Clay* (New York: Picador, 2001).

50. See Weinstein, *Up, Up, and Oy Vey!*, 26; Les Daniels, *Superman: The Complete History* (New York: Chronicle Books, 1998), 19. On the diffusion of the myth of the hero who is abandoned, set adrift, or exposed as a baby, see Campbell, *The Hero with a Thousand Faces*, 276–77.

51. See Weinstein, *Up, Up, and Oy Vey!*, 27.

52. Ibid.

53. Louise Simonson and Jon Bogdanove, *Man of Steel* #81, July 1998.

54. Something similar also happens in another commemorative episode, *Superman* #400, October 1984, edited by Julius Schwartz, which contains various stories on the character's heritage and legend in future centuries in the DC Universe, where we see Superman being celebrated as a sort of religious figure on a holiday much like Passover (for more on this, see Weinstein, *Up, Up, and Oy Vey!*, 20). Here, in effect, we have come full circle: if the original Superman came at least in part out of the Jewish tradition, in this story it is the Judaism of the future to be influenced by Superman.

55. Paul Simpson et al., ed., *The Rough Guide to Superheroes* (London: Haymarket Customer Publishing, 2004), 5.

56. This is applicable even if this factor ends up being less important in Superman's specific case, since his superhero public image involves the *loss* of an attribute of civil identity rather than the addition of a mask. Still, the famous removing of his glasses (along with him tousling his hair) constitutes the recognizable and iconic sign we want to emphasize here. Furthermore, the fact that Clark Kent wears glasses that Superman doesn't need spurred Jules Feiffer to write in the 1960s that Superman's real identity is his alien identity and Clark Kent is the mask, the façade (in *The Great Comic Book Heroes*, [New York: Bonanza Books, 1965], 18–19, and also referenced—or rather, plagiarized—by Quentin Tarantino in the film *Kill Bill*, Vol. 2). As a side note, I personally disagree with this reading, which in a way interprets Superman from Lex Luthor's perspective, seeing him as an alien disguised as a human. This view ignores the fact that Kal-El was adopted by human beings and raised with values of the Earth. If his powers are of extraterrestrial origin, still Superman's ethics and psychology are based on what the young Clark Kent absorbed in the years before adopting the costume and the title of superhero. In other words, Superman is what he is and does what he does because there is always something of Clark Kent's earthly upbringing inside him.

57. Kurt Busiek and Fabian Nicieza, *Superman* #659, February 2007, now in the volume *Superman: Redemption* (New York: DC Comics, 2007).

58. Greg Potter and George Pérez, *Wonder Woman*, vol. 2, #1, February 1987, now in the collection *Gods and Mortals* (New York: DC Comics, 2004), 33.

59. I obviously refer to stories without indications to the contrary, or rather stories not external to the "canon" of the narrative universe, such as unauthorized parodies, instances of plagiarism, or homages, "What Ifs" and "Elseworlds," which are clearly external to the main continuity (based as they are on working hypotheses such as: what would happen if Peter Parker hadn't become Spider-Man? What if Bruce Wayne had lived in the Middle Ages?). So forgive me the tautology, but to avoid any misunderstandings I prefer to specify that only the stories not excluded a priori from the "standard" narrative universe in question have the same degree of reality within such narrative universe. In other words, one need not do anything specific to include a new Marvel Spider-Man story in the character's multidecade story. In absence of indications to the contrary, the readers take it as a given that each new addition builds on to the previous narrative continuum. On the basis of this (and what they know of that continuum), they construct their own interpretation of narrative events and change their own perception of the entire timeline.

60. The fact that Captain America's authors were Jewish—and that Captain America's protection of the Jews was implicit in his battle against the Nazis—actually

elicited death threats from American Hitler sympathizers. In the early forties, one incensed voice shouted "Death to the Jews!" in front of the Timely (later Marvel) offices. See Joe Simon and Jim Simon, *The Comic Book Makers* (Lebanon, NJ: Vanguard Productions, 2003), 45.

61. See Joe Simon and Jack Kirby, *Captain America Comics* #2, April 1941, reprinted in *Marvel Masterworks: Golden Age Captain America* (New York: Marvel Comics, 2005).

62. Weinstein, *Up, Up, and Oy Vey!*, 50–51. These symbolic-visual parallels are reinforced further when one thinks about how the patriotic symbols and their position on Captain America's costume could have been done in countless other ways that would not have had the double meaning I note in the text above. Just think of Shield, a superhero created the year before Captain America, whose chest armor also bore flag symbols, or Wonder Woman, Captain America's contemporary, who has the stars from the flag on her skirt (later pants) and the American eagle on her chest, and has bracelets for defense instead of a shield.

63. The difference may seem specious: why should the average person in the Marvel Universe trust Iron Man, who can shoot rays of energy from his armor, but fear Cyclops, whose power (shooting optical rays) is practically identical but obtained naturally? Still, it is worth talking about this specious division, insofar as in the real world it lies at the root of a sadly common discriminatory mentality, according to which the problem isn't the existence or the nature of a certain power—physical, military, political, economic, etc.—but the fear of the "different" being able to use it.

64. This element, fundamental to the modern version of the character, is depicted at the beginning of the *X-Men* film (Bryan Singer, 2000). See also the stories of Chris Claremont and John Bolton, "A Fire in the Sky," in *Classic X-Men* #19, March 1988, reprinted in *Magneto* #0 (New York: Marvel Comics, 1993), and Ralph Macchio and John Byrne, "That I Be Bound in a Nutshell," in *X-Factor Annual* #4, 1989, 31–41. See also essays by Marie-Catherine Caillava, "Magneto the Jew," in *The Unauthorized X-Men*, edited by Len Wein and Leah Wilson (Dallas: BenBella Books, 2005), 99–109, and by Cheryl Alexander Malcolm, "Witness, Trauma, and Remembrance: Holocaust Representation and *X-Men* Comics," in *The Jewish Graphic Novel: Critical Approaches*, edited by Samantha Baskind and Ranen Omer-Sherman (New Brunswick, NJ: Rutgers University Press, 2008), 144–60.

65. Chris Claremont and John Bolton, "I, Magneto," in *Classic X-Men* #12, August 1987, reprinted in *Magneto* #0.

66. Karl Kesel and Stuart Immonen, *Fantastic Four*, vol. 3, #56, August 2002. *Remembrance of Things Past* is one of the standard English titles of Proust's *À la recherche du temps perdu*, thus the story includes a nice play of words with "things."

67. This parallel is explicated in Bill Mantlo and Bob Brown, *Marvel Two-In-One* #11, September 1975, where the Thing is shown in battle with an actual golem brought to life from the pages of *Strange Tales* (Len Wein and John Buscema, *Strange Tales* #174 and 176–77, June–December 1974). A few years ago, in the sequel to "Remembrance of Things Past," the Thing encountered a golem that had been long buried underground, and he felt a curious connection between his own "monstrosity" and the clay giant's (see the illustration of this in the chapter). See Roberto Aguirre-Sacasa and Valentine De Landro, *Marvel Knights 4* #22, September 2005, reprinted in

the volume *Marvel Knights 4: Impossible Things Happen Every Day* (New York: Marvel Comics, 2006). Batman meets a classic golem in Peter Milligan and Jim Aparo, *Detective Comics* #631–32, July 1991; Superman faces a cosmic golem in Kurt Busiek et al., *Superman* #675, June 2008, later reprinted in the volume *Shadows Linger* (New York: DC Comics, 2009).

68. See also *Ultrachrist!,* Kerry Douglas Dye, 2003, another independent film that depicts Jesus as a superhero (complete with costume) in action in the contemporary world.

69. At most it comes to an unstated, uncompromising representation of major Christian figures. In one old story, Ghost Rider is saved from Satan's clutches by a stranger in modern clothes who vaguely recalls the Jesus of traditional iconography. When Ghost Rider asks the stranger his name, he says only: "I'm . . . a friend." See Tony Isabella and Jim Mooney, *Ghost Rider* #9, December 1974, now in *Essential Ghost Rider*, 1 (New York: Marvel Comics, 2006). In an anomalous story, Spider-Man meets God, who is represented as a homeless man and never referred to by name. See Roberto Aguirre-Sacasa and Clayton Crain, *Sensational Spider-Man* #40, August 2007, later reprinted in *Back in Black*, 2 (New York: Marvel Comics, 2007).

70. In this list of superheroes whose religion is known, I have in mind the Catholics Daredevil and Nightcrawler (who both, oddly, have demoniac connotations, the former in name and costume, the latter in physical appearance) or the mutant Dust in the New X-Men, a rare instance of a Muslim character described as a superhero and not as a criminal.

71. See Glenn Herdling and Craig Brasfield, *Illuminator* #1–3, February–June 1993. These phrases are the slogans that appear on the cover of issues 1 and 2, respectively.

72. On the relationship between angels and superheroes, see Lisa Beaven, "Someone to Watch over Me: The Guardian Angel as Superhero in Seicento Rome," in *Super/Heroes from Hercules to Superman*, edited by Haslem et al., 251–61.

73. Morrison may not have been the first to see this analogy of Hawkman as a type of angel. In 1961 Gardner Fox and Joe Kubert relaunched the Hawkman character after a decade of oblivion (*The Brave and the Bold* #34, February–March 1961, in *Hawkman Essential*, vol. 1 [New York: DC Comics] 2007). Just two years later, in 1963, Stan Lee and Jack Kirby added Angel, a human with bird wings representing the Marvel version of DC's Hawkman, to the ranks of their X-Men (*The X-Men Omnibus*, vol. 1 [New York: Marvel Comics, 2009]).

74. Grant Morrison explained in an interview: "Zauriel started out as an attempt by Mark Millar and I to create a completely new and updated Hawkman. Instead of the science-fiction origin of Katar Hol, we gave him a heavenly background to explain the wings and the crusading. He was originally intended to appear in the JLA under the name Hawkman, and I imagined a sense-strangling battle of the Hawkmen between Zauriel and Katar Hol at some point down the line. The Hawkman name was seen as a biohazard after the numerous continuity maulings the character had sustained. We were asked to retain the angel concept and simply call him Zauriel. I felt it took away the mythic power of the name Hawkman from the team, but I grew to like Zauriel when, as you say, I decided to write him as DC's Thor but with a Judeo-Christian/Muslim background to replace the halls of Asgard, et cetera." The

interview can be read at https://sites.google.com/site/deepspacetransmissions/inter views-1/1990-s/199911-next-planet-over.

75. Grant Morrison and Howard Porter, *JLA* #6, June 1997, reprinted in *JLA: American Dreams* (New York: DC Comics, 1998); Mark Millar and Ariel Olivetti, *JLA: Paradise Lost* #1–3, January–March 1998.

76. Charlie Houston et al., *Marvel One-Shot: Horror*, October 2005, reprinted in *Legion of Monsters* (New York: Marvel Comics, 2007). A previous official statement was nearly identical: "Mephisto is an extradimensional demon, his nature and origins unknown. He is the ruler of a fiery dimension he calls Hell, and has a number of lesser demons serving him. His domain also houses the astral bodies of certain deceased human beings, trapped in the bodies of demons." See Mark Sanderson et al., *The Official Handbook of the Marvel Universe*, #7, July 1983, now reprinted in the volume *Essential Official Handbook of the Marvel Universe* (New York: Marvel Comics, 2006).

77. Charlie Houston et al., *Marvel One-Shot: Horror*, entry "Hellstorm."

78. Daniel Way, Javier Saltares, and Max Texeira, *Ghost Rider* #1–5, July–November 2006, now in the volume *Vicious Cycle* (New York: Marvel Comics, 2007). Ghost Rider stories, however, are an exception in the boldness of their representation of the Christian supernatural (or, if one accepts the game above that Mephisto is not really the devil but merely acts like him, of the doubles of the Christian supernatural).

79. Jim Starlin, *The Death of Captain Marvel* (New York: Marvel Comics, 1994).

80. This is also reminiscent of the image of Clark Kent bound to a scarecrow pole as if he had been crucified during a scene in the pilot of the television series *Smallville* (2001), as well as in the show's promotional material. See Gustav Peebles, "God, Communism, and the WB," in *The Man from Krypton*, edited by Glenn Yeffeth, 77–92.

81. In fact, when Octopus returns to attack the passengers trying to defend Spider-Man, they are brutally and effortlessly defeated. Certainly the passengers knew right from the beginning that they had no hope of besting the supervillain, but they nonetheless chose to be loyal to the one who had saved them.

82. On Superman as Christ metaphor, see in particular Stephen Skelton, *The Gospel According to the World's Greatest Superhero* (Eugene, OR: Harvest House Publishing, 2006), and Ken Schenck, "Superman: A Popular Messiah," in *The Gospel According to Superheroes*, edited by Oropeza, 33–48.

83. See Skelton, *The Gospel According to the World's Greatest Superhero*, 47–48. The same symbolism returns at the end of *Superman II* (1980), where Zod believes that Superman has lost his powers and he forces the hero to kneel before him, thinking he is at last exacting on the son the threat that he had made to the father.

84. Skelton, *The Gospel According to the World's Greatest Superhero*, 55–56.

85. Again with a notable scriptural parallel, given that in the Bible there is no news of Joseph after Jesus is twelve years old. Therefore, it seems reasonable to assume that he died when his adoptive son was still fairly young (as noted by Skelton).

86. The idea of Superman as being sent from the sky for a mission to save humanity is also very present in the recent film *Superman Returns* (Bryan Singer, 2006), in which Superman comes back down to Earth after a long absence, in what is truly a second coming. The messianic symbolism is clearly expressed in the original film

poster, with Superman suspended in flight over Earth, his cape swelling as if simulating angel wings, his pose and facial expression showing him in absorbed contemplation (about the ills of the world, it might seem).

87. See Schenk, "Superman: A Popular Messiah," 33 and 44, where it is noted that this Superman enters the Fortress of Solitude for the first time at eighteen and is instructed there by his father for twelve years before putting on the hero's cape.

88. In the comic, the connection between Superman and Jesus reached its most obvious parallel in 1992–1993, with the story arc that saw the hero's death and resurrection. The fact that the characters are reinserted into the narrative world after death is nowadays commonplace in the superhero genre, but this rarely involves a genuine return from the dead. More often we come to learn that the character wasn't really dead, or that the body had died but the psyche was transferred to another body (perhaps a clone's), or maybe other characters travel back in time or change the fabric of reality in such a way that the deceased never actually died, and so on. Superman's corpse, however, was literally regenerated and brought back from the dead by the alien machines in the Fortress of Solitude. See Dan Jurgens et al., *The Death of Superman* (New York: DC Comics, 1993); Louise Simonson et al., *The Return of Superman* (New York: DC Comics, 1993).

89. See Baio, *Supereroi*TM, 76–80.

90. Note also that the star symbol on Captain Marvel's chest, if placed within the context of other Christian signs, as on the cover of *The Death of Captain Marvel*, can take on the significance of the flaming heart.

91. In superhero comics, the Catholic reader may also see modern versions of other traditional figures who receive miraculous powers such as flight or invulnerability: the saints. No disrespect is intended in such a comparison—the religious themselves have noted it. Reverend Lawrence G. Lovasik, for example, composed a series of booklets for children on the lives of the saints called *The Book of Saints: "Super-Heroes of God"* (New York: Catholic Book Publishing, 1985). Since he chose superheroes rather than something else familiar to children in order to attract young readers to hagiography, this suggests that he found the affinities between saints and superheroes significant and not shameful.

92. Stan Lee and Jack Kirby, *Fantastic Four*, vol. 1, #48–50, March–May 1966, now collected in *Fantastic Four Omnibus*, 2 (New York: Marvel Comics, 2007).

93. Stan Lee, *Son of Origins of Marvel Comics* (New York: Simon & Schuster, 1997), 230. This statement is also cited and discussed in B. J. Oropeza, "The God-Man Revisited: Christology through the Blank Eyes of the Silver Surfer," in *The Gospel According to Superheroes*, edited by Oropeza, 154–69.

94. Silver Surfer is completely naked in the original stories of the Galactus trilogy and in recent incarnations, whereas he wears a sort of swimsuit (in the same silver color as his body) in his own series starting from 1968.

95. Stan Lee and John Buscema, *Silver Surfer* #1, July 1968, now in *Silver Surfer Omnibus*, vol. 1 (New York: Marvel Comics, 2007).

96. Stan Lee and John Buscema, *Silver Surfer* #2, October 1968, now in *Silver Surfer Omnibus*, vol. 1.

Notes to Pages 49–52

97. Stan Lee and John Buscema, *Silver Surfer* #7, August 1969, now in *Silver Surfer Omnibus*, vol. 1.

98. Stan Lee and John Buscema, *Silver Surfer* #3, December 1968, now in *Silver Surfer Omnibus*.

99. In the special story *Judgement Day*, Mephisto makes Silver Surfer an offer he can't refuse: if the hero gives him his soul, in exchange Mephisto will allow him to save millions of people who would otherwise be killed by Galactus. And even in protecting others Silver Surfer goes beyond the typical risk in superhero adventure (getting killed) to voluntarily choose condemning himself to the fires of Hell. Stan Lee and John Buscema, *Silver Surfer: Judgement Day* (New York: Marvel Comics, 1988).

100. Now in J. Michael Straczynski and Esad Ribic, *Requiem* (New York: Marvel Comics, 2008).

101. Simon Spurrier and Tan Eng Huat, *In Thy Name* #1–4, January–April 2008, reprinted as a volume of the same name (New York: Marvel Comics, 2008).

102. Bill Mantlo and Frank Robbins, "There's a Mountain on Sunset Boulevard," *Marvel Premier* #28, February 1976, now reprinted in *Ghost Rider Team-Up* (New York: Marvel Comics, 2007), and *Legion of Monsters*.

103. The undecidability between different religious perspectives thus makes superhero comics a perfect starting point for dialogue. The shaman, the priest, and the rabbi, based on the above, have to admit that Superman incarnates something that they can all identify with, a meeting point that shows how much they have in common.

104. Chris Claremont and Brent Anderson, *X-Men: God Loves, Man Kills* (New York: Marvel Comics, 1982, thereafter regularly reprinted).

105. Joe Casey and Chuck Austen, *Uncanny X-Men* #395–399, July–November 2001, now collected in the volume *Uncanny X-Men: Poptopia* (New York: Marvel Comics, 2001). Also see a Fantastic Four story from 2005 in which the heroes try to defend an alien being hunted as a heretic by his planet's repressive religious culture—in J. Michael Straczynski and Mike McKone, *Fantastic Four* #530–531, August–September 2005, reprinted in *Fantastic Four by J. Michael Straczynski* (New York: Marvel Comics, 2006).

106. The story develops starting from Jim Starlin and Ron Lim, *Infinity Crusade* #1–6, June–November 1993 but also includes chapters that appeared in different periodicals. The saga can be read in its entirety in the collections *Infinity Crusade*, vol. 1–2 (New York: Marvel Comics, 2008–2009).

Chapter 2. Ethics and Society

1. Dennis O'Neil, Dick Dillin, and Joe Giella, *Justice League of America*, vol. 1, #77, December 1969, now reprinted in the volume *JLA: The Greatest Stories Ever Told* (New York: DC Comics, 2006). The name "John Dough," referring both to the generic "John Doe" and the slang term for money, is thus an apt name for a character without much personality besides an interest in money. The "dictatorship of the center/center-right" that Dough wants to establish is particularly interesting considering that at the time social homogenization and loss of individuality tended to be understood only as possible effects of communism, not Western capitalism.

2. For this reason, even if the visual conventions of superhero comics predate the Cold War, one can maintain that during that period the freedom of forms and colors of the superhero costume contributed to sustaining the official idea of a West as the seat of individuality against an East that was seen as the realm of imposed uniformity. In order to understand the extent to which the artistic expression of such concepts can be politicized, recall that in the Cold War era the CIA secretly supported the promotion of Jackson Pollock, the artist of the unique and unrepeatable gesture, but showed suspicion toward Andy Warhol and his realistic art of mass-production. On this and other related issues, see Frances Stonor Saunders, *The Cultural Cold War: The CIA and the World of Arts and Letters* (New York: New Press, 1999).

3. See Gary Engle, "What Makes Superman So Darned American?," in *Superman at Fifty!*, edited by Dooley et al., 79–87.

4. Later on, the same happens with the aliens Martian Manhunter (whose name is changed from J'onn J'onzz to John Jones) and Hawkman (whose name went from Katar Hol to Carter Hall).

5. Originally, all Kryptonians were endowed with superstrength on their planet, which made their superpower a true ethnic trait. The idea that Superman receives his superpowers from Earth's yellow sun was only introduced later. See Jerry Siegel and Joe Shuster, *Superman: The Dailies, Strips 1–966, 1939–1942* (New York: Sterling Publishing, 2006), strip 1, 1939, 13.

6. In addition to Gary Engle's essay, cited in note 3, see Aldo Regalado, "Modernity, Race, and the American Superhero," in *Comics as Philosophy*, edited by Jeff McLaughlin (Jackson: University of Mississippi Press, 2005), 84–99, especially 92.

7. Geoff Johns and Gary Frank, *Action Comics* #859, January 2008, now reprinted in *Superman and the Legion of Super-Heroes* (New York: DC Comics, 2008). The idea of a future society that joins deep racism with a distorted Superman cult has a precedent in the 2004 story arc by Michael Turner, Joe Kelly, and Talent Caldwell, now in the volume *Superman: Godfall* (New York: DC Comics, 2004).

8. See Engle, "What Makes Superman So Darned American?," 83.

9. See Jeffrey A. Brown, *Black Superheroes, Milestone Comics, and Their Fans* (Jackson: University of Mississippi Press, 2001).

10. Len Wein and Dave Cockrum, *Giant-Size X-Men*, vol. 1, May 1975, now in *The Uncanny X-Men Omnibus*, vol. 1 (New York: Marvel Comics, 2007).

11. Chris Claremont and Bob McLeod, *Marvel Graphic Novel*, 4, *The New Mutants*, 1982, now reprinted in *New Mutants Classic*, vol. 1 (New York: Marvel Comics, 2006).

12. On the question of ethics in superhero comics, see the sections about the topic in Mark D. White, ed., *Watchmen and Philosophy: A Rorschach Test* (Hoboken, NJ: Wiley, 2009); Mark D. White and Robert Arp, eds., *Batman and Philosophy: The Dark Knight of the Soul* (Hoboken, NJ: Wiley, 2008); Tom Morris and Chris Ryall, eds., *Superheroes and Philosophy: Truth, Justice, and the Socratic Way* (Peterborough, NH: Carus Publishing, 2008); Roz Kaveney, *Superheroes! Capes and Crusaders in Comics and Films* (New York: I. B. Tauris, 2008), 4–14; Danny Fingeroth, *Superman on the Couch: What Superheroes Really Tell Us about Ourselves and Our Society* (New York: Continuum, 2005), 155–68; Peter Coogan, *Superhero: The Secret Origin of a Genre* (Austin:

Monkey Brain Books, 2006), 135–39; Richard Reynolds, *Superheroes: A Modern Mythology* (Jackson: University of Mississippi Press, 1992), 74–83.

13. I mean "positive" or "negative" in the broadest sense apart from the content to which these labels are often applied. The catechism portrays the obedient child as "positive" whereas Beat literature depicts the rebel and those under the influence of drugs and alcohol as "positive," but in both cases the exemplifying function presents itself to each product's particular elective audience. On this issue in general, see Ryan Indy Rhodes and David Kyle Johnson, "What Would Batman Do? Bruce Wayne as Moral Exemplar," in White and Arp, eds., *Batman and Philosophy*, 114–25.

14. This passion of Barack Obama's was widely discussed in the media in early 2009, for example in the *USA Today* piece "Obama, Spider-Man on the Same Comic-Book Page" (at http://www.usatoday.com/life/books/news/2009-01-07-obama -spiderman-comic_N.htm).

15. Some superheroes, like Gardner Fox's Hawkman and Hawkgirl or Eric Larsen's Savage Dragon are also police officers employed as actual law enforcement agents, while the Green Lantern Corps is an official intergalactic police force of thousands of agents.

16. Robert Jewett and John Shelton Lawrence, *The Myth of the American Superhero* (Grand Rapids, MI: Eedermans, 2002); Robert Jewett and John Shelton Lawrence, *Captain America and the Crusade against Evil* (Grand Rapids, MI: Eedermans, 2004).

17. Jewett and Lawrence, *The Myth of the American Superhero*, 362–63.

18. Valentina Semprini, *Bam! Sock! Lo scontro a fumetti: Dramma e spettacolo del conflitto nei comics d'avventura* [Bam! Sock! The Fight in Comics: Drama and Spectacle in Adventure Comics] (Latina, Italy: Tunué, 2006), 294–304.

19. Chuck Dixon and Graham Nolan, *Detective Comics* #665, August 1993, reprinted in *Knightfall Part Two: Who Rules the Night* (New York: DC Comics, 1993).

20. Bill Finger and Bob Kane, "The Case of the Chemical Syndicate," in *Detective Comics* #27, May 1939, now in *The Batman Chronicles*, vol. 1 (New York: DC Comics, 2005).

21. Gardner Fox and Harry Lampert, in *Flash Comics* #1, January 1940, reprinted in *Golden Age Flash Archives*.

22. Joe Simon and Jack Kirby, "Meet Captain America," in *Captain America Comics* #1, March 1941, now reprinted in *Marvel Masterworks: Golden Age Captain America*.

23. Gardner Fox and Jack Burnley, *Adventure Comics* #61, April 1941, now reprinted in *The Golden Age Starman Archives* (New York: DC Comics, 2000).

24. Jerry Siegel and Joe Shuster, *Superman* #2, Fall 1939, reprinted in *Superman Chronicles*, 2 (New York: DC Comics, 2007). See Peter B. Lloyd, "Superman's Moral Evolution," in *The Man from Krypton*, edited by Yeffeth, 181–98, especially 188–89.

25. Roger Stern and John Byrne, *Captain America*, vol. 1, #254, February 1981.

26. Jerry Ordway and Tom Grummett, *The Adventures of Superman* #497, December 1992, reprinted in *The Death of Superman*.

27. Chuck Austen and Ron Garney, *JLA* #101–106, September–November 2004, now in the volume *Pain of the Gods* (New York: DC Comics, 2005).

28. Michael Green and Denys Cowan, *Batman Confidential* #12, February 2008, now in *Batman: Lovers and Madmen* (New York: DC Comics, 2008). The captions

read: "With him in the world there is no possibility of order. He has no fears. Unmoved by anything except suffering. He'll never stop. Not until he's dead. All I need to do is let it happen. And I end all this insanity. I save all the lives I know he'll take. Let it happen ... let chaos prevail for the six more seconds it will take for madman to meet pavement ... or the rest of my life will be spent picking up the pieces."

29. Roger Stern and John Byrne, *Captain America*, vol. 1, #249, September 1980.

30. Paul Jenkins and Mark Buckingham, *Peter Parker: Spider-Man* #28, April 2001, now in *Peter Parker: Spider-Man: One Small Break* (New York: Marvel Comics, 2002).

31. Stuart Moore and Carlos Pagulayan, *Iron Man, Director of S.H.I.E.L.D.* # 32, August 2008, now in *Iron Man, Director of S.H.I.E.L.D.: With Iron Hands* (New York: Marvel Comics, 2009).

32. The character was created by Dwayne McDuffie and John Paul Leon in *Static*, which debuted in April 1993 with Milestone, an imprint of DC.

33. Dwayne McDuffie, Denys Cowan, and Prentis Rollins, "Static Shock: Wednesday Afternoon," in *9-11, September 11th 2001: The World's Finest Comic Book Writers and Artists Tell Stories to Remember*, edited by Steven T. Seagle (New York: DC Comics, 2002), 31–32.

34. The other modern cases are rare and include *Wonder Woman* #189 from August 1969, written and drawn by Mike Sekowsky, in which the heroine shoots down a Chinese plane that is attacking innocent civilians, yet without any reference to the moral consequences of the fact that the pilot was surely killed. This was perhaps the effect of a realistic turn that the publisher had recently imposed on the series, with the addition of the psychological effect of the ongoing war in Vietnam, which gave a dark tone to an episode with military-political content (Wonder Woman tries to help the inhabitants of a Chinese village to escape the oppression of the communist government). The story is now reprinted in *Diana Prince: Wonder Woman, 2* (New York: DC Comics, 2008).

35. Mark Gruenwald and Paul Neary, *Captain America* #321, September 1986.

36. Gruenwald and Neary, *Captain America* #322, October 1986.

37. Greg Rucka and Rags Morales, *Wonder Woman*, vol. 2, #219, July 2005, reprinted in *Mission's End* (New York: DC Comics, 2006).

38. See Geoff Johns et al., *Infinite Crisis* #1–7, December 2005–June 2006, now in the volume *Infinite Crisis* (New York: DC Comics, 2006).

39. Stan Lee and Steve Ditko, "Spider-Man!," in *Amazing Fantasy* #15, August 1962, now in *Amazing Spider-Man Omnibus*, vol. 1 (New York: Marvel Comics, 2007), 9–19. This scene is on page 19.

40. Paul Jenkins and Paolo Rivera, *Mythos: Spider-Man*, August 2007, now reprinted in *Mythos* (New York: Marvel Comics, 2008).

41. See also *The Dark Knight* (Christopher Nolan, USA 2008): One would say that Harvey Dent dying the usual death and Batman saving the Joker occurs primarily so that the directors and screenwriters can include Joker in later films in the series.

42. Jewett and Lawrence, *The Myth of the American Superhero*, 6.

43. Dennis O'Neil and Neal Adams, *Green Lantern* #76–89, April 1970–May 1972 and *The Flash* #217–219, June–August 1972, now in *Green Lantern/Green Arrow Collection*, #1–2 (New York: DC Comics, 2004).

Notes to Pages 83–95

44. Robert M. Peaslee insists on superhero comics' ability to both support and critique the status quo in "Superheroes, 'Moral Economy,' and the 'Iron Cage': Morality, Alienation, and the Super-Individual," in *Super/Heroes from Hercules to Superman*, edited by Haslem et al., 37–50.

45. Patrick L. Eagan, "A Flag with a Human Face," in *Superman at Fifty!*, edited by Dooley et al., 88–95, especially 89.

46. Alan Burnett and Ed Benes, *Justice League of America*, vol. 2, #17, January 2008, reprinted in *Justice League of America: Sanctuary* (New York: DC Comics, 2009).

47. Please note that the word "democrat" here is used in the broader sense of "someone who loves freedom," and not according to the Democrat/Republican dichotomy with which it is commonly associated in American English.

48. Steve Englehart and Sal Buscema, *Captain America* #175, July 1974, reprinted in *Captain America: Secret Empire* (New York: Marvel Comics, 2005).

49. Captain America reflects: "There was a time [the Second World War], yes, when the country faced a clearly hideous aggressor, and her people stood united against it! But now nothing's that simple. Americans have many goals . . . some of them quite contrary to others! . . . So when people the world over look at me, which America am I supposed to symbolize?" Steve Englehart and Sal Buscema, *Captain America* #176, August 1974, reprinted in *Captain America: Secret Empire* (New York: Marvel Comics, 2005).

50. Note that when the critique involves not the government but a general value, Captain America jumps into action. A famous example is *Captain America* #267, March 1982, by J. M. DeMatteis and Mike Zeck, which introduces the criminal Everyman, who has turned to terrorism in protest of the idea of the American dream and the attention paid solely to the few citizens considered "winners" as opposed to the masses of "losers." The story seems to express a widespread bitterness, to the point that multiple characters, on three separate occasions, spit at Captain America to show their contempt for what his costume represents. In the end, in addition to defeating Everyman, Cap manages to bring some hope to even the most disillusioned.

51. Mark Millar and Steve McNiven, *Civil War* #1–7, May 2006–January 2007, now in the volume *Civil War* (New York: Marvel Comics, 2007).

52. Steve Darnall and Alex Ross, *U.S.: Uncle Sam* (New York: DC Comics, 1997).

53. Justin Gray, Jimmy Palmiotti, and Daniel Acuña, *Uncle Sam and the Freedom Fighters* #1–8, September 2006–April 2007, now in the volume *Uncle Sam and the Freedom Fighters* (New York: DC Comics, 2007).

54. Umberto Eco, "The Myth of Superman," in *The Role of the Reader: Explorations in the Semiotics of Texts* (Bloomington: Indiana University Press, 1979), 107–24.

55. Ibid., 123.

56. For this and other examples of Superman's intervention in societal problems, see Jerry Siegel and Joe Shuster's stories now collected in *The Superman Chronicles*, vol. 1–2 (New York: DC Comics, 2006–2007).

57. They also fight enemies such as the Russian astronaut Ivan Kragoff, a.k.a. the Red Ghost, who has the power to dematerialize (thus representing the fear of the "impalpable" communist invasion) and who commands super-apes who indicate the dehumanization to which, according to capitalist societies, the communist regime

would lead. This character is introduced in Stan Lee and Jack Kirby, *Fantastic Four*, vol. 1, #13, April 1963, now in the volume *Fantastic Four Omnibus*, vol. 1 (New York: Marvel Comics, 2005). As to the significance of the super-apes, Sue Richards makes the explicit comment that "they are like the Communist masses, innocently enslaved by their evil leaders" (341).

58. Robert Kanigher and Ross Andru, *Metal Men*, 5, December 1963–January 1964, now reprinted in *Showcase Presents: Metal Men* (New York: DC Comics, 2007).

59. Zeb Wells and Todd Nauck, *Amazing Spider-Man* #583, January 2009.

60. See Paul Levinson's similar conclusions in "Superman, Patriotism, and Doing the Ultimate Good: Why the Man of Steel Did So Little to Stop Hitler and Tojo," in *The Man from Krypton*, edited by Yeffeth, 211–19.

61. In reality, this mechanism still enables the representation of monumental events, as long as they are posited as pure additions to the present political scenario. The aliens or the Mole Man can attack Earth whenever they want, as long as they don't kill any real public figures, end wars that are currently going on in our world, and so on.

62. On close examination, we find that even the most fantastic adventures in distant worlds and parallel dimensions are always framed within an accurate political-historical setting that remains implicit, even when not represented directly. In other words, even if heroes can travel to the outer reaches of the universe (and often beyond), the situation on their Earth continues to evolve in the meantime parallel to the situation in our world. Thus, if the heroes leave Andromeda for Washington, D.C., in 2007 they find Bush in the White House but if they come in 2009 they find Obama, even if that transition never appeared at any point in the stories.

63. J. Michael Straczynski et al., *Rising Stars* #1–24, August 1999–May 2005, now in the eponymous volume (Orange, CA: Image Comics, 2005).

64. This remains true even if at points one notices a narrative progression of events initially conceived to be developed in serial form rather than over the course of a properly novelistic plotline.

65. Elliot S. Maggin, Curt Swan, and Vince Colletta, *Superman* #273, March 1974.

66. Booster Gold is initially a satirical character who fights crime to get rich off of publicity, movie rights, toys, and television appearances—a distorted version of Superman who does the right things (altruistically) for the wrong reasons (selfishly), and who represented the unchecked materialism of the eighties. The entire series conveyed the message that it took more than performing a superhero's typical deeds to be a real superhero; see Dan Jurgens's introduction to Geoff Johns, Jeff Katz, and Dan Jurgens, *Booster Gold: 52 Pick-Up* (New York: DC Comics, 2008). The character seems to take up an old Superman story in which Kal-El loses his powers and gets substituted by a Kryptonian who is only concerned with building monuments to himself and fabricating incidents so that he can "heroically" step in and increase his fame. See Edmond Hamilton and Curt Swan, *Superman* #172, October 1964.

67. Dan Jurgens, *Booster Gold* #7, August 1986, now in the volume *Showcase Presents: Booster Gold* (New York: DC Comics, 2008).

68. Kelley Puckett and Jon Bogdanove, *Batman* #566, June 1999, now in *No Man's Land*, vol. 3 (New York: DC Comics, 2000).

69. Paul Dini and Alex Ross, *Superman: Peace on Earth* (New York: DC Comics, 1999), later reprinted in the volume *The World's Greatest Superheroes* (New York: DC Comics, 2005).

70. Brian Azzarello and Jim Lee, *Superman*, vol. 2, #206, August 2004, now in *For Tomorrow*, vol. 1 (New York: DC Comics, 2005).

71. Superman's decision to cooperate with Nox doesn't mean that the hero thinks any power approved of by the masses is necessarily good, especially if such masses do not examine the ways in which that power came into being (whether from the mass media, religious fundamentalism, propaganda, and political policing). The story is simply about the limit to the legitimacy of the power to change the living conditions of other people. In other words, Superman does not conclude that Nox's power or that of rulers like him should go unquestioned, but rather, he realizes that it is not up to him, as Superman, to decide for others what sort of government they should have; that he cannot resolve the issue by himself, even if he would undoubtedly be happy to lend a hand to the population should they express a desire to depose their ruler.

72. Roger Stern and John Byrne, *JLA Classified* #50–54, March–May 2008, now in the volume *That Was Now, This Is Then* (New York: DC Comics, 2008).

73. Cited in Theodore Sorensen, *Let the Word Go Forth: The Speeches, Statements, and Writings of John F. Kennedy 1947 to 1963* (New York: Delta, 1991), 282.

74. Gerry Conway and Dick Dillin, *Justice League of America*, vol. 1, #167, June 1979, now reprinted in the volume *JLA: The Greatest Stories Ever Told*.

75. Edmond Hamilton and Curt Swan, *World's Finest* #142, June 1964.

76. Philip Wylie, *Gladiator* (1st ed. 1930; Westport, CT: Hyperion Press, 1974), 112.

77. Ibid., 188.

Chapter 3. Epic and Neobaroque

1. Sergio Zatti, *Il modo epico* (Rome: Laterza, 2000), 7. Translated as *The Quest for Epic: From Ariosto to Tasso* (Toronto, Ontario: University of Toronto Press, 2006).

2. Ibid., 15.

3. Ibid., 19.

4. The opposite, however, is not necessarily true—that is, it isn't a given that superhero comics have a *closer* or an exclusive affinity to epic than they do to any other literary or narrative genre of the past. This means that superhero comics are more indebted to the epic than to any other genre, whereas obviously I realize that they also draw on many other concomitant sources (like the adventure novel or the soap opera). In practice, therefore, the superhero comic constitutes the closest version of the epic genre within the panorama of contemporary genres, but that does not mean that the epic is the only model that defines the superhero genre.

5. William Moulton Marston and Harry G. Peter, *All Star Comics* #8, December 1941–January 1942, now in *Wonder Woman Archives*, vol. 1 (New York: DC Comics, 1998).

6. Michael Avon Oeming and Andrea DiVito, *The Mighty Thor: Disassembled* (New York: Marvel Comics, 2004).

7. See Dennis O'Neil and Dick Dillin, *Justice League of America*, vol. 1, #78, February 1970, and Gerry Conway and Chuck Patton, *Justice League of America Annual*, vol. 1, #2, 1984.

8. See Grant Morrison and Howard Porter, *JLA* #4, April 1997, reprinted in *JLA: New World Order*, vol. 1 (New York: DC Comics, 1997), and Geoff Johns, Alan Heinberg, and Chris Batista, *JLA* #120, December 2005, now in the volume *JLA: Crisis of Conscience* (New York: DC Comics, 2006).

9. Brad Meltzer and Ed Benes, *Justice League of America*, vol. 2, #7, May 2007, reprinted in *Justice League of America: Tornado's Path* (New York: DC Comics, 2007).

10. Brian Michael Bendis and Frank Cho, *The Mighty Avengers* #1, March 2007, now in the volume *The Mighty Avengers: The Ultron Initiative* (New York: Marvel Comics, 2007).

11. Zatti, *Il modo epico*, 98. And just as this device in the epic poem served to gratify the patron's desire for representation, or the politician who wanted to see himself mentioned in the text through a reference to his ancestors, group scenes in superhero comics create the same gratifying effect for today's "patron": the devoted reader, the only person with the necessary competence to interpret all the implications of the image.

12. Craig Kyle, Christopher Yost, and Skottie Young, *New X-Men* #37–41, April–August 2007, reprinted in *New X-Men: Childhood's End* (New York: Marvel Comics, 2007).

13. Marc Guggenheim and Howard Chaykin, *Wolverine*, vol. 3, #57–61, November 2007–March 2008, now in the volume *The Death of Wolverine* (New York: Marvel Comics, 2008).

14. Kurt Busiek and Carlos Pacheco, *Superman* #654–658, September 2006–January 2007, now in the volume *Superman: Camelot Falls*, vol. 1 (New York: DC Comics, 2007).

15. Kurt Busiek and Carlos Pacheco, *Superman* #662–664 and 667–668, May–August and November–December 2007, and annual 13, 2008, now in the volume *Superman: Camelot Falls*, 2 (New York: DC Comics, 2008).

16. Walter Simonson, *The Mighty Thor* #338, December 1983, now reprinted in the volume *Thor Visionaries: Walter Simonson* (New York: Marvel Comics, 2001).

17. For lines in comics that don't indicate movement, see Marco Pellitteri, *Sense of Comics. La grafica dei cinque sensi nel fumetto* (Roma: Castelvecchi, 1998), 68–73.

18. Stan Lee and Jack Kirby, *Fantastic Four*, vol. 1, #7, October 1962, now in *Fantastic Four Omnibus*, vol. 1.

19. On the theme of battle, see also Semprini, *Bam! Sock!*

20. See Eco, "The Myth of Superman," 259.

21. An example of this can be found in Leo Dorfman and Neal Adams, "The Superman-Batman Revenge Squads" in *World's Finest* #175, May 1968, now republished in *Superman in the Sixties* (New York: DC Comics, 1999).

22. Bill Finger and Wayne Boring, *Superman* #155, August 1962.

23. Dennis O'Neil and Neal Adams, *Superman vs. Muhammad Ali* (New York: DC Comics, 1978).

24. Mark Gruenwald et al., *Contest of Champions #1–3*, June–August 1982, later in the eponymous volume. The Marvel heroes return to fight in a contest in Chris Claremont, Oscar Jimenez, and Michael Ryan, *Contest of Champions II #1–5*, May–November 1999, later reprinted in the volume of the same title (New York: Marvel Comics, 2001).

25. Jim Shooter, Mike Zeck, and Bob Layton, *Secret Wars #1–12*, May 1984–April 1985, later collected in the eponymous volume (New York: Marvel Comics, 2005).

26. Ron Marz et al., *Marvel Comics Versus DC #1–4*, February–May 1996, reprinted in the volume with the mirroring title *DC Versus Marvel Comics* (New York: DC Comics, 1996).

27. Greg Pak and John Romita Jr., *World War Hulk #1–5*, August–December 2007, now in the eponymous volume (New York: Marvel Comics, 2008).

28. Zatti, *Il modo epico*, 27.

29. Ibid., 28.

30. See Giulio Strozzi, *Il Barbarigo, o l'amico sollevato* (Venice: Piuti, 1626); Guidubaldo Benamati, *Il Trivisano, poema eroicivico* (Frankfurt: Beyer, 1630).

31. On the topic of architecture, Gillo Dorfles discussed the neobaroque as early as 1951 in *Barocco nell'architettura moderna* [The Baroque in Modern Architecture] (Milan: Libreria Editrice Politecnica Tamburini) and returned to the concept in subsequent decades in essays collected in *Architetture ambigue: Dal Neobarocco al Postmoderno* [Ambiguous Architectures: From Neobaroque to Postmodern] (Bari, Italy: Dedalo, 1984). An important extension of the idea of the neobaroque to general cultural discourse can be found in Omar Calabrese, *L'età neobarocca* (translated as *Neo-Baroque: A Sign of the Times* [Princeton: Princeton University Press, 1992]). Especially useful for its bibliography is Angela Ndalianis, *Neo-Baroque Aesthetics and Contemporary Entertainment* (Cambridge, MA: MIT Press, 2004). Other contributions to the topic can be found in: Omar Calabrese, *Caos e bellezza: Immagini del Neobarocco* [Chaos and Beauty: Images of the Neobaroque] (Milan: Domus, 1991); Ezio Raimondi, "Lo specchio del barocco e le immagini del presente" [The Mirror of the Baroque and the Images of the Present], in *Il colore eloquente: Letteratura e arte barocca* [The Eloquent Color: Literature and Baroque Art] (Bologna: Il Mulino, 1995), 3–19; Ezio Raimondi, *Barocco moderno: Roberto Longhi e Carlo Emilio Gadda* [Modern Baroque: Roberto Longhi and Carlo Emilio Gadda] (Milan: Bruno Mondadori, 2003), especially the chapter "Raccontare le forme" [Narrating Forms], 1–18; Simonetta Chessa Wright, *La poetica neobarocca in Calvino* [Neobaroque Poetics in Calvino] (Ravenna, Italy: Longo, 1998); Bartolomeo Massimo D'Azeglio, *Neobarocco e architettura* [Neobaroque and Architecture] (Milan: Lampi di stampa, 2005); Micaela Giovannotti et al., ed., *Neo Baroque!* (Milan: Charta, 2005); Lucinda Spera, "Il Barocco che è in noi" [The Baroque in Us], in *Verso il moderno: Pubblico e immaginario nel Seicento italiano* [Toward the Modern: Audience and Imagination in Seventeenth-Century Italy] (Rome: Carocci, 2008), 200–208; Stephen Calloway, *Baroque Baroque* (London: Phaidon, 2000); Cristina Degli-Esposti, "Federico Fellini's *Intervista* or the Neo-Baroque Creativity of the Analysand on Screen," *Italica* 73, 2 (1996):157–72; Peter Wollen, "Baroque and Neo-Baroque in the Age of Spectacle," *Point of Contact* 3 (1993): 9–21; Janet Pérez and Genaro J. Pérez, eds., *Hispanic Contemporary Baroque* (Odessa: University

of Texas of the Permian Basin, 1994); Fabio Benincasa, *Barocco e Neo-barocco: Percorsi autoriali nel cinema italiano: Fellini, Antonioni, Pasolini* [Baroque and Neobaroque: Authorial Paths in Italian Cinema: Fellini, Antonioni, Pasolini], Ph.D. dissertation, Indiana University, Bloomington, October 2008.

32. Calabrese, *Neo-Baroque*, vol. 6.

33. See Raimondi, "Lo specchio del barocco," 3.

34. Is it necessary to state that a comparison of styles does not imply value judgment? If we compare the devices and objectives of one of baroque poet Giambattista Marino's marvelous sonnets with a bad example by one of his early imitators, we can legitimately say that both compositions are baroque in nature even if the strategies used by both authors differ significantly in quality. For this reason, one can note the presence of neobaroque *modes* in the prose of great modern writers such as Carlo Emilio Gadda or Umberto Eco just as easily as in an Indiana Jones movie, a Lady Gaga video, a Wii videogame, or, in our case, a superhero comic.

35. Raimondi, *Barocco moderno*, 43.

36. See Raimondi, "Lo specchio del barocco."

37. Galileo Galilei, *Dialogo dei massimi sistemi* (Milan: Mondadori, 1996), vol. 4, 475. Among the many bibliographical references, I would recommend the detailed summary in Michele Camerota, *Galileo Galilei e la cultura scientifica nell'età della Controriforma* [Galileo Galilei and Scientific Culture in the Age of the Counter-Reformation] (Rome: Salerno, 2004), 430–32.

38. As Gillo Dorfles writes in *Barocco nell'architettura moderna* [The Baroque in Modern Architecture]: "The contrast between individual and society, between private and public life, between historical and existential fact, finds in the Baroque age its first truly conflictual manifestation. [. . .] Today, in fact, we are living in such an era" (20).

39. Respectively, in Grant Morrison and Frank Quitely, *New X-Men* #115, August 2001, now in the collection *New X-Men Ultimate Collection*, vol. 1 (New York: Marvel Comics, 2008), and in Brian Michael Bendis and Mike Deodato, *New Avengers* #16–20, April–August 2006, now in the volume *New Avengers: The Collective* (New York: Marvel Comics, 2008).

40. The concept of hierarchical continuity is explained in Reynolds, *Superheroes*, 40–41.

41. The inextricable complexity that the superhero comic has developed is sometimes contextualized as such in playful metatextual and self-referential jokes. For example, in a recent Spider-Man story, a video of a villain called Basher appears on YouTube where he states that he has fought Spider-Man before and wants to challenge the hero to a rematch. The most interesting element lies in the fact that none of the characters seems to remember this villain (including Peter Parker himself) and that even the publisher of *Spider-Man* seems struck by amnesia, as he "admits" in an explanatory caption that he can't recall the episode with the original fight. Thus the reader is left wondering whether Basher is really referring to some obscure forgotten digression in the previous continuity or whether the authors aren't good-naturedly teasing the reader by sending him in search of a nonexistent source. In other words, the story *thematizes* the reader's uncertainty in the face of the vast

quantity of citable materials, and the difficulty of knowing the extent of the narrative background that has accumulated in the Marvel universe. The story in question is in Bob Gale and Mike McKone, *The Amazing Spider-Man* #562, June 2008, now in the volume *The Amazing Spider-Man: Brand New Day*, vol. 3 (New York: Marvel Comics, 2008).

42. Jerry Siegel and Joe Shuster, "Superman," in *Action Comics* #1, June 1938, reprinted in *Superman Chronicles*, vol. 1 (New York: DC Comics, 2006).

43. Jerry Siegel and Joe Shuster, "Superman," in *Superman* #1, July 1939, reprinted in *Superman Chronicles* 1.

44. Leo Dorfman and Al Pastino, "The Last Days of Ma and Pa Kent," in *Superman* #161, May 1963, now in *Superman in the Sixties*.

45. John Byrne, *Man of Steel* #1–6, July–September 1986, then in the volume *Superman: The Man of Steel*, vol. 1 (New York: DC Comics, 1991).

46. Mark Waid and Leinil Francis Yu, *Superman: Birthright*, September 2003–September 2004, now in the eponymous volume (New York: DC Comics, 2005).

47. Calabrese returns to this example several times in *Neo-Baroque*.

48. Purely for the sake of economy, I am leaving out other forms of art, such as film, television, music, and dance.

49. J. M. DeMatteis and Mike Zeck, *Web of Spider-Man* #31–32, *Amazing Spider-Man* #293–294, *Spectacular Spider-Man* #131–132, October–November 1987, now in the volume *Kraven's Last Hunt* (New York: Marvel Comics, 2007): "Spyder! Spyder! burning bright / in the forests of the night, / what immortal hand or eye / could frame thy fearful symmetry," where "Spyder" obviously replaces poet William Blake's "Tyger." It is hard to decide whether to include in this category the cases in which comics authors translate the content of a literary extract in visual form, without necessarily reproducing the exact verbal form—which could range from a single character (like Bram Stoker's *Dracula* for Marvel's *Tomb of Dracula* series) to a scene or an entire work. In such cases, it is perhaps better to speak of transposition or adaptation. Generally, however, this practice also contributes to shaping works with rich intertextual backgrounds, thus forming part of the schema I have outlined here.

50. Keith Giffen et al., *Invasion! #2: Battleground Earth*, 1988, now in the volume *Invasion!* (New York: DC Comics, 2008).

51. Dan Slott and Marcos Martin, *The Amazing Spider-Man* #560, May 2008, now in the volume *The Amazing Spider-Man: Brand New Day* (New York: Marvel Comics, 2008), vol. 3.

52. Note that, perhaps not coincidentally, at the same time when this story came out, New York's Metropolitan Museum of Art opened an exhibition called *Superheroes: Fashion and Fantasy* devoted to superhero costumes and their influence on modern fashion. See the exhibition catalogue: *Superheroes: Fashion and Fantasy*, edited by Harold Koda and Andrew Bolton (New Haven: Yale University Press, 2008).

53. Stan Lee and Jack Kirby, *Fantastic Four*, vol. 1, #5, July 1962, now in *Fantastic Four Omnibus*, vol. 1. In a slightly later episode, Stan Lee and Jack Kirby, the authors, appear as characters in the Marvel Universe, taken hostage by Doctor Doom. See Stan Lee and Jack Kirby, *Fantastic Four*, vol. 1, #10, January 1963, later in *Fantastic Four Omnibus*, vol. 1.

54. This idea reaches a new level of conceptual complexity (and playfulness) in a commemorative series of stories in which Stan Lee, founder of the modern Marvel style, appears as a character alongside his creations, such as Spider-Man and Doctor Strange. See Stan Lee et al., *Stan Lee Meets*, September–December 2006, now in the eponymous volume (New York: Marvel Comics, 2007).

55. Brad Meltzer and Ed Benes, *Justice League of America*, vol. 2, #1, October 2006, now in the volume *Justice League of America: Tornado's Path* (New York: DC Comics, 2007).

56. Dwayne McDuffie and Ed Benes, *Justice League of America*, vol. 2, #13, November 2007, now in the volume *Justice League of America: The Injustice League* (New York: DC Comics, 2008).

57. David Michelinie and John Romita Jr., *Iron Man*, vol. 1, #150, September 1981, now in the volume *Iron Man: Doomquest* (New York: Marvel Comics, 2008); David Michelinie and Bob Layton, *Iron Man*, vol. 1, #250, December 1989, now in the volume *Iron Man: Doomquest*. The parallel is also found in tables 2 and 3 in that comic, which have identical graphic structures in both stories.

58. See Giovanni Pozzi's commentary in Giambattista Marino, *L'Adone* [Adonis] (Milan: Adelphi, 1988).

59. On the neobaroque effects of serial production, see Ndalianis in *Neo-Baroque Aesthetics*, especially 25 and 31, where she explains how it is typical of neobaroque expression to complicate a linear storyline through serial publications that divide the narrative into several branches, "drawing the audience into a series of potentially infinite, or at least multiple, directions," due to which, "closed forms are replaced by open structures that favor a dynamic and expanding poly-centrism" (25).

60. Roberto Aguirre-Sacasa and Mizuki Sakakibara, *Marvel Knights 4* #23, December 2005, reprinted in the volume *Marvel Knights 4: Impossible Things Happen Every Day*. Note the reference to the Fantastic Four having "chosen" the author of their comic, and that develops the idea that certain superheroes are directly involved in the production of their own comics . . . here even to the point that they can decide their own author!

61. Mike W. Barr and Daerick Gross, *Batman: Two-Face Strikes Twice* (New York: DC Comics, 1993).

62. Roberto Aguirre-Sacasa et al., *Marvel Knights 4* #21, August 2005, reprinted in the volume *Marvel Knights 4: Impossible Things Happen Every Day*.

63. Greg Rucka and Matthew Clark, *Adventures of Superman* #638, May 2005, reprinted in the volume *Superman: That Healing Touch* (New York: DC Comics, 2005).

Conclusion

1. Kwame Anthony Appiah, *Cosmopolitanism: Ethics in a World of Strangers* (New York: Norton, 2007), 78.

Bibliography

Comics and Graphic Novels

Aguirre-Sacasa, Roberto, and Clayton Crain. *Sensational Spider-Man* #40, August 2007. In *Back in Black*, vol. 2. New York: Fawcett Comics, 2007.

Aguirre-Sacasa, Roberto, and Valentine De Landro. *Marvel Knights 4* #22, September 2005. In *Marvel Knights 4: Impossible Things Happen Every Day*. New York: Marvel Comics, 2006.

Aguirre-Sacasa, Roberto, and Mizuki Sakakibara. *Marvel Knights 4* #23, December 2005. In *Marvel Knights 4: Impossible Things Happen Every Day*. New York: Marvel Comics, 2006.

Aguirre-Sacasa, Roberto, et al. *Marvel Knights 4* #21, August 2005. In *Marvel Knights Fantastic Four 4: Impossible Things Happen Every Day*. New York: Marvel Comics, 2006.

Austen, Chuck, and Ron Garney. *JLA* #101–106, September–November 2004. In *Pain of the Gods*. New York: DC Comics, 2005.

Azzarello, Brian, and Jim Lee. *Superman*, 2, #206, August 2004. In *For Tomorrow*, vol. 1. New York: DC Comics, 2005.

Barr, Mike W., and Daerick Gross. *Batman: Two-Face Strikes Twice*. New York: DC Comics, 1993.

Bendis, Brian Michael, and Frank Cho. *The Mighty Avengers* #1, March 2007. In *The Mighty Avengers: The Ultron Initiative*. New York: Marvel Comics, 2007.

Bendis, Brian Michael, and Mike Deodato. *New Avengers* #16–20, April–August 2006. In *New Avengers: The Collective*. New York: Marvel Comics, 2008.

Binder, Otto, and Marc Swayze. *Captain Marvel Adventures* #18, December 1942. New York: Fawcett Comics, 1942.

Burnett, Alan, and Ed Benes. *Justice League of America*, vol. 2, #17, January 2008. In *Justice League of America: Sanctuary*. New York: DC Comics, 2009.

Burstein, Martin A., and Jack Kirby. "Mercury in the 20th Century." *Red Raven Comics* #1, August 1940. In *The Complete Jack Kirby*, vol. 1. New York: Pure Imagination, 1997.

Busiek, Kurt, et al. *Superman* #675, June 2008. In *Shadows Linger*. New York: DC Comics, 2009.

Busiek, Kurt, and Jesus Merino. *Superman* #673, April 2008. In *Shadows Linger*. New York: DC Comics, 2009.

Busiek, Kurt, and Fabian Nicieza. *Superman* #659, February 2007. In *Superman: Redemption*. New York: DC Comics, 2007.

Busiek, Kurt, and Carlos Pacheco. *Superman* #662–664 and 667–668, May–August, November–December 2007, and annual #13, 2008. In *Superman: Camelot Falls*, vol. 2. New York: DC Comics, 2008.

———. *Superman* #654–658, September 2006–January 2007. In *Superman: Camelot Falls*, vol. 1. New York: DC Comics, 2007.

Busiek, Kurt, and Alex Ross. *Marvels*. New York: Marvel Comics, 1995.

Byrne, John. *Avengers West Coast* #52, December 1989. In *Avengers West Coast: Darker than Scarlet*. New York: Marvel Comics, 2008.

———. *Man of Steel* #1–6, July–September 1986. In *Superman: The Man of Steel*, vol. 1. New York: DC Comics, 1991.

———. *Alpha Flight*, vol. 1, #5, December 1983. In *Alpha Flight Classic*, vol. 1. New York: Marvel Comics, 2007.

Casey, Joe, and Chuck Austen. *Uncanny X-Men* #395–399, July–November 2001. In *Uncanny X-Men: Poptopia*. New York: Marvel Comics, 2001.

Claremont, Chris, and Brent Anderson. *X-Men: God Loves, Man Kills*. New York: Marvel Comics, 1982.

Claremont, Chris, and John Bolton. *Classic X-Men* #19, March 1988. In *Magneto* #0. New York: Marvel Comics, 1993.

———. *Classic X-Men* #12, August 1987. In *Magneto* #0. New York: Marvel Comics, 1993.

Claremont, Chris, and John Byrne. *Uncanny X-Men* #120, April 1979. In *Uncanny X-Men Omnibus*, vol. 1. New York: Marvel Comics, 2006.

Claremont, Chris, Oscar Jimenez, and Michael Ryan. *Contest of Champions II* #1–5, May–November 1999. In *Contest of Champions II*. New York: Marvel Comics, 2001.

Claremont, Chris, and Bob McLeod. *Marvel Graphic Novel*, vol. 4, *The New Mutants*. In *New Mutants Classic*, vol. 1. New York: Marvel Comics, 2006.

Claremont, Chris, and Mark Silvestri. *Uncanny X-Men* #227, March 1988.

Conway, Gerry, and Dick Dillin. *Justice League of America*, vol. 1, #167, June 1979. In *JLA: The Greatest Stories Ever Told*. New York: DC Comics, 2006.

Conway, Gerry, and Bob Oksner. *Action Comics* #521, July 1981.

Conway, Gerry, and Chuck Patton. *Justice League of America Annual*, vol. 1, #2, 1984.

Darnall, Steve, and Alex Ross. *U.S.: Uncle Sam*. New York: DC Comics, 1997.

DeMatteis, J. M., and Mike Zeck. *Amazing Spider-Man* #293–294, October–November 1987. In *Kraven's Last Hunt*. New York: Marvel Comics, 2007.

———. *Spectacular Spider-Man* #131–132, October–November 1987. In *Kraven's Last Hunt*. New York: Marvel Comics, 2007.

———. *Web of Spider-Man* #31–32, October–November 1987. In *Kraven's Last Hunt*. New York: Marvel Comics, 2007.

———. *Captain America* #267, March 1982.

Dini, Paul, and Alex Ross. *The World's Greatest Superheroes*. New York: DC Comics, 2005.

———. *Superman: Peace on Earth*. New York: DC Comics, 1999.

———. *Wonder Woman: The Spirit of Truth*. New York: DC Comics, 1999.

Dixon, Chuck, and Graham Nolan. *Detective Comics* #665, August 1993. In *Knightfall Part Two: Who Rules the Night*. New York: DC Comics, 1993.

Dorfman, Leo, and Neal Adams. "The Superman-Batman Revenge Squads," in *World's Finest* #175, May 1968. In *Superman in the Sixties*. New York: DC Comics, 1999.

Dorfman, Leo, and Al Pastino. "The Last Days of Ma and Pa Kent," in *Superman* #161, May 1963. In *Superman in the Sixties*. New York: DC Comics, 1999.

Englehart, Steve, and Sal Buscema. *Captain America* #175, July 1974. In *Captain America: Secret Empire*. New York: Marvel Comics, 2005.

Everett, Bill. "The Sub-Mariner." *Marvel Comics* #1, October 1939. In *The Golden Age of Marvel Comics*. New York: Marvel Comics, 1997.

Finger, Bill, and Wayne Boring. *Superman* #155, August 1962.

Finger, Bill, and Bob Kane. "The Case of the Chemical Syndicate," in *Detective Comics* #27, May 1939. In *The Batman Chronicles*, 1. New York: DC Comics, 2005.

Fox, Gardner, and Jack Burnley. *Adventure Comics* #61, April 1941. In *The Golden Age Starman Archives*. New York: DC Comics, 2000.

Fox, Gardner, and Joe Kubert. *The Brave and the Bold* # 34, February–March 1961. In *Hawkman Essential*, vol. 1. New York: DC Comics, 2007.

Fox, Gardner, and Harry Lampert. *Flash Comics* #1, January 1940. In *The Golden Age Flash Archives*, vol. 1. New York: DC Comics, 1999.

Fox, Gardner, and Howard Sherman. *More Fun Comics* #56, June 1940. In *The Golden Age Doctor Fate*, vol. 1. New York: DC Comics, 2007.

———. *More Fun Comics* #55, May 1940. In *The Golden Age Doctor Fate*, vol. 1. New York: DC Comics, 2007.

Friedrich, Gary, and Tom Sutton. *Marvel Spotlight* #8–11, February–August 1973. In the volume *Essential Ghost Rider*, vol. 1. New York: Marvel Comics, 2005.

Gale, Bob, and Mike McKone. *The Amazing Spider-Man* #562, June 2008. In *The Amazing Spider-Man: Brand New Day*, vol. 3. New York: Marvel Comics, 2008.

Gerber, Steve, and Jim Mooney. *Marvel Spotlight: Son of Satan* #17, September 1974. In *Essential Marvel Horror*, vol. 1. New York: Marvel Comics, 2006.

Giffen, Keith, et al. *Invasion! #2: Battleground Earth*, 1988. In *Invasion!* New York: DC Comics, 2008.

Gray, Justin, Jimmy Palmiotti, and Daniel Acuña. *Uncle Sam and the Freedom Fighters* #1–8, September 2006–April 2007. In *Uncle Sam and the Freedom Fighters*. New York: DC Comics, 2007.

Green, Michael, and Denys Cowan. *Batman Confidential* #12, February 2008. In *Batman: Lovers and Madmen*. New York: DC Comics, 2008.

Gruenwald, Mark, and Paul Neary. *Captain America* #322, October 1986.

———. *Captain America* #321, September 1986.

Gruenwald, Mark, et al. *Contest of Champions* #1, June 1982. In *Contest of Champions*. New York: Marvel Comics, 1999.

Guggenheim, Marc, and Howard Chaykin. *Wolverine*, vol. 3, #57–61, November 2007–March 2008. In *The Death of Wolverine*. New York: Marvel Comics, 2008.

Hamilton, Edmond, and Curt Swan. *World's Finest* #142, June 1964.
———. *Superman* #172, October 1964.
Herdling, Glenn, and Craig Brasfield. *Illuminator* #1–3, February–June 1993.
Houston, Charlie, et al. *Marvel One-Shot: Horror*, October 2005. In *Legion of Monsters*. New York: Marvel Comics, 2007.
Isabella, Tony, and Jim Mooney. *Ghost Rider* #9, December 1974. In *Essential Ghost Rider*, vol. 1. New York: Marvel Comics, 2006.
Jenkins, Paul, and Mark Buckingham. *Peter Parker: Spider-Man* #28, April 2001. In *Peter Parker: Spider-Man: One Small Break*. New York: Marvel Comics, 2002.
Jenkins, Paul, and Paolo Rivera. *Mythos: Spider-Man*, August 2007. In *Mythos*. New York: Marvel Comics, 2008.
Johns, Geoff, and Gary Frank. *Action Comics* #859, January 2008. In *Superman and the Legion of Super-Heroes*. New York: DC Comics, 2008.
Johns, Geoff, Alan Heinberg, and Chris Batista. *JLA* #120, December 2005. In *JLA: Crisis of Conscience*. New York: DC Comics, 2006.
Johns, Geoff, Jeff Katz, and Dan Jurgens. *Booster Gold: 52 Pick-Up*. New York: DC Comics, 2008.
Johns, Geoff, et al. *Infinite Crisis* #1–7, December 2005–June 2006. In *Infinite Crisis*. New York: DC Comics, 2006.
Jones, Gerard, et al. *Batman: Legends of the Dark Knight* #0, October 1994.
Jurgens, Dan. *Booster Gold* #7, August 1986. In *Showcase Presents: Booster Gold*. New York: DC Comics, 2008.
Jurgens, Dan, et al. *The Death of Superman*. New York: DC Comics, 1993.
Jurgens, Dan, Eric Larsen, and Klaus Janson. *The Mighty Thor*, vol. 2, #28, October 2000. In *Across All Worlds*. New York: Marvel Comics, 2001.
Kanigher, Robert, and Ross Andru. *Metal Men*, vol. 5, December 1963–January 1964. In *Showcase Presents: Metal Men*. New York: DC Comics, 2007.
Kesel, Karl, and Stuart Immonen. *Fantastic Four*, vol. 3, #56, August 2002.
Kyle, Craig, Christopher Yost, and Skottie Young. *New X-Men* #37–41, April–August 2007. In *New X-Men: Childhood's End*. New York: Marvel Comics, 2007.
Lee, Stan. *Son of Origins of Marvel Comics*. New York: Simon & Schuster, 1997.
Lee, Stan, et al. *Stan Lee Meets*, September–December 2006. In *Stan Lee Meets*. New York: Marvel Comics, 2007.
Lee, Stan, and John Buscema. *Silver Surfer: Judgement Day*. New York: Marvel Comics, 1988.
———. *Silver Surfer* #7, August 1969. In *Silver Surfer Omnibus*, vol. 1. New York: Marvel Comics, 2007.
———. *Silver Surfer* #3, December 1968. In *Silver Surfer Omnibus*, vol. 1. New York: Marvel Comics, 2007.
———. *Silver Surfer* #2, October 1968. In *Silver Surfer Omnibus*, vol. 1. New York: Marvel Comics, 2007.
———. *Silver Surfer* #1, July 1968. In *Silver Surfer Omnibus*, vol. 1. New York: Marvel Comics, 2007.
Lee, Stan, and Steve Ditko. "Spider-Man!," in *Amazing Fantasy* #15, August 1962. In *Amazing Spider-Man Omnibus*, vol. 1. New York: Marvel Comics, 2007.

Bibliography

Lee, Stan, and Jack Kirby. *The X-Men Omnibus*, vol. 1. New York: Marvel Comics, 2009.

———. *Fantastic Four*, vol. 1, #72, March 1968. In *Fantastic Four Omnibus*, vol. 2. New York: Marvel Comics, 2007.

———. *Fantastic Four*, vol. 1, #48–50, March–May 1966. In *Fantastic Four Omnibus*, vol. 2. New York: Marvel Comics, 2007.

———. *Fantastic Four*, vol. 1, #13, April 1963. In *Fantastic Four Omnibus*, vol. 1. New York: Marvel Comics, 2005.

———. *Fantastic Four*, vol. 1, #10, January 1963, later in *Fantastic Four Omnibus*, vol. 1. New York: Marvel Comics, 2005.

———. *Fantastic Four*, vol. 1, #7, October 1962. In *Fantastic Four Omnibus*, vol. 1. New York: Marvel Comics, 2005.

———. *Fantastic Four*, vol. 1, #5, July 1962. In *Fantastic Four Omnibus*, vol. 1. New York: Marvel Comics, 2005.

Macchio, Ralph, and John Byrne. *X-Factor Annual* #4, 1989.

Maggin, Elliot S., Curt Swan, and Vince Colletta. *Superman* #273, March 1974.

Mantlo, Bill, and Bob Brown. *Marvel Two-In-One* #11, September 1975.

Mantlo, Bill, George Pérez, and Jack Abel. "An Ending!" In *The Deadly Hands of Kung Fu* #19, December 1975.

Mantlo, Bill, and Frank Robbins. "There's a Mountain on Sunset Boulevard," *Marvel Premier* #28, February 1976. In *Ghost Rider Team-Up*. New York: Marvel Comics, 2007.

Marz, Ron, et al. *Marvel Comics Versus DC* #1–4, February–May 1996. In *DC Versus Marvel Comics*. New York: DC Comics, 1996.

McDuffie, Dwayne, and Ed Benes. *Justice League of America*, vol. 2, #13, November 2007. In *Justice League of America: The Injustice League*. New York: DC Comics, 2008.

McDuffie, Dwayne, Denys Cowan, and Prentis Rollins. "Static Shock: Wednesday Afternoon." In *9-11, September 11th 2001: The World's Finest Comic Book Writers and Artists Tell Stories to Remember*, edited by Steven T. Seagle. New York: DC Comics, 2002.

Meltzer, Brad, and Ed Benes. *Justice League of America*, vol. 2, #7, May 2007. In *Justice League of America: Tornado's Path*. New York: DC Comics, 2007.

———. *Justice League of America*, vol. 2, #1, October 2006. In *Justice League of America: Tornado's Path*. New York: DC Comics, 2007.

Michelinie, David, and Bob Layton. *Iron Man*, vol. 1, #250, December 1989. In *Iron Man: Doomquest*. New York: Marvel Comics, 2008.

Michelinie, David, and John Romita Jr. *Iron Man*, vol. 1, #150, September 1981. In *Iron Man: Doomquest*. New York: Marvel Comics, 2008.

Mill, John Stuart. *The Spirit of the Age*. New Haven: Yale University Press, 2007.

Millar, Mark, and Steve McNiven. *Civil War* #1–7, May 2006–January 2007. In *Civil War*. New York: Marvel Comics, 2007.

Millar, Mark, and Ariel Olivetti. *JLA: Paradise Lost* #1–3, January–March 1998.

Miller, Frank, Klaus Janson, and Lynn Varley. *The Dark Knight Returns*. New York, DC Comics: 1986.

Milligan, Peter, and Jim Aparo. *Detective Comics* #632, July 1991.

———. *Detective Comics* #631, July 1991.

Mills, Tarpe. *Miss Fury*. New York: Pure Imagination Publishing, 2007.

Moore, Alan, and Dave Gibbons. *Watchmen*. New York, DC Comics: 1987.

Moore, Stuart, and Carlos Pagulayan. *Iron Man, Director of S.H.I.E.L.D.* # 32, August 2008. In *Iron Man, Director of S.H.I.E.L.D.: With Iron Hands*. New York: Marvel Comics, 2009.

Morrison, Grant, and Howard Porter. *JLA* #6, June 1997. In *JLA: American Dreams*. New York: DC Comics, 1998.

———. *JLA* #4, April 1997. In *JLA: New World Order*, vol. 1. New York: DC Comics, 1997.

Morrison, Grant, and Frank Quitely. *New X-Men* #115, August 2001. In *New X-Men Ultimate Collection*, vol. 1. New York: Marvel Comics, 2008.

Moulton Marston, William, and Harry G. Peter. *Wonder Woman* #1, Summer 1942. In *Wonder Woman Archives*, vol. 1. New York: DC Comics, 1998.

———. *Sensation Comics* #1, January 1942. In *Wonder Woman Archives*, vol. 1. New York: DC Comics, 1998.

———. *All Star Comics* #8, December 1941 and January 1942. In *Wonder Woman Archives*, vol. 1. New York: DC Comics, 1998.

Oeming, Michael Avon, and Andrea DiVito. *The Mighty Thor: Disassembled*. New York: Marvel Comics, 2004.

O'Neil, Dennis, and Neal Adams. *The Flash* #217–219, June–August 1972. In *Green Lantern/Green Arrow Collection*, #1–2. New York: DC Comics, 2004.

———. *Green Lantern* #76–89, April 1970–May 1972. In *Green Lantern/Green Arrow Collection*, #1–2. New York: DC Comics, 2004.

———. *Superman vs. Muhammad Ali*. New York: DC Comics, 1978.

O'Neil, Dennis, and Dick Dillin. *Justice League of America*, vol. 1, #78, February 1970.

O'Neil, Dennis, Dick Dillin, and Joe Giella. *Justice League of America*, 1, #77, December 1969. In *JLA: The Greatest Stories Ever Told*. New York: DC Comics, 2006.

O'Neil, Dennis, and Edward Hannigan. *Batman: Legends of the Dark Knight* #1–5, November 1989–March 1990. In *Batman: Shaman*. New York: DC Comics, 1998.

O'Neil, Dennis, and Mike Sekowsky. *Wonder Woman* #183, August 1969. In *Diana Prince: Wonder Woman*, vol. 1. New York: DC Comics, 2008.

———. *Wonder Woman* #179, December 1968. In *Diana Prince: Wonder Woman*, vol. 1. New York: DC Comics, 2008.

Orlando, Joe, ed. *Cancelled Comic Cavalcade*, vol. 2. New York: DC Comics, 1978.

Ordway, Jerry, and Tom Grummett. *The Adventures of Superman* #497, December 1992. In *The Death of Superman*, by Dan Jurgens et al. New York: DC Comics, 1993.

Ostrander, John, and Tom Mandrake. *The Kents* #4, November 1997. In *The Kents*. New York: DC Comics, 1999.

Pak, Greg, and John Romita Jr. *World War Hulk* #1–5, August–December 2007. In *World War Hulk*. New York: Marvel Comics, 2008.

Parker, Bill, and C. C. Beck. *Whiz Comics* #2, February 1940. In *Shazam! The Greatest Stories Ever Told*. New York: DC Comics, 2008.

Potter, Greg, and George Pérez. *Wonder Woman,* vol. 2, #1, February 1987. In *Gods and Mortals.* New York: DC Comics, 2004.

Puckett, Kelley, and Jon Bogdanove. *Batman* #566, June 1999. In *No Man's Land,* vol. 3. New York: DC Comics, 2000.

Rucka, Greg, and Matthew Clark. *Adventures of Superman* #638, May 2005. In *Superman: That Healing Touch.* New York: DC Comics, 2005.

Rucka, Greg, and Drew Johnson. *Wonder Woman,* vol. 2, #210, November 2004. In *Eyes of the Gorgon.* New York: DC Comics, 2005.

Rucka, Greg, and Rags Morales. *Wonder Woman,* vol. 2, #219, July 2005. In *Mission's End.* New York: DC Comics, 2006.

Sanderson, Mark, et al. *The Official Handbook of the Marvel Universe* #7, July 1983. In *Essential Official Handbook of the Marvel Universe.* New York: Marvel, 2006.

Schwartz, Julius, ed. *Superman* #400, October 1984.

Sekowsky, Mike. *Wonder Woman* #189, August 1969. In *Diana Prince: Wonder Woman,* vol. 2. New York: DC Comics, 2008.

Shooter, Jim, Mike Zeck, and Bob Layton. *Secret Wars* #1–12, May 1984–April 1985. In *Secret Wars.* New York: Marvel Comics, 2005.

Siegel, Jerry, and Bernard Baily. *The Spectre* #3, in *More Fun Comics* #54, April 1940. In *Golden Age Spectre Archives,* vol. 1. New York: DC Comics, 2003.

Siegel, Jerry, and Joe Shuster. *The Superman Chronicles,* vol. 1. New York: DC Comics, 2007.

———. *Superman* #2, Fall 1939. In *Superman Chronicles,* vol. 2. New York: DC Comics, 2007.

———. *Superman: The Dailies, Strips 1–966, 1939–1942.* New York: Sterling Publishing, 2006.

———. "Superman," in *Superman* #1, July 1939. In *Superman Chronicles,* vol. 1. New York: DC Comics, 2006.

———."Superman," in *Action Comics* #1, June 1938. In *Superman Chronicles,* vol. 1. New York: DC Comics, 2006.

Simon, Joe, and Jack Kirby. *Captain America Comics* #2, April 1941. In *Marvel Masterworks: Golden Age Captain America.* New York: Marvel Comics, 2005.

———. "Meet Captain America," in *Captain America Comics* #1, March 1941. In *Marvel Masterworks: Golden Age Captain America.* New York: Marvel Comics, 2005.

Simon, Joe, and Jim Simon. *The Comic Book Makers.* Lebanon, NJ: Vanguard Productions, 2003.

Simonson, Louise, and Jon Bogdanove. *Man of Steel* #81, July 1998.

Simonson, Louise, et al. *The Return of Superman.* New York: DC Comics, 1993.

Simonson, Walter. *The Mighty Thor* #338, December 1983. In *Thor Visionaries: Walter Simonson.* New York: Marvel Comics, 2001.

Slott, Dan, and Juan Bobillo. *She-Hulk: Single Green Female.* New York: Marvel Comics, 2007.

Slott, Dan, and Marcos Martin. *The Amazing Spider-Man* #560, May 2008. In *The Amazing Spider-Man: Brand New Day,* vol. 3. New York: Marvel Comics, 2008.

Spiegelman, Art. *Maus: A Survivor's Tale.* New York: Pantheon Books, 1986 and 1991.

Spurrier, Simon, and Tan Eng Huat. *In Thy Name* #1–4, January–April 2008. In *In Thy Name*. New York: Marvel Comics, 2008.

Starlin, Jim. *The Death of Captain Marvel*. New York: Marvel Comics, 1994.

Starlin, Jim, and Ron Lim. *Infinity Crusade*, #1–2. New York: Marvel Comics, 2008–2009.

Stern, Roger, and John Byrne. *JLA Classified* #50–54, March–May 2008. In *That Was Now, This Is Then*. New York: DC Comics, 2008.

———. *Captain America*, 1, #254, February 1981.

———. *Captain America*, 1, #249, September 1980.

Straczynski, J. Michael, et al. *Rising Stars* #1–24, August 1999–May 2005. In *Rising Stars*. Orange, CA: Image Comics, 2005.

Straczynski, J. Michael, and Mike McKone. *Fantastic Four* #530–531, August–September 2005. In *Fantastic Four by J. Michael Straczynski*. New York: Marvel Comics, 2006.

Straczynski, J. Michael, and Esad Ribic. *Requiem*. New York: Marvel Comics, 2008.

Straczynski, J. Michael, and John Romita Jr. *Amazing Spider-Man* #507, July 2004. In *The Book of Ezekiel*. New York: Marvel Comics, 2004.

———. *Amazing Spider-Man*, vol. 2, #31, July 2001. In *Coming Home*. New York: Marvel Comics, 2002.

Turner, Michael, Joe Kelly, and Talent Caldwell. *Superman: Godfall*. New York: DC Comics, 2004.

Waid, Mark, and Leinil Francis Yu. *Superman: Birthright*, September 2003–September 2004. In *Superman: Birthright*. New York: DC Comics, 2005.

Way, Daniel, Javier Saltares, and Max Texeira. *Ghost Rider* #1–5, July and November 2006. In *Vicious Cycle*. New York: Marvel Comics, 2007.

Wein, Len, and John Buscema. *Strange Tales* #177, December 1974.

———. *Strange Tales* #176, October 1974.

———. *Strange Tales* #174, June 1974.

Wein, Len, and Dave Cockrum. *Giant-Size X-Men*, 1, May 1975. In *The Uncanny X-Men Omnibus*, vol. 1. New York: Marvel Comics, 2007.

Wells, Zeb, and Todd Nauck. *Amazing Spider-Man* #583, January 2009.

Willow Wilson, G., and CAFU. *Return of the Lion* #1–5, December 2008–April 2009.

Secondary Sources

Appiah, Kwame Anthony. *Cosmopolitanism: Ethics in a World of Strangers*. New York: Norton, 2007.

Baio, Ivan. *Supereroi™. Araldica e simbologia dell'eroismo dai miti classici a Superman e The Authority*. Latina, Italy: Tunué, 2006.

Beaven, Lisa. "Someone to Watch over Me: The Guardian Angel as Superhero in Seicento Rome." In *Super/Heroes from Hercules to Superman*, edited by Wendy Haslem, Angela Ndalianis, and Chris Mackie, 251–61. Washington, DC: New Academia Publishing, 2007.

Beck Kehoe, Alice. *Shamans and Religion: An Anthropological Exploration in Critical Thinking*. Long Grove, IL: Waveland Press, 2000.

Benamati, Guidubaldo. *Il Trivisano, poema eroicivico*. Frankfurt: Beyer, 1630.

Benincasa, Fabio. "Barocco e Neo-barocco: Percorsi autoriali nel cinema italiano: Fellini, Antonioni, Pasolini." Ph.D. dissertation, Indiana University, Bloomington, October 2008.

Benton, Mike. *Superhero Comics of the Golden Age: The Illustrated History*. Dallas: Taylor Publishing Company, 1992.

———. *Superhero Comics of the Silver Age: The Illustrated History*. Dallas: Taylor Publishing Company, 1991.

Brown, Jeffrey A. *Black Superheroes, Milestone Comics, and Their Fans*. Jackson: University of Mississippi Press, 2001.

Buhle, Paul, ed. *Jews and American Comics: An Illustrated History of an American Art Form*. New York: New Press, 2008.

Caillava, Marie-Catherine. "Magneto the Jew." In *The Unauthorized X-Men*, edited by Len Wein and Leah Wilson, 99–109. Dallas: BenBella Books, 2005.

Calabrese, Omar. *Caos e bellezza: Immagini del Neobarocco*. Milan: Domus, 1991.

———. *Neo-Baroque: A Sign of the Times*. Princeton: Princeton University Press, 1992.

Calloway, Stephen. *Baroque Baroque*. London: Phaidon, 2000.

Camerota, Michele. *Galileo Galilei e la cultura scientifica nell'età della Controriforma*. Rome: Salerno, 2004.

Campbell, Joseph. *The Hero with a Thousand Faces*. Novato, CA: New World Libra, 2008.

———. *The Masks of God: Primitive Mythology*. New York: Viking Press, 1959.

Chabon, Michael. *The Amazing Adventures of Kavalier & Clay*. New York: Picador, 2001.

Chessa Wright, Simonetta. *La poetica neobarocca in Calvino*. Ravenna, Italy: Longo, 1998.

Coogan, Peter. *Superhero: The Secret Origin of a Genre*. Austin: Monkey Brain Books, 2006.

Daniels, Les. *DC Comics: Sixty Years of the World's Favorite Comic Book Heroes*. Boston: Bulfinch Press, 1995.

———. *Marvel: Five Fabulous Decades of the World's Greatest Comics*. New York: Abrams, 1991.

———. *Superman: The Complete History*. New York: Chronicle Books, 1998.

D'Azeglio, Bartolomeo Massimo. *Neobarocco e architettura*. Milan: Lampi di stampa, 2005.

Degli-Esposti, Cristina. "Federico Fellini's *Intervista* or the Neo-Baroque Creativity of the Analysand on Screen." *Italica* 73, no. 2 (1996): 157–72.

Dorfles, Gillo. *Architetture ambigue: Dal Neobarocco al Postmoderno*. Bari, Italy: Dedalo, 1984.

———. *Barocco nell'architettura moderna*. Milan: Libreria Editrice Politecnica Tamburini, 1951.

Eagan, Patrick L. "A Flag with a Human Face." In *Superman at Fifty! The Persistence of a Legend!*, edited by Dennis Dooley and Gary Engle, 88–95. New York: Macmillan, 1988.

Eco, Umberto. "The Myth of Superman." In *The Role of the Reader: Explorations in the Semiotics of Texts*, 107–24. Bloomington: Indiana University Press, 1979.

Egolf, Jamie. "Dreaming Superman: Exploring the Action of the Superhero(ine) in Dreams, Myth, and Culture." In *Super/Heroes from Hercules to Superman*, edited by Wendy Haslem, Angela Ndalianis, and Chris Mackie, 139–51. Washington, DC: New Academia Publishing, 2007.

Eliade, Mircea. *Shamanism: Archaic Techniques of Ecstasy*. London: Penguin Arkana, 1988.

Engle, Gary. "What Makes Superman So Darned American?" In *Superman at Fifty! The Persistence of a Legend!*, edited by Dennis Dooley and Gary Engle, 79–87. New York: Macmillan, 1988.

Feiffer, Jules. *The Great Comic Book Heroes*. New York: Bonanza Books, 1965.

Fingeroth, Danny. *Disguised as Clark Kent: Jews, Comics, and the Creation of the Superhero*. New York: Continuum, 2007.

———. *Superman on the Couch: What Superheroes Really Tell Us about Ourselves and Our Society*. New York: Continuum, 2005.

Galilei, Galileo. *Dialogo sopra i due massimi sistemi del mondo*. Florence: Geo. Batista Landini, 1632. Published in English as *Dialogue Concerning the Two Chief World Systems*. New York: Modern Library, 2001.

Garrett, Greg. *Holy Superheroes! Exploring the Sacred in Comics, Graphic Novels, and Film*. Louisville, KY: Westminster John Knox Press, 2008.

Giovannotti, Micaela, and Joyce B. Korotkin, ed. *Neo Baroque!* Milan: Charta, 2005.

Hajdu, David. *The Ten-Cent Plague: The Great Comic-Book Scare and How It Changed America*. New York: Farrar, Straus and Giroux, 2008.

Harper, Stephen. "Supermyth!" In *The Man from Krypton: A Closer Look at Superman*, edited by Glenn Yeffeth, 93–100. Dallas: Benbella Books, 2006.

Jewett, Robert, and John Shelton Lawrence. *Captain America and the Crusade against Evil*. Grand Rapids, MI: Eedermans, 2004.

———. *The Myth of the American Superhero*. Grand Rapids, MI: Eedermans, 2002.

Jones, Gerard, and Will Jacobs. *The Comic Book Heroes*. Roseville, CA: Prima Publishing, 1997.

Kaplan, Arie. *From Krakow to Krypton: Jews and Comic Books*. Philadelphia: Jewish Publication Society, 2008.

Kaveney, Roz. *Superheroes! Capes and Crusaders in Comics and Films*. New York: I. B. Tauris, 2008.

Klock, Geoff. *How to Read Superhero Comics and Why*. New York: Continuum, 2002.

Knowles, Chris. *Our Gods Wear Spandex: The Secret History of Comic Books Heroes*. San Francisco: Weiser Books, 2007.

Koda, Harold, and Andrew Bolton, eds. *Superheroes: Fashion and Fantasy*. New Haven: Yale University Press, 2008.

Levinson, Paul. "Superman, Patriotism, and Doing the Ultimate Good: Why the Man of Steel Did So Little to Stop Hitler and Tojo." In *The Man from Krypton: A Closer Look at Superman*, edited by Glenn Yeffeth, 211–19. Dallas: Benbella Books, 2006.

Lloyd, Peter B. "Superman's Moral Evolution." In *The Man from Krypton: A Closer Look at Superman*, edited by Glenn Yeffeth, 181–98. Dallas: Benbella Books, 2006.

LoCicero, Don. *Superheroes and Gods: A Comparative Study from Babylonia to Batman.* Jefferson, NC: McFarland & Co., 2008.

Lovasik, Lawrence G. *The Book of Saints: Super-Heroes of God.* New York: Catholic Book Publishing, 1985.

Mackie, C. J. "Men of Darkness." In *Super/Heroes from Hercules to Superman,* edited by Wendy Haslem, Angela Ndalianis, and Chris Mackie, 83–95. Washington, DC: New Academia Publishing, 2007.

Malcolm, Cheryl Alexander. "Witness, Trauma, and Remembrance: Holocaust Representation and *X-Men* Comics." In *The Jewish Graphic Novel: Critical Approaches,* edited by Samantha Baskind and Ranen Omer-Sherman, 144–60. New Brunswick, NJ: Rutgers University Press, 2008.

Marino, Giambattista. *L'Adone.* Milan: Adelphi, 1988.

Morris, Tom, and Chris Ryall, ed. *Superheroes and Philosophy: Truth, Justice, and the Socratic Way.* Peterborough, NH: Carus Publishing, 2008.

Ndalianis, Angela. *The Contemporary Comic Book Superheroes.* London: Routledge, 2009.

———. *Neo-Baroque Aesthetics and Contemporary Entertainment.* Cambridge, MA: MIT Press, 2004.

Nyberg, Amy Kyste. *Seal of Approval: The History of the Comics Code.* Jackson: University of Mississippi Press, 1998.

O'Neil, Dennis. "The Man of Steel and Me." In *Superman at Fifty! The Persistence of a Legend!,* edited by Dennis Dooley and Gary Engle, 46–58. New York: Macmillan, 1988.

Oropeza, B. J. "The God-Man Revisited: Christology through the Blank Eyes of the Silver Surfer." In *The Gospel According to Superheroes,* edited by B. J. Oropeza, 154–69. New York: Peter Lang, 2005.

———, ed. *The Gospel According to Superheroes: Religion and Pop Culture.* New York: Peter Lang, 2005.

Peaslee, Robert M. "Superheroes, 'Moral Economy,' and the 'Iron Cage': Morality, Alienation, and the Super-Individual." In *Super/Heroes from Hercules to Superman,* edited by Wendy Haslem, Angela Ndalianis, and Chris Mackie, 37–50. Washington, DC: New Academia Publishing, 2007.

Peebles, Gustav. "God, Communism, and the WB." In *The Man from Krypton,* edited by Glenn Yeffeth, 77–92. Dallas: Benbella Books, 2006.

Pellitteri, Marco. *Sense of Comics. La grafica dei cinque sensi nel fumetto.* Rome: Castelvecchi, 1998.

Pérez, Janet, and Genaro J. Pérez, eds. *Hispanic Contemporary Baroque.* Odessa: University of Texas of the Permian Basin, 1994.

Raimondi, Ezio. *Barocco moderno: Roberto Longhi e Carlo Emilio Gadda.* Milan: Bruno Mondadori, 2003.

———. "Lo specchio del barocco e le immagini del presente." In *Il colore eloquente: Letteratura e arte barocca,* 3–19. Bologna: Il Mulino, 1995.

Regalado, Aldo. "Modernity, Race, and the American Superhero." In *Comics as Philosophy,* edited by Jeff McLaughlin, 84–99. Jackson: University of Mississippi Press, 2005.

Reynolds, Richard. *Superheroes: A Modern Mythology.* Jackson: University of Mississippi Press, 1992.

Rhodes, Ryan Indy, and David Kyle Johnson. "What Would Batman Do? Bruce Wayne as Moral Exemplar." In *Batman and Philosophy: The Dark Knight of the Soul,* edited by Mark D. White and Robert Arp, 114–25. Hoboken, NJ: Wiley, 2008.

Robbins, Trina. *The Great Women Superheroes.* Northampton, MA: Kitchen Sink Press, 1996.

Sanderson, Peter. *Classic Marvel Superheroes: The Story of Marvel's Mightiest.* New York: Barnes & Noble Books, 2005.

Schenck, Ken. "Superman: A Popular Messiah." In *The Gospel According to Superheroes: Religion and Pop Culture,* edited by B. J. Oropeza, 33–48. New York: Peter Lang, 2005.

Semprini, Valentina. *Bam! Sock! Lo scontro a fumetti: Dramma e spettacolo del conflitto nei comics d'avventura.* Latina, Italy: Tunué, 2006.

Simpson, Paul, Helen Rodiss, and Michaela Bushell, ed. *The Rough Guide to Superheroes.* London: Haymarket Customer Publishing, 2004.

Skelton, Stephen. *The Gospel According to the World's Greatest Superhero.* Eugene, OR: Harvest House, 2006.

Sorensen, Theodore. *Let the Word Go Forth: The Speeches, Statements, and Writings of John F. Kennedy 1947 to 1963.* New York: Delta, 1991.

Spera, Lucinda. "Il Barocco che è in noi." In *Verso il moderno: Pubblico e immaginario nel Seicento italiano,* 200–208. Rome: Carocci, 2008.

Stonor Saunders, Frances. *The Cultural Cold War: The CIA and the World of Arts and Letters.* New York: New Press, 1999.

Strazdins, Estelle. "Conqueror of Flood, Wielder of Fire: Noah the Hebrew Superhero." In *Super/Heroes from Hercules to Superman,* edited by Wendy Haslem, Angela Ndalianis, and Chris Mackie, 275–87. Washington, DC: New Academia Publishing, 2007.

Strozzi, Giulio. *Il Barbarigo, o l'amico sollevato.* Venice: Piuti, 1626.

Tesauro, Emanuele. *The Aristotelian Telescope.* Turin: Zavatta, 1670.

Vitebsky, Piers. *Shamanism.* Norman: University of Oklahoma Press, 2001.

Walsh, Roger. *The World of Shamanism: New Views of an Ancient Tradition.* Woodbury, MN: Llewellyn Publications, 2007.

Weinstein, Simcha. *Up, Up, and Oy Vey! How Jewish History, Culture and Values Shaped the Comic Book Superhero.* Baltimore: Leviathan Press, 2006.

White, Mark D., ed. *Watchmen and Philosophy: A Rorschach Test.* Hoboken, NJ: Wiley, 2009.

White, Mark D., and Robert Arp, ed. *Batman and Philosophy: The Dark Knight of the Soul.* Hoboken, NJ: Wiley, 2008.

Wolk, Douglas. *Reading Comics: How Graphic Novels Work and What They Mean.* Cambridge, MA: Da Capo Press, 2007.

Wollen, Peter. "Baroque and Neo-Baroque in the Age of Spectacle." *Point of Contact* 3 (1993): 9–21.

Wright, Lucy. "Shamans vs. (Super)heroes." In *Super/Heroes from Hercules to Superman*, edited by Wendy Haslem, Angela Ndalianis, and Chris Mackie, 127–37. Washington, DC: New Academia Publishing, 2007.

Wylie, Philip. *Gladiator*. Westport, CT: Hyperion Press, 1974.

Zatti, Sergio. *Il modo epico*. Rome and Bari: Laterza, 2000. Published in English as *The Quest for Epic: From Ariosto to Tasso*. Toronto, Ontario: University of Toronto Press, 2006.

Index

Note: Italicized page numbers indicate text in captions to illustrations.

Adventure Comics #1, 160n6
Aguirre-Sacasa, Roberto, 150
Ali, Muhammad, *129*, 130
Ama, 55–56
Amazons, 14, 15, *16*, 60, 120, 129
Amazons Attack, 41
American society: assimilation to, 68;
  increased tolerance in, 154; and
  Judeo-Christian belief, 27; present
  time in, 132–34; values of, 119. *See
  also* society; United States
American War of Independence, 119
Angel, 168n73
Angel of Death, 125
angels, 30, 32, 41, 47, 60, 168n73
Animal Man, 19
animals, traits of, 19
Ant-Man, 19
Appiah, Kwame Anthony, 157–58
Aquaman, 19, 160n6
archetypes, 12, 117–19
Arion, 126
Aristotle, 136
Armadillo, 19, 137
Arthur, King, 126, 148
Astro City, 5, 160–61n8
Atlas (publishing company), 159n3
authors: collaborative writing by, 13;
  and epic length, 119; and ethical
  norms, 86; ethnic or religious
  background of, 29–32, 165n47; and
  evolving narratives, 136–37, 139, 144,

149–53; readers as potential, 153; and
  seriality, 4, 8; stylistic differences
  among, 2
Avengers, 120, *123*, 154, 159–60n3
Avengers, The, 137
Azrael, 75–76, *77*, 133

Badoon, 53
Baily, Bernard, 160n6
Bane, 75
Banshee, 68
Baron Blood, 79
baroque, 135, 139–40, 149. *See also*
  neobaroque
Batman (Bruce Wayne), *82*, 130, 160n6;
  and American individualism, 65; and
  Azrael, 133; chest symbol of, 145,
  146; and council of gods, 121; and
  golem, 167–68n67; and government,
  96; and Judaism, 29; and killing, 78,
  79, 89, 90, 92, 94; and Miss Fury, 21;
  motivation of, 85; origin stories of,
  23; and pictorial style, 150–52; and
  political intervention, 107; and
  respect for life, 82–83; and seriality,
  4; and shamanism, 19, 23–24; and
  violence, 75–77; as Bruce Wayne, 23,
  24, 75; and Wonder Woman, 89, 90
Batman Begins (film), 94
Batman: Legends of the Dark Knight
  #0, 151
Batman: Year One, 23

197

battles, 118, 129, 130
Bauer, Jack, 89
Beast, 19, *61*
Beast Boy, 134
Beta Ray Bill, 126, *127*
Beyonder, 130
Bible, 39, 52, 60; Exodus, 30; Genesis, 32; Matthew, 48, 53, 61; Sermon on the Mount, 53; and Superman, 29–30
Bin Laden, Osama, 57, 112
Black Panther, 19, 151, *152*
Blake, William, 141, 148, 181n49
Bobbio, Norberto, 96–97
Brekk, 55–56
Brother Eye, 89
Buffy the Vampire Slayer (film and television series), 4
Bullseye, 94
Burstein, Martin A., 13
Buscema, John, Sr., 52
Bush administration, 57
Busiek, Kurt, 32, 160–61n8

Cable, 76
Camelot Falls, 126
Campbell, Joseph, 12, 18, 95, 161–62n4
Cannonball, 68
capitalism, 97, 120, 171n1, 175–76n57
Captain America, *61*, 130, 159n3; and American culture, 32; and American individualism, 65; costume of, 32, 34, 87–88, 96, 167n62; and democracy, 97; and government, 97–98, 99, 100; and Hitler, 103; in *Infinity Crusade,* 62; and Judaism, 29, 32, 34, 166–67n60; and killing, 79, 86–89, 94, 95; as Nomad, 98, 120; and past values, 119; and patriotism, 96, 98; and Pop Art, 142; and respect for life, 83; return of, 154; shield of, 32, 34, *35;* symbols of, 32, 34; and Watergate scandal, 97–98, *98;* and World War II, 132
Captain Marvel, 13, 18, 42–44, 53, 142, 170n90
Catholicism, 40, 51, 168n70, 170n91
Catwoman, 19, 21
Cervantes, Miguel de, 144
Chameleon, 105
Cheetah, 146

Christianity, 22, 39–59, 60, 62, 71–72, 136, 168n69; Eucharist, 54; Mary, 48; Protestantism, 40; religious practices of, 40–41; and Superman, 32; supernatural elements of, 41; symbolism of, 59, 94. *See also* Catholicism; Christology; God; Jesus; Judeo-Christian belief
Christology, 42–59; and Silver Surfer, 51–57; and Spider-Man, 44–46, *45, 46, 47;* and Superman, 47–51. *See also* Jesus
Church of Humanity, 62
Civil War, 98–99, 100, 129
Claremont, Chris, 29
Cold War, 36, 97, 103, 119, 120, 132, 172n2
collective, the, 64, 70; historical memory of, 117, 119. *See also* community; society
Colossus, 19, 68
comics: daily strips, 3–4; definition of, 3; parameters of discussion of, 8–10; selection of, 5–7; sources of, 9
Comics Code, 102, 144
communism, 97, 120
community: and American monomyth, 95; and epic, 118; heroic, 120; and hero's journey, 12–13; as saved by superhero, 44; and shamans, 18. *See also* collective, the; social context; society
Composite Superman, 114, *115*
conservatism, 71, 72, 73, 105
Constitution of the United States, 133
Contest of Champions, 130
copyright, 11
costumes, 133; and American individualism, 65; of Captain America, 32, 34, 87–88, 96, 98, 167n62; hero transfigured by, 44; and New Mutants, 68, 69–70; and secret identity, 20; and shamans, 19–21; of Spider-Man, 46, 96, 133; and superhero groups, 68–71; of Superman, 49–51; of Wonder Woman, 167n62. *See also* masks
crime, 130; and Umberto Eco, 102–3; legitimacy of fighting, 84–85

Index

criminals: and conservatism, 71; and demons, 41; and killing, 79, 80, 84, 85, 86, 89, 92–94; religious proselytizing by, 62; and Superman, 78; and Watergate scandal, 97–98
crucifixion, 45–46, 56–57
culture(s), 111, 136; coexistence of, 154; differences in, 154; high vs. low, 142; and plurality, 134; and relativity, 108. *See also* multiculturalism; social context; society
current events, 103, 104, 132–34
Cyberforce, 160n5
Cyclops (X-Men), 19, 68, 167n63

Daredevil, 18, 52, 62, 94, 159–60n3, 168n70
Daredevil (film), 94
Dark Horse, 5, 160n7
Dark Knight Returns, The, 5, 7, 75, 160n6
Darnall, Steve, 99
David (biblical hero), 34, *35*
Dazzler, 19
DC Comics: and Christian supernatural elements, 41; founding of, 160n6; and Image, 2; and killing, 79; number of issues published by, 6; and seriality, 4; and shamans, 23; unifying narrative of, 136–37; and violence, 75–77
DC Universe, 4, 166n54, 166n59; reboot of, 138–39. *See also individual characters and comics*
DC/Wildstorm, 160–61n8
death: and Batman, 85; and Captain Marvel, 42–44, 142; and katabasis, 125; revival from, 40; and shamans, 18; and Silver Surfer, 53–55, 57; and Spider-Man, 92; and Superman, 49. *See also* killing
Death of Captain Marvel, The, 42–44, 170n90
Death of Superman, The, 80
Demarbre, Lee, 39
democracy, 71–75, 96–97, 111
demons/devils, 41–42, 60
Detective Comics, 160n6. *See also* DC Comics
discrimination, 156

diversity, 65, 156. *See also* multiculturalism
Doctor Doom, 128, 148
Doctor Fate, 13, 165n45
Doctor Octopus, 45, 169n81
Doctor Strange, 129, 142
Donne, John, 136
Donner, Richard, 47
Doomsday, 80, *81*
Dough, John, 64, 67, 171n1
Dylan, Bob, 1

Eagan, Patrick, 96
Eco, Umberto, 102–3, 140
Eisner, Will, 29
Eliade, Mircea, 19, 27
Elongated Man, 134
Engle, Gary, 65
epic(s), 117–34, 137, 139, 154, 155, 177n4
equality, 67, 73, 96, 111, 114
escapism, 2, 59, 71–72, 156
ethics, codes of, 73, 92–93, 156–57; and killing, 78–91, 95; and violence, 74–78
ethics/morality, 1, 71–74, 111, 156; and absolute obligation, 45; and Batman, 76–77; and Captain America, 86–89, 97; and democracy, 97; and killing, 93; and *Legion of Monsters,* 59; and motivation, 84–85; and readers, 91; reductive vs. complex definition of, 87–88; remorse for transgressions of, 86–91; and respect for life, 80, 82–83; and Silver Surfer, 53, 57; and *Spider-Man 2,* 44–46; and Superman, 72, 73; and Wylie, 115
ethnicity, 9, 154, 158. *See also* diversity; multiculturalism
Everett, Bill, 159–60n3
Everyman, 175n50
Excalibur, 126
Ezekiel, 26

Falcon, 19
Fantastic Four, *144*, 160n4; and Cold War, 103; and high-tech tools and weapons, 128; and identity, 20; and Judaism, 37, 38, 39; as mutates, 34; and pictorial style, 151; and Silver Surfer, 51; and uniforms, 68–69

Fantastic Four, The: citations and references in, 143; and Judeo-Christian belief, 27; launch of, 159n3; as self-reflexive, 150
fascism, 71, 73
fate, 44, 58, 59, 119, 121
films, 2, 4–5, 44–46, 78, 91–95, 100. *See also individual directors and films*
Finger, Bill, 29, 160n6
fire fighters, 73
Flag-Smasher, 86–89, 95
Flash, 13, 65, 78–79, 160n6
Flight 93, 74
folkloric process, 13, 32
Fox, Gardner, 160n6
Frankenstein, Dr., 53
freedom, 65, 73, 96, 111, 112, 119, 125, 133
Friedrich, Gary, 159–60n3

Galactus, 51, 52, 78
Galileo, 136
Gambit, 40
games and contests, 118, 129–30
Gandalf, 103
General Nox, 108, 111, 177n71
Genosha, 137
Ghost Rider, 21–23, 42, 58, 59, 159–60n3, 168n69, 169n78
Gilgamesh, 12
Gladiator (Wylie), 114–15
Glenowen, Mary, 25
God, 27–30, 40, 41, 47, 48, 60, 165n45. *See also* Jesus; *individual faiths*
Goddess, the, 62
gods, council of, 118, 120–21
Gold, Booster, 106, 176n66
golem, 29, 30, 32, 34, 37, 47, 60, 167–68n67
Goliath, 154
Goodman, Martin, 159n3
government, 95–102, 112. *See also* politics/political context; society
graphic novels, 3, 6. *See also individual authors and titles*
Great Depression, 119, 132
Greek and Roman mythology: Aeneas and Dido, 125; Aphrodite, 14, 15; Ares (Mars), 11, 15, *16*, 129; Athena, 14;

Cerberus, 125; Eros (Cupid), 11; Galatea, 15; Hercules, 11, 14, 15, 39, 120, 125, 154; Hermes, 14; Hippolyta, 14, 15; Jupiter, 13–14; Medusa, 16–17, 79; Mercury, 13–14, 162n10; Orpheus and Eurydice, 125; Pluto, 13–14; Pygmalion, 15, 32
Green Arrow, 64, 95, 114, 160n6
Green Lantern, 95, 160n6
Grimm, Ben. *See* Thing, the
Grundy, Solomon, 40

Hades, 16
Hand, the, 40
Harkness, Agatha, 28
Hawkgirl, 19, 173n15
Hawkman, 19, 41, 160n6, 168n73, 172n4, 173n15
Heck, Don, 159–60n3
Hellstorm, 27, *28*
Hendler, Rudolph, 14
Heroes Reborn, 75
heroic adventure/quest, 12–13, 118, 120
heroic vision, 117, 119
history: alternative, 103; events of, 118, 120; fantasy, 104; interchangeability of epochs of, 16; and memory, 117, 119
Hitler, Adolf, 14, 30, 103, 166–67n60
Holocaust, 35, 37
Homage, 160–61n8
Homer, 132
horror, 2
hubris, 118
Hulk, 18, 130, 137, 154, 160n4
Hulk, 143
Human Torch (Johnny Storm), 19, 143, *144,* 159n3

"I, Magneto," 35
identity/identities: and American culture, 133; as dual, 44; and hero's journey, 12; and immigrant culture, 65–68; and masks and costumes, 20; multiple, 134; redefinition of, 133, 134; secret, 20, 23; and Superman, 31, 65–68; and the Thing, 38; and X-Men, 68
Illuminator, 41

Image Comics, 2, 5, 75, 160n5, 160–61n8
immigrants, 65–68, 154
Indiana Jones, 140
individualism, 64–65, 68–71, 125
Infinite Crisis, 90
Infinity Crusade, 62
Injustice League, 145–47
intertextuality, 143
In Thy Name, 55–57, 59, 60
Invasion!, 142
Invisible Woman (Sue Storm, Sue Richards), 20, 27, 69, 151, *152*
Iraq, 111
Iraq War, 57, 101, 112
Iron Man (Tony Stark), 18, 52, 83, 128, 147–48, *148*, 154, 159–60n3
Iron Man, 83
Islam, 40, 62
Iwo Jima, flag raising at, *141*, 142

Japanese manga and animation, 63
Jesus: age of, 49; deposition of, 46; as human and divine, 44; Jor-El as, 47–48; as mediator, 52; Sacred Heart of, *50*, 51; as shaman, 153; and *Spider-Man 2,* 45, 46; as superhero, 39–40; and Superman, 32, 47, 48–51; third temptation of, 48. *See also* Christianity; Christology; God
Jesus Christ Vampire Hunter (film), 39–40, 49
Jewett, Robert, 95; *Captain America and the Crusade against Evil,* 74; *The Myth of the American Superhero,* 74
Jews, 30, 34, 35, 37. *See also* Judaism
JLA: That Was Now, This Is Then, 111–12
Johnson, Mark Steven, 94
Joker, *82,* 82–83, 92, 146
Jor-El, 47–48, *48, 49*
Judah Loew ben Bezalel, 29
Judaism, 29–39, 47, 60, 166n54, 166–67n60. *See also* God; Jews
Judeo-Christian belief, 27, 41, 60. *See also* Christianity; Judaism
justice, 73, 91, 96
Justice League of America, 64, 80, 111–12, *113,* 114, 121, 145
Justice Society of America, 160n6

Kal-El. *See* Superman
Kane, Bob, 29
Karma, 68
katabasis, 118, 124–25
Kennedy, John F., 112
Kent, Clark. *See* Superman (Clark Kent)
Kent, Jonathan, 48, 138
Kent, Martha, 48, 138
Kent, Mary, 138
Kent, Nathaniel, 24–25
Kents, The, 24–25
killing: and Batman, 78, 79, 89, 90, 92, 94; and Captain America, 79, 86–89, 94, 95; and code of ethics, 78–91, 95; and Daredevil, 94; and euthanasia, 83; in films, 91–95; and Spider-Man, 92–93; and Superman, 4, 79, 89, 90, 94; and Wonder Woman, 79, 89–90. *See also* death; violence
Kingpin, 94
Kirby, Jack, 13, *14,* 29, 32, 51, 128, 151, *152,* 159–60n3, 162n10
Kraven, 141
Kraven's Last Hunt, 148
Krypton, 65, 66
Kryptonians, 29–30, 47, 172n5
kryptonite, 29

labyrinth, 149, 150
Lampert, Harry, 160n6
Lane, Lois, 49, 66, 151
Larsen, Erik, 160n5
Lawrence, John Shelton, 95; *Captain America and the Crusade against Evil,* 74; *The Myth of the American Superhero,* 74
Lee, Jim, 160n5
Lee, Stan, 20, 29, 51, 52, 159–60n3
Legion of Monsters, 57–59
Legion of Super-Heroes, 114
Lester, Richard, 94
Lichtenstein, Roy, 142
Lieber, Larry, 159–60n3
Liefeld, Rob, 160n5
Limbaugh, Rush, 100
Limbo, 125
literature, citations from, 140–41
Littletrees, Linda, 21–23
Lord, Maxwell, 89

Lovasik, Lawrence G., 170n91
Lovers and Madmen, 82–83, 94
Luthor, Lex, 49, 132, 146

Machine Man, 154
Machinesmith, 83
macrotext, 7, 8, 137, 149, 157. *See also*
    metatext; series/seriality
Magneto (Max Eisenhardt), 35–36, 64
Mamma Mia! (musical), 140
mannerism, 139
Man-Thing, 58, 59
Marino, Giambattista, 140, 149
Marrina, 19
Marston, William Moulton, 14
Martian Manhunter, 112, 172n4
Marvel Comics, 159–60n3; audience of,
    1; and Christian supernatural
    elements, 41; and Image, 2; and
    killing, 79; number of issues pub-
    lished by, 6; and Pop Art, 142–43; and
    seriality, 4; and shamans, 23; and
    violence, 75
Marvel Versus DC, 130
Marvels, 5
Marvel Universe, 4, 18, 20, 60, 98,
    166n59; comics referenced as
    historically accurate in, 144; and
    demons, 41–42; intertextuality in,
    143; proof correction by heroes in,
    144; unifying narrative of, 136–37. *See
    also individual characters and comics*
masks: and American individualism, 65;
    of Captain America, 34; and secret
    identity, 20; and shamans, 19–21; in
    Spider-Man 2, 46. *See also* costumes
Masters, Alicia, 51
Mayer, Sheldon, 160n6
Mazzucchelli, David, 23
McFarlane, Todd, 160n5
media, 97, 136
Melville, Herman, 132
Mephisto, 41–42, 53, 54, 57, 169n76,
    169n78, 171n99
"Mercury in the 20th Century," 13–14
Metal Men, 103, 134
Metamorpho, 134
metatext, 7, 119, 138, 150, 180n41. *See
    also* macrotext; series/seriality

Michael the archangel, 30
Michelangelo, 42–44, 141–42
Mighty Avengers, The, 122
Mighty Thor, The, 126–27
Mill, John Stuart, 9–10
Miller, Frank, 23, 151; *The Dark Knight
    Returns,* 5, 7, 75, 160n6
Mills, Tarpe, 20
minorities, 35, 40, 67–68, 136
Miss Fury (Marla Drake), 20–21
Mister Fantastic (Reed Richards), 20, 69,
    128, 134
Mister Mxyzptlk, 151, *153*
mobility, social and geographic, 133
monomyth: American, 95; classic, 12–13
monotheism, 29, 60
Moonstar, 68–70
morality. *See* ethics/morality
Morbius the Living Vampire, 58, 59
Morrison, Grant, 41
Moses, 30, 32, 47, 153
multiculturalism, 60–61, 68–71, 156,
    158. *See also* culture(s); diversity
Multiple Man (Jamie Madrox), 40
mutants, 18, 34–37, 62, 167n63
myths, 2, 11–17, 118; allegorical
    possibilities of, 17; ancient, 120; and
    contemporary world, 16–17;
    Egyptian, 11; and epic, 132; pagan, 41.
    See also Greek and Roman mythol-
    ogy; Norse mythology; Thor

Namor the Sub-Mariner, 159n3, 162n6
narrative, 105; baroque, 149; length of,
    118–20; and loss of center, 149–50;
    and myth, 11, 12; proliferation of
    elements of, 136–37; self-contained,
    3, 4; serial, 3–4, 125; structure of, 5;
    universe, 4, 6–7, 32, 138–39. *See also*
    series/seriality
National Allied Publications, 160n6
nationalism, 96
Native Americans, 11, 22–23, 25, 68, 99
Nazis, 14, 15, 30, 35, 103
neobaroque, 134–55; characteristics of,
    135; and citation, 140–49; historical
    development of, 136; and loss of
    center, 149–55. *See also* baroque
New Fun, 160n6

New Mutants, 68–70
New X-Men, 125
New X-Men: Childhood's End, 125
Nightcrawler, 68, 168n70
Nixon, Richard, 98
Nodell, Martin, 160n6
Nolan, Christopher, 94
No Man's Land, 107, 109, 114
Norris, Paul, 160n6
Norse mythology, 15, 39, 41, 60; Asgard, 29, 120; Loki, 11; Ragnarök (Twilight of the Gods), 120; Valkyries, 15, 16, 60, 129. See also Thor

Obama, Barack, 72, 103, 104, 105
Octopus, 19
O'Neil, Dennis, 12, 13, 23–24, 32
optimism, 64, 66

Pain of the Gods, 80
paladins, 15, 16, 60, 129
Paperdoll, 142–43
Papp, George, 160n6
Paradise Island, 14
Parker, Peter. See Spider-Man (Peter Parker)
patriotism, 65, 95–96, 98, 100, 112, 167n62
"Peace on Earth," 107–8
Pérez, George, 16
pictorial style, 150–52; graphic excess, 2. See also neobaroque; individual artists and styles
Plastic Man, 134
Ploog, Mike, 159–60n3
police officers, 73–74, 75, 77–78, 173n15
politics/political context, 59, 71, 72–74, 96, 102–16, 176n62; addition to and substitution for, 104–5; Umberto Eco on, 102–3; and epic, 132; and immigrants, 66; intervention in, 106–16; limitations from, 103; and religion, 60; and Watergate scandal, 98. See also government; social context; society
polytheism, 60
Pop Art, 142–43
Portacio, Whilce, 160n5

Prince, Diana. See Wonder Woman (Diana, Diana Prince)
Professor X (Charles Francis Xavier), 68
progressivism, 72
prophecy, 25, 118, 125–26
Pulsar, 154
Punisher, 79
Pym, Hank, 154

race/racism, 9, 67, 156
Raimi, Sam, 44, 92
Raimondi, Ezio, 135
Rambo (film), 4, 5
Ra's al Ghul, 94
readers/audience, 17, 148, 156; actual reality of, 104; adolescent boys as, 2; adults as, 2; avoiding offending, 29, 39, 49, 59–60; and catalogue of warriors, 122–24; and Christological symbols, 42, 43; and democracy and violence, 74; and escapism, 71–72; and ethics, 91; external, 144; individual knowledge of, 137–38, 180–81n41; and Judeo-Christian belief, 27; as potential authors, 153; preadolescent, 1
Red Ghost, 175–76n57
Red Skull, 79, 132
relativism, 149, 156
religion(s), 2, 156, 158; coexistence of, 154; fundamentalist, 62, 100, 158; indirect references to, 42, 59–60; rituals of, 118; traditions of, 153. See also individual faiths
"Remembrance of Things Past" (Fantastic Four), 37–39
Renaissance, 135, 139, 140
Republican party, 100
Requiem, 53–54, 57
Reynolds, Richard, 11
Rhino, 19
Richardson, Mike, 160n7
Rising Stars, 105
Robin, 75
Rocca, Antonino, 130
Roland, 15, 16, 129
Roman mythology. See Greek and Roman mythology
Romita, John, Sr., 159–60n3

Rorschach, 75
Rosenthal, Joe, 142
Ross, Alex, 99
Rucka, Greg, 16

sacrifice, 118, 129; and Silver Surfer, 52,
    57; and *Spider-Man 2,* 45–46; and
    superhero's identity, 44; and
    Superman, 72
Samson, 29
Satan, 22, 42, 49, 94, 168n69
Savage Dragon, 173n15
Savage Dragon, 160n5
Scarlet Witch, 27–28, 154
Scorpion, 19
Seagal, Steven, 74
Secret Empire, 97–98, 120
Secret Wars, 130
secularism, 60, 125
September 11, 2001, 74, 85, 103, 119
series/seriality, 153; characteristics of,
    3–5; and Jewish religion of Ben
    Grimm (The Thing), 38, 39; and loss
    of center, 149–50; and myth, 13;
    neobaroque effects of, 182n59; and
    social and political intervention,
    103–5, 112–13; and Superman, 31,
    102–3. *See also* macrotext; metatext;
    narrative
Serpent Squad, 19
ShadowHawk, 160n5
shaman/shamanism, 18–27, 60, 153,
    163n17, 163n19, 163n27; and Batman,
    19, 23–24; and Jesus, 153; and masks,
    19–21; powers of, 18–19; and Silver
    Surfer, 19; and Spider-Man, 18–20,
    26–27, 96; and Superman, 18, 24–25, 32
Shaman (Michael Twoyoungmen), 23,
    164n34
Shaman, 23–24
Sheckerberg, 37–38
She-Hulk (Jenny Walters), 144, *145*
She-Hulk, 145
Shuster, Joe, 1, 11, 20, 29, 30, 160n6
Siegel, Jerry, 1, 11, 20, 29, 30, 160n6
Silver Surfer (Norrin Radd), 27, *54, 55,*
    56, 78, 159–60n3, 171n99; appear-
    ance of, 51, 52, 170n94; and Christol-
    ogy, 51–57; illness of, 53–54; and

Legion of Monsters, 58; and shamanism,
    19; superpowers of, 52
Silver Surfer: Judgement Day, 171n99
Silvestri, Marc, 160n5
Simon, Joe, 29, 32, 159n3
Simpsons, The (television series), 140
Smallville (television series), 138
Snake Dance, 21–23, 163–64n29
Snowbird, 19
social context, 102–16; addition to and
    substitution for, 104–5; Umberto Eco
    on, 102–3; intervention in, 106–16;
    limitations from, 103; and *In Thy
    Name,* 57
society, 2, 3, 13; and epic, 132; multieth-
    nic and multicultural, 68–71, 158;
    multireligious, 158; and mutants,
    34–35; problems of, 102–3, 105, 106,
    107–8; responsibility to, 71–74; and
    Superman, 66, 67, 102, 103. *See also*
    American society; community;
    cultures; government; politics/
    political context
Soviet Union, 97, 103
Spawn, 160n5
Spectre, 160n6, 165n45
Spider-Man (Peter Parker), 26, 160n4;
    and Christological symbols, 44–46,
    47; civilian rescue vs. crimefighting
    by, 80; costume of, 96, 133; and God,
    168n69; identity of, 44–46; and
    killing, 92–93; and Kraven, 141; and
    Obama, 72, 103, 105; and Paperdoll,
    142–43; as Peter Parker, 26, 44–46;
    and respect for life, 83, *84, 93*; and
    shamanism, 18, 19, 20, 26–27;
    superpowers of, 26–27, 52
Spider-Man, 120
Spider-Man (film), 92–93
Spider-Man 2 (film), 44–46, 80
Spider-Woman, 19
Spiegelman, Art, 6, 161n10
Spirit, The, 29
Spirit of Truth, 108
Stark, Tony. *See* Iron Man
Starman, 79, *80*
Star of David, 34, 37, 39
Starseed, 57–59, *58*
Static, 85, 95, 103

Index

Storm, 68, 130, *131*
Straczynski, J. Michael, 27, 105
Stromm, Mendell, 83, *84*
Stryker, Reverend, 62
Sunfire, 68
Sunspot, 68, 69
Superhuman Registration Act, 98–99
Superman (Clark Kent), 130, 161–62n4; age of, 49; and Muhammad Ali, *129*, 130; and American culture, 65–68; arrival on Earth of, 25, 29–30, 32, 47; and authoritarianism, 114; and Bible, 29–30; chest symbol of, 24–25, *25*, 49–51, 145, 146; and Christianity, 32, *33*, 47, 94; and Christology, 47–51; civilian rescue vs. crimefighting by, 80, *81*; as Clark Kent, 24, 65–66, 67, 107–8, 166n56, 169n80; collaborative writing of stories of, 13; and copyright, 11; costume of, 24–25, *25*, 49–51, 145, 146; and council of gods, 121; and Umberto Eco, 102–3; and fall from Paradise, 47; first story of, 1, 7, 138; and God, 94; and golem, 47, 167–68n67; and government, 96, 97, 102; and heroic code of ethics, 73; iconicity and flexibility of, 31; as immigrant, 65–68; and Jesus, 32, 47, 48–51, 94, 169n85, 169–70n86, 170n88; and Judaism, 29–32, 166n54; as Kal-El, 30, 48, 65–66, 166n56; and Kent family, 48, 66, 138–39, *153*, 166n56; and killing, 4, 79, 89, 90, 94; Kryptonian parents of, 30, 47–48; and Mister Mxyzptlk, 151; and Moses, 30, 32, 47, 153; and Nazis, 30; original name of, 65–66; and past values, 119; and pictorial style, 151–52; and political intervention, 106–12, *110*, 177n71; powers of, 25, 29–30, 172n5; and private property, 102; and prophecy, 126; and Rocca, 130; and seriality, 4, 31; and shamanism, 18, 24–25, 32; and society, 66, 67, 102, 103; superhuman strength of, 29–30; and technological modernization, 132; values of, 72; and violence, 78; weakness of, 29; and Wonder Woman, 89, 90

Superman, 106, 160n6
Superman and the Legion of Super-Heroes, 67
Superman, Man of Steel, 30
Superman Returns (film), 169–70n86
Superman: The Movie (film), 47–51, *48*, *49*
Superman II (film), 94, 169n83
superpolice, 73, 77, 78, 97
superpowers/powers: acquisition of, 52; of Batman, 23–24; of Jesus, 39–40; and shamans, 18–19; and Spider-Man, 26–27, 44–46, 52; and superhero's identity, 44; of Superman, 25, 29–30, 172n5; and Wonder Woman, 14–15; of X-Men, 52

Talisman, 23
Tesauro, Emanuele, 149
Thing, the (Ben Grimm), 37–39, 51, 129, 160n4, 167–68n67
Thomas, Roy, 159–60n3
Thor, 11, 159–60n3, 162n10; and Christianity, 39, 40; consistent depiction of, 137; and epic, 120; and God, 42; hammer of, 126–27; and Judeo-Christian belief, 28–29; and monotheism, 60; and religious pluralism, 154; and Zauriel, 41
Thunderbird, 68
Tigra, 19, 154
Timely Publications, 159n3
Timm, Bruce, 151
Titus, 111–12
Trevor, Steve, 14
24 (television series), 89
Two-Face Strikes Twice, 151

Uncle Sam, 96, 99–102
Uncle Sam and the Freedom Fighters, 100–101
United Kingdom, 63
United States, 3, 57, 63–71, 154–55; culture of, 64–65; geography of, 133, 134; and literary canon, 154; military intervention by, 110–12; production of comics in, 63–64; way of life in, 116. *See also* American society
Urban VIII, 136, 139
U.S. Patriot Act, 99

Valentino, Jim, 160n5
Vermin, 19
Vertigo, 6, 160–61n8
Vietnam War, 1
violence, 2, 17, 73–79, 86. *See also*
    killing
Vision, 154
"Visitor, The," 107
visual art, 140, 141–43
Vixen, 23, 164n32
Vulture, 19

war, 12, 14, 15
Warhol, Andy, 142
warriors, catalogue of, 118, 122–24
Wasp, 19, 154
Watcher, 27, 40
Watchmen, 5, 6, 75, 160n6
Watergate scandal, 97–98, 120
Watson, Mary Jane, 44
Watterson, Bill, 151; *Calvin and Hobbes,*
    153
weapons, 118, 126–29
weddings and funerals, 40–41
Wein, Len, 159–60n3
Weinstein, Simcha, 29, 32, 34
Weisinger, Mort, 160n6
Werewolf, 58, 59
West Coast Avengers, 27–28
Wetworks, 160n5
Wheeler-Nicholson, Malcolm, 160n6
White Tiger, 19, 23
WildC.A.T.s, 160n5

Wolfsbane, 68, 69
Wolk, Douglas, 161n10
Wolverine, 19, 68, 125, 159–60n3
Wonder Woman (Diana, Diana Prince),
    130, *131,* 160n6, 174n34; and Bible,
    32; birth of, 15, *34;* chest symbol of,
    145, 146; costume of, 167n62; and
    council of gods, 121; creation of,
    14–16; debut story of, 120; as Diana,
    14, 15; and killing, 79, 89–90, *90;*
    lasso of, 126; and Medusa, 16–17; and
    past values, 119; and political
    intervention, 108, *109;* and seriality,
    32; superpowers of, 14–15
Wonder Woman: Diana Prince, 129
World War Hulk, 130
World War II, 1, 4, 78, 96, 103, 119, 120,
    130, 132
Wylie, Philip, *Gladiator,* 114–15

Xavier, Charles Francis. *See* Professor X
X-Men, 29, 34–37, 52, 62, 64, 68, *69,*
    120, 160n4
X-Men, 137
X-Men (film), 167n64
X-Men: God Loves, Man Kills, 62

Youngblood, 160n5

Zatti, Sergio, 117, 124, 132
Zauriel, 41, 168–69n74
Zenn-La, 52, 53–54
Zod, 47, *48,* 94

Index